Will Carling won his first cap ~~for the England~~ team in 1988, and went on t~~o play for them over~~ fifty times, many of them as captain. He led the team during their Grand Slam-winning seasons of 1991, 1992 and 1995, and to the World Cup Final against Australia in 1991. Educated at Sedburgh School and Durham University, Carling is a former Army officer who has since gone on to achieve a rare double by succeeding in both the sporting and business worlds. He has worked in a marketing role for an international oil company and is now Managing Director of the management training company Insights Ltd. He was awarded an OBE in 1991.

Robert Heller is one of the country's leading authorities on management. He was the founding editor of *Management Today* and took it rapidly to the position of Britain's pre-eminent business magazine. He is the author of many acclaimed and best-selling books, including *The Naked Manager, The Supermanagers, The Fate of IBM* and *The Naked Manager for the Nineties*. He writes a monthly newsletter with Edward de Bono, 'Letter to Thinking Managers', and is a frequent visitor to management groups all over the world. He lives in London.

THE WAY TO WIN

Strategies for Success in Business and Sport

Will Carling
and
Robert Heller

WARNER BOOKS

A *Warner* Book

First published in Great Britain in 1995
by Little, Brown and Company
This edition published in 1996 by Warner Books

A CIP catalogue record for this book
is available from the British Library.

ISBN 0 7515 1567 1

Typeset by Palimpsest Book Production Limited,
Polmont, Stirlingshire
Printed and bound in Great Britain by
Clays Ltd, St Ives plc

Warner Books
A Division of
Little, Brown and Company (UK)
Brettenham House
Lancaster Place
London WC2E 7EN

Contents

V: Integrity – How to Create Credibility

VI: Team-Work – How to Build Effective Teams

VII: Visibility – How to Lead by Example

VIII: Communicating – How to Open the Channels

IX: Attention – How to Listen and Respond

X: Commitment – How to Settle for Success

Acknowledgements

This book was originally suggested by Clive Williams of Ernst & Young, who also initiated our collaboration in management seminars at Insights Ltd, and can justly be named godfather of this project. Jim Foley, a founder of Insights, played a key – and much appreciated – role in formulating the concepts on which the book is based.

We owe a debt to some outstanding management thinkers. Some are cited in the Bibliography, but Manfred Perlitz, Peter M. Senge, Michael J. Kami, Edward de Bono, Ricardo Semler, James Champy and Richard Pascale have personally provided perceptions of great value. Several outstanding publications, through their commissions and content, have been vital to this book: including *Management Today*, *Worldlink*, *Business Solutions*, the *Observer*, *Customer Service Management*, *Intercity*, *The Engineer*, *Fortune* and *Business Week*. We are very grateful to their editors.

Sven-Erik Gunnervall of Norden Publishing, by commissioning the book *The Quality Makers*, launched the series of interviews which have been a powerful influence on this book. Two other books, *The State of Industry* and *Unique Success Proposition*, were also important in shaping *The Way to Win*'s content. Two admirable management consultants, Michael de Kare-Silver of Kalchas and William Hextall of Kepner-Tregoe, were catalysts and sources of excellent information. Ronald Cohen of venture capitalists Apax Partners & Co. kindly allowed us to use material on entrepreneurs originally developed at his request.

Above all, we are grateful to the interviewees from the worlds of both business and sport: Will Carling offers special thanks to the sports interviewees 'who showed amazing patience as well as humour at my interviewing technique'. This book would not have been possible without them: the virtues are all theirs, and the faults all ours.

Finally, we are deeply indebted to everybody involved with Insights; that includes the team members, the many managers who have attended the seminars, and especially Caroline Whicker for her heroic typing. At the Highgate end of the enterprise, Anne McKenzie fully deserves equal thanks.

Introduction:

The Way to Win

Success in management and success in sports have the same roots. In business as in games, players must master two critical aspects: the techniques (including those of strategy and tactics) and themselves. Self-mastery, making the best of your abilities, is the foundation of achievement in both fields. But there are also clear and important analogies in the approaches taken by winning managers and winners in sports to an equally vital matter: working with and through others to achieve success.

Yet the analogy between management and games has seldom been stressed. Far more often, writers have sought management lessons in warfare. Many books have dipped into military history, going as far back as the Middle Ages of Japan, to discover the secrets of business success. In highly competitive markets, strategists and tacticians can learn much useful lore (like never to attack the enemy head-on unless you have at least a 3–1 advantage). But the ability to compete at all rests on qualities and attributes that are even clearer (because of the greater focus) in sport than they are in war.

The vital qualities and attributes can be summed up in one word: leadership. Obviously, and as everybody knows, that's crucial for sporting achievement. Once again, though, the sports analogy is far less commonly used. When John F. Kennedy entertained a group of businessmen in the White House early in his presidency, one told him bluntly that the United States needed a 'man on horseback'. But Kennedy rightly shot him down with a burst of spontaneous eloquence. Leadership in time of peace, even of cold war, is not properly exercised by riding roughshod over opposition.

Even better informed people persist in identifying great leadership with military models. When William Rees-Mogg was berating John Major for lack of leadership in *The Times*, the heroes with which the luckless Premier was lashed were Roosevelt, Churchill and de Gaulle – all victors in the Second World War. However, the military contribution of de Gaulle, the only certified soldier, was small, while his civilian contribution to France was huge. Roosevelt, too, achieved military leadership only because of his prior success in reversing America's civilian slide into slump and despair. Of the trio, only Churchill depends largely on wartime achievements for his Titanic reputation. The adjective is significant. These men (like their vile contemporaries, Hitler and Stalin) were Titans. But if leadership depended on supermen, most of the world would be leaderless – anyway, Titans who, like Hitler, lead their followers to destruction are grotesque failures: who wants to join the Charge of the Light Brigade?

The question 'What makes a great leader?' thus has a simple answer, as any sacked football manager knows: success. It doesn't necessarily require the man-on-horseback quality of charisma, the aura that generates worship in lesser creatures. Charisma counts only because it reinforces the leader's ability to generate support for successful action. Successes in sport clearly demonstrate that this leadership ability is founded on five strengths that are *inward*. These personal strengths – **vision**, **self-belief**, **results focus**, **courage**, **integrity** – are what people must develop to close the gap between their potential and their achievement.

These five strengths, while vital, are not enough in themselves. They achieve their effect through **team-work**, **visibility**, **communication**, **attention**, **commitment**. These five *outward* processes, common to all organisations, but badly executed in most, enable everybody to maximise their contribution to closing that same gap on a larger scale: between what the organisation could achieve, and what actually results. Note that the need for these qualities and attributes is general: all managers, at all levels, like all players in all sports, will succeed more the more they develop these assets.

Because he (or she) is literally above all, the ultimate leader needs these ten strengths and processes above all. They lie behind the charisma of the flamboyant leader, in war, politics, business or sport. But provided the leader can deploy the ten, image becomes far less important. Alf Ramsay, who led the England football team to World Cup victory, had the charisma of a quartermaster-sergeant. Churchill virtually defined charisma, English-style, but was outdone in most respects in peace (so the historical consensus holds) by Clement Attlee. The latter's small size, dry manner and crisp style suggested a pedagogue rather than a leader of men – and of powerful, obstinate men like Ernest Bevin, at that.

Excessive charisma can have the reverse effect: the Light Brigade rides again, right into the Russian guns. The late, unlamented Robert Maxwell is a horrible example, charisma oozing from every pore as he bankrupted his businesses and pillaged his pensioners. He is merely an extreme and extremely obnoxious example of the Great Leader disease. Maxwell is alleged to have observed that boards should always contain an odd number of directors, and three was too many.

That sentiment, inimical to true leadership, is secretly shared by many would-be horseback-riders. The identification of leadership with total power, supreme authority and horsemen goes back deep into the fog of history. Early rulers were either warriors (like Charlemagne) or served by warriors (like Elizabeth I). Tribal chiefs, and feudal ones, maintained their positions by fighting, just as many dominant males must still fight to maintain their places in the animal kingdom. So the identification of leaders with commanders is easily understood.

That identification set up a leadership model which has

outlived its value. The peerless, supreme commander stood at
the apex of the hierarchical pyramid, served by loyal staff, laying
down the strategy which sub-commanders converted into tactics.
To this day, in the standard Western model, the chief executive
and the government minister occupies the same exalted position.
His word is law, and his decision (or indecision) is final. The same
used to be true of captains in sport, notably in primeval cricket,
where the captain, sometimes a very moderate performer, was
the leader of the amateur 'gentlemen' and the best batsman or
bowler in England a mere 'player'.

What worked, more or less, in simple times and situations
bears no useful relation to the complex institutions of the
modern world. The leadership which (if you believe his critics)
John Major fails to exercise would, if he were to produce it,
contain little of Churchill, Roosevelt or de Gaulle. Reducing
unacceptable unemployment and raising the living standards
of the underclass poses technocratic challenges of the highest
order, and none of the Titans would have relished that kind
of task.

Yet Titans do display, writ super-large, characteristics which
all successful leaders share. First, they know absolutely what they
want to achieve. Second, they maintain absolute concentration
on that aim through all vicissitudes. Thus Sergei Diaghilev,
through a life of messy entanglements and crackpot finances,
never lost sight of his determination to create the world's greatest
ballets, no matter what devious twists and turns he performed.
Indeed, the third common characteristic of great leaders is
that they are apt to believe that the end justifies the means:
they deploy the attributes, in Isaiah Berlin's famous phrase,
of both the lion and the fox. Unfortunately, this carelessness
about means is shared with the sociopaths who have disfigured
human history, from Genghis Khan to Pol Pot.

So what marks the difference between leaders and sociopaths?

The answer lies in a fourth characteristic. Great leadership
expresses the will of the led, and leaves them better for its

contribution. Nobody in Geoff Cooke's rugby squad initially shared the convictions which led him to turn upside-down the organisation of the team and the game in England. But his main purpose, to raise the side's performance to the world's best levels, was undeniably the popular will, among both the team and its supporters. Not that all Cooke's moves were popular with all those affected – but courting popularity is not part of the leadership deal.

Sir Georg Solti led the Covent Garden orchestra from the pits, so to speak, to the heights. He did not, in the process, win his musicians' love. You can't generalise about leadership styles. The martinet, as exemplified by the rough-and-tough, General Patton model of the American football manager, can be sharply effective, but not necessarily more so than the encouraging leader who is 'compassionate, versatile, sweet-natured, courageous and temperate'. That description of Field-Marshal Alexander, 'a highly competent supreme commander', comes from Norman Dixon's brilliant *On the Psychology of Military Incompetence*. Dixon argues that 'afflictions of the ego' underlie authoritarianism, which is the disease of psychological misfits and born blunderers. In contrast, splendid warrior-leaders are psychologically whole, warm-hearted and even (Napoleon, for example) intensely amorous.

They also (Napoleon again, de Gaulle and the under-rated Eisenhower) convert ably into peacetime leaders. That's partly because of the military system described above. The general lays down his strategy, and then goes peacefully to sleep (like General Montgomery before El-Alamein or Norman Schwarzkopf in Desert Storm), confident that his army is superbly trained and armed and that all subordinates know their tasks and will carry them out.

In sports and business alike, effective delegation is indispensable to modern leadership, in which objectives must be agreed and shared. The leader musters all available resources of brainpower, knowledge and experience to come up with a feasible game plan. Leadership further entails ensuring that the plan is turned into action by combined operations. Finally, the leader must monitor the results, and instigate further action if the plan needs modifying or if U-turns need turning (without making them a habit).

This trio of steps demands something else: the ability to form teams and sustain a high level of morale and achievement. None of this can be managed on horseback. The leader has to be on foot, moving among the organisation's members and interacting with them. Shakespeare's 'little touch of Harry in the night' before Agincourt has never outlived its usefulness – as Montgomery showed to famous effect when taking command of a demoralised Eighth Army. His takeover speech to his officers has passed into legend as a crisp 400-word summation of great leadership. The credo started with two-way trust, team-work and the 'culture' created by the boss ('One of the first duties,' snapped Monty, 'is to create what I call atmosphere'). The objective, to smash Rommel, was sharp and sharply communicated with absolute self-confidence. The confident leader gives his people the confidence and tools needed to finish the job – and absolutely insists on high performance.

But he also walks a couple of tightropes: one between discipline (which binds the led together) and the human touch (which enlists their hearts); and another between the out-and-out urge to outdistance all competitors and the rational intellect which keeps the competitive drive under control. The crashes of men on horseback (or bankers' backs) like Alan Bond and Maxwell show many examples of overweening ambition: 'the deal too far'.

That's one great problem with great leadership. Even in more enlightened circles, the feeling is that excellent achievement can only result if a single person takes charge with clear and total authority. That style of authority can all too easily be abused. The principle is further weakened in the West by the insistence that the said person must also be the most senior (which generally means the oldest). In sports that insistence has dwindled away for the good and sufficient reason that great captaincy requires experience, and playing careers end too early for players to start their on-the-job learning late in the day. Neither age nor long service has anything to do with ability to lead in the modern sense: identifying the need, mobilising the power to identify the solution, effecting and controlling the execution. The mysterious East, which has caused the transparent West so much economic pain, has never shared this faith in peerless leadership, despite the ferocious military traditions of *shoguns* and *samurai.*

Behind the warriors lay a different tradition, summed up by the constitution promulgated in 604 by Shotoku Tiashi. Among fourteen injunctions, 'all the nobles, greater and lesser' were told to 'be at their posts from the early morning and go home late', and in 'important affairs', never to 'act alone on the basis of your own judgement, but discuss the matter first with several others'. All this fits in perfectly with the concept of the inward strengths and outward processes which we have described.

The modern Japanese leader is still just as industrious, still practises on the basis of consensus, and still exists to serve the organisation, not the other way round. If the leader's weaknesses endanger the long-term interests of the corporation, he is swiftly dispatched: preferably before lasting damage has been done, and not afterwards (as in the recent enforced departures of the bosses of General Motors and IBM). Both these failed leaders followed in Titanic footsteps taken between the wars, when one man could mentally embrace an entire corporation. Those days are gone forever. Making these stumbling businesses pick up their feet and run demands new collegiate forms of leadership, and replacing old with new over such vast organisations is a fiendishly difficult task, with only one factor in its favour. When you inherit a shambles, you have a licence to cure.

That's why, so often, the great sports sides – like Wigan in Rugby League – rise from the ashes of failure. The cure will demand another attribute of leadership: stubborn persistence in a winning cause. By definition, great leaders never give up. Like Mao on the Long March, they may retreat, but only to fight, and win, another day. Such invincible determination is essential in sustaining morale among your followers when there's precious little food for encouragement. Indeed, great leaders deliberately use adversity as a springboard to success. When Ian McGeechan's British Lions were savaged by Australia, the outcome was a stunning win in the Second Test and the series. Similarly, ICI's first-ever quarterly loss was used by Sir John Harvey-Jones as his leverage to jack up the entire group and raise its sights to another first: the first billion-pound profit made by a British industrial company. Analyse the Harvey-Jones achievement and you find a programme that bears a close resemblance to Monty's maxims – which isn't surprising, for leadership knows no boundaries. It can be exercised in any profession and by any personality.

Those who believe that leaders are born, not made, will wrongly challenge that statement. True, there are natural leadership qualities, dependent on genes and early life experience, that elevate gifted personalities above the pack. But those with lesser gifts can also achieve greater results if they systematically and intelligently obey clear-cut rules, which start with taking clear charge and unifying the group, team, company or institution behind clear and agreed objectives.

Be ready to challenge and re-examine anything and everything in the process of clarifying ends and means, and determining which are right. Don't take any longer over that process than you need. Be prepared for instant changes in plan, people and anything else that requires altering, because circumstances will change. 'Never fail to reward merit,' to quote a great Japanese business leader, Seisei Kato of Toyota, 'but never let a fault go unremarked,' or uncorrected. Make sure that everybody knows exactly what's happening, why, and what his or her role is, and help everybody to contribute to the full.

The case histories in this book use great business and sporting successes to demonstrate how great performers have used the five *inward* strengths and five *outward* processes to achieve their triumphs. The concept is the foundation of the seminars which, working together at Insights Ltd, we have conducted with many managers in many companies. The cases are accompanied by chapters which draw together the themes of the inward strengths and outward processes. Like the Insights seminars, the chapters show how managers can apply the lessons of both sporting and business success to build much more successful organisations, outperforming not only the competition, but – an equally satisfying part of the game – their own previous best standards.

Not one of these leadership techniques is inborn, and all are easily grasped. Using them to achieve well-chosen objectives is what ultimately makes a great leader, or a leader great. That is a matter of choice rather than birth. But while many leaders are chosen, few choose to learn the lessons of leadership. That is why so few are great; but it's also why anybody can aspire to rise towards greatness – and maybe achieve it.

I

Vision – How to Turn Ambition into Reality

1

'We Can Win the World Cup'

To achieve anything, you must have a direction, a purpose, an aim. Without that fundamental bearing, you can never know how to channel your resources and energy. To have a vision in sport is crucial, and very likely far more common than in business. Looking through the remarkable achievements of the personalities featured in this book, it's immediately obvious that they were all driven by their vision, their ultimate goal.

For Tracy Edwards, her goal was to lead the first all-female crew into the Whitbread Round the World Yacht Race, and to win. The vision was that ultimate moment of crossing the finishing line in first place. That image is what she carried in her mind as she dragged herself from one office to another, seeking not only sponsorship, but a boat as well. It also motivated her as she ploughed through hundreds of applications to join her crew. She had a purpose, a direction. It was the foundation for her eventual success.

Adrian Moorhouse, too, had a vision. It was cemented in his mind at the age of twelve while he watched the Olympics on a black-and-white TV upstairs in secret (his parents wouldn't let him watch in colour downstairs because he was too young). That night he saw David Wilkie win the gold medal, and Adrian decided that this was something he, too, wanted to achieve. His

vision was born. He knew his ultimate goal. All he had to do was
fill in the remaining eight or nine years!

Communicating the vision

All visions vary, and all visions must evolve. Like Jonah
Barrington's vision of developing himself into the best squash
player in the world, the world champion, number one. And
like the vision of Seb Coe, who also desired to be number one,
and nothing less, in his chosen track events. Or that of Mike
Brearley, whose vision was to win an Ashes series with a group of
individuals of varying and difficult talents. But however different
their ambitions, the stars all shared the ability to conceptualise a
vision. That led to their motivation, their commitment and their
eventual triumphs.

Geoff Cooke, the England Rugby Union manager, presented
his vision to the national squad in 1988 in a room in the
Petersham Hotel overlooking the Thames. It was that England
were capable of reaching the 1991 World Cup final and would
do so. At the time of this somewhat startling announcement,
England were far from a successful side. Their record in the
1980s made for unhappy reading, unless you were a supporter
of the other home Union sides. Yet Cooke delivered his vision
with belief, with honesty, and, most important of all, in detail.

It was the articulation of his vision to the squad that achieved
their commitment. He explained the change that England would
have to go through as a squad and as a management in order
to achieve that vision. The change would encompass not only
the physical but the mental side of the game, and, crucially, the
structure of English rugby generally and the physical structure
of the players themselves. A fitness programme was introduced
which would monitor players on a regular basis.

The programme tested not only their basic cardiovascular
fitness, but their speed over varying distances, their strength,
their fat content, their blood content, their leg power, their
arm power – and their ability to smile through it all. Instead

of delivering this package as a *fait accompli*, Cooke explained exactly why the players needed to go through this physical change. They needed to become fitter, stronger and faster if they wanted to compete with the top countries in world rugby. Each player was shown how fitness would benefit him in the long run. The huge men in the scrum could quite rightly be proud of their immense strength, scrummaging ability and bulk; now they had to be persuaded of the need to alter the focus of their training. They had to retain their strength, but they had to lose fat content; they had to add enormous explosive power through new methods of training; their speed off the mark, as well as their maximum speed, had to be increased.

Change is always resented, in whatever environment people operate, but this new regime of fitness and the changed focus of training almost took away everything in which these men took immense pride. It was as though what they had trained for and practised for years was no longer important. They had to be persuaded that they needed to retain their existing skills and basic ability, but also to broaden their horizons in terms of what else they could add to the side. Only then could the team achieve its vision.

The success of that friendly persuasion must have been the key to England's wins on the field. Whether the side was as successful as it should have been will be debated for many years to come, but one of the most useful benchmarking tours during this period actually occurred shortly before the World Cup itself – and England were beaten. All the European sides in the Five Nations Championship travelled to Australia for a four-and-a-half-week tour. Its purpose and necessity were debated heatedly in England.

Many experts said that the players would benefit more from a rest than from a tour. The trip, it was argued, would intensify pressure on the team only months before the World Cup. The players themselves, however, were keen to tour; keen to measure themselves against Australia, recognised as one of the best sides in the world; keen to see how strong the team really was and at the same time to discover where its weaknesses lay. In the event, the side that had won the Grand Slam in Europe lost three out of four games on tour. Its frailties were cruelly exposed and the tour was labelled a disaster by many observers.

From the squad's point of view, though, it was regarded as an immense success. The side arrived home feeling that there was enough time to change areas of its game, and areas of approach, to negate the exposed weaknesses. Had the team sat back in England, basking in the glory of their first Grand Slam for eleven years, these vulnerabilities would never have been acknowledged. Certainly there wouldn't have been time, once the World Cup itself had started, to rectify the faults. Being benchmarked against the best gave the team a far greater chance of success in the tournament.

The players had to change mentally as well. They were given tapes on relaxation, tapes on concentration, tapes to help them visualise; they played them either in their cars on the way to squad training or on headphones. The players had to develop their ability to concentrate in match situations in front of crowds of 60,000 to 70,000, under intense pressure from the opposition, at times under the over-critical eye of the referee. They had to be able to concentrate on their roles and their team direction, one area which England believed wasn't strong enough. They also had to learn to concentrate in the build-up to internationals. Each player had to be able to switch on, maybe for only half-an-hour or an hour each week, to the task of winning the next international amid the chaos of club training, club matches, work, family life and, somewhere in the middle, relaxation. They had to learn to switch on as well as off.

Geoff Cooke also explained how the new structure, the new league system and the new management set-up would contribute to success on the field. He had, for the first time, looked not only at the twenty-one players who were picked for the World Cup squad but at the clubs which produced them; the management that selected them; the medical staff who looked after them; and the technical personnel who provided the analytical data on the players. Everyone came under scrutiny for the first time, and everyone was provided with this focus on the 1991 World Cup final.

It was obvious, throughout the explanation, that certain members of the squad would not meet these new and higher standards. But this, far from demotivating the squad, had the reverse effect: their aspirations had been raised and their desire intensified. They wanted to be part of this new and testing set-up. They accepted the challenge of achieving the vision outlined for them that day in 1988.

Since all visions must evolve, progress towards goals must be monitored along the way. For England this was achieved by going on tours to the southern hemisphere, whose teams provided the standard against which the players wanted to measure themselves. Yet it was frustrating that there were not enough of such tours, and the squad had to make do with what limited southern hemisphere opposition could be found. But the valuable lessons learned on the few expeditions did allow continual fine tuning, not only of playing style, but of fitness targets and mental approach.

There were many major lessons learned from the 1991 World Cup and the attempt to achieve Cooke's vision. The most important was that his vision of reaching the final was achievable – and was achieved. True, the game itself was lost. The team believes that Australia had a different vision, that England's opponents in the final went into the tournament with the sole aim of winning. It is no use being wise in hindsight, but this lesson is certainly something England took on board for the 1995 tournament. Being in the final was not the vision chosen for 1995: winning was.

Many people make the mistake of believing that experienced, successful individuals and teams do not need a vision, an ultimate goal. They believe that such teams and people will be self-motivated. Here we disagree: experience teaches otherwise. In the 1993 season, England had a phenomenally experienced side containing many players who had contributed to the back-to-back

Grand Slams in the two previous years. After their performance in the World Cup Final, England entered 1993 as overwhelming favourites to win another Grand Slam, and to provide the bulk of the British players on the forthcoming Lions tour of New Zealand.

More than one objective is no objective

Herein lay the problem. It's been wisely said that in management more than one objective is no objective. Given the cyclical nature of the competition, England needed to view the 1993 season as the bedding-in process for the new side that would contest the 1995 World Cup. But Geoff Cooke, the England manager, and Dick Best, the England coach, were to take on the same positions for the 1993 British Lions. We're both sure they will agree that this involvement with the Lions deflected the management from the aim of rebuilding the side for 1995. To make matters even more confusing, a number of rules had been changed in the off-season. The changes had helped to alter the emphasis of the game in ways that negated the influence and success of many of the key England players who had the experience and knowledge to be successful in New Zealand.

The desire to do justice to both England and the Lions eventually proved too much. The outcome provides a classic proof that a team, and certainly an individual, cannot have two visions, two long-term goals. The focus either had to be on rebuilding England with a view to the 1995 World Cup, or totally upon the British Lions tour. Unfortunately, the side fell between the two stools. The minds of some players wandered during the domestic season, dwelling on the possibility of a swansong tour to New Zealand. This led to a lack of focus in the England side of that year, and to an almost directionless season.

Not enough new players had been brought into the squad to provide the edge of internal competition that was needed, and too few minds were concentrated on the task of winning a third Grand Slam. As a result, England played four, lost two – the worst season since 1988. At the end of that deeply disappointing year, Will Carling sat down with Peter Winterbottom, one of the most experienced players and a straight-talking Yorkshireman, and asked where he had gone wrong as a captain. One of Winterbottom's major points was that the captain hadn't given the team a direction for that year, hadn't raised their aspirations, hadn't forced them to look for a new challenge.

The goal was just another Grand Slam – the same again, and that is never enough. It didn't excite the players and, worse, allowed the opposition to catch up and beat England. The vision had not evolved. Because sights had not been raised, commitment wavered: the England players were unsure of their direction and of what they should commit themselves to. Lack of a vision, lack of a direction, and lack of an ultimate goal on which to pin commitment, direction, training and desire led to the season's disappointments. It was a sorry contrast to the transformation that could be seen in English rugby from 1988 to 1992.

In that period, England, the so-called under-achievers of the northern hemisphere, were transformed into the strongest side in Europe. Players who had staggered from game to game, hoping to win just one more cap, hoping not to make mistakes and thereby forfeit their place, suddenly pictured in their minds playing in a World Cup final. They suddenly had a management who had that belief in them and told them so.

The effect was dramatic. Their eyes, their focus, had been raised from just the next game, the next mistake, to looking into the future. They had been given the processes, the building blocks, which enabled them to visualise progress to this goal. The fitness programmes, the mental focus, the club rugby – all provided the necessary supports which would enable them to achieve this vision. They could start to plan long-term in their fitness training: a detailed fitness programme and wall chart was given to each of them eighteen months before the World Cup.

With this injection of physical and mental confidence, they could start to plan their development as players, and as a team, believing that they would be together for more than just one game. They would have time to get to know each other as people, rather than just as players; to learn about each other's families; to take interest in each other and develop friendships, forming a bond that would actually be decisive in winning many of the extremely close games that were to come. It allowed them to break out of the shackles and restrictions of the no-risk games and blame culture that had stifled English rugby. Vision gave the players the foundation and direction for England's most successful period.

2

The Start-Up
that Started Right

The start-up is among the most exciting and demanding of management tasks. It begins with an enormous advantage: the entrenched habits that are the greatest obstacle to organisational change don't exist. A company like National Westminster Life Assurance – which was announced in September 1991 and started business on New Year's Day in 1993 – is a 'green-field' operation, free to build 'an excellent company by any test' in its own way, and thus to realise its vision.

Total Quality Management

The method chosen by NatWest Life was TQM – total quality management. It's a cause which several leading British companies have adopted in recent years. Using this approach British Telecom thus set out to prove that:

(1) We put our customer first.
(2) We are professional.
(3) We respect each other.

    (4) We work as one team.

    (5) We are committed to continuous improvement.

Likewise, Honeywell (UK) launched a drive 'to envelop all aspects of quality and its subsequent impact on business success'. For Rank Xerox, the task was 'providing our external and internal customers with innovative products and services that fully satisfy their requirements'.

In sum, the TQM visionaries seek perfection, even though part of the quality gospel is that perfection is never achieved. In top-level sport, every team and every player shares the same almost impossible vision – to play a perfect game. Even when an individual champion reaches the seemingly absolute heights, like Pete Sampras at Wimbledon in 1994, defeating an in-form and brilliant opponent with decisive power, unforced errors creep in and unjustified criticism follows: Sampras was so good that he was 'boring'. What's hard for individuals is fifteen times more difficult for rugby players. How can all members of an international team play perfectly?

Reality must fall short of the vision. To say that perfection is fifteen times harder for a rugby team to achieve actually under-estimates the difficulty, since the permutation of possible and indispensable connections between the fifteen amount to a mind-boggling total. Every pass has to be correctly weighted and aimed, every ball caught at the right speed and correct angle of run, etc. Impossible. And the difficulties are, of course, vastly greater in a business unit, let alone a whole company. The numbers aren't limited to fifteen. NatWest Life had ten times that many sales people operating out of bank branches, plus 650 head office staff: the possible combinations require a super-computer's calculations.

Moreover, while a start-up gains from being brand-new, it also has disadvantages: it's a scratch side, few of whose members have ever worked together. The scratch side rarely succeeds in sports. Sometimes, magically, an established team does play as one superb collective champion. Graham Mourie's All Blacks defeated Wales with one such legendary performance. You might expect that from a thoroughly drilled touring side coming from a deep, shared tradition, but not from a scratch team. Yet on one occasion when the Southern Hemisphere played the Rest of the World at Twickenham, fifteen players who had never all been on the same side clicked into an irresistible combination.

Chance played its part, but there was an underlying cause. Every player possessed high and highly trained skills: each knew exactly what to do in any situation; each, moreover, trusted all the other fourteen to be equally expert. Everybody shared the same objective, to move forward towards the try-line with maximum speed and power. Above all, each player acted decisively on the instant when action was demanded. Much the same thing happened when the scratch Barbarians side, drawn from ten nations, defeated the powerful Springboks in 1994. Shared purpose and commitment magically overcame the odds.

Interestingly, another green-field start-up, Nissan Motors UK in Sunderland, stresses that very need in its vision statement: 'To give a common sense of direction and purpose for the whole company and its suppliers.' That follows on from: 'To improve every aspect of our business and our products . . . To improve the future security and prosperity of NMUK, its employees and its suppliers . . . To improve the quality of life at work for all employees.' These aims clearly interlock. But the cement lies in the 'shared purpose and commitment' that can turn a scratch side into a major industry force.

Keep improving

The two drivers are the essence of vision and of TQM. They are evidently difficult to achieve, given that TQM's disappointments probably outnumber its successes. The disappointments, however, enshrine a fundamental misunderstanding: TQM is founded on the facts, not of perfection, but of imperfection. Progress towards the vision arises from meticulously measuring where any operation is now and plotting how it can be improved.

Then you go on improving. In fact, continuous improvement is really an unspoken part of the vision, just as when a very young Sampras decides to become a champion, or an infant NatWest Life decides on this aim:

> We will be a leading provider in our chosen sectors of financial services . . . first choice for customers throughout their lives for outstanding services, straightforward products and superior investment returns.

Lawrence Churchill, the managing director, used this vision statement as a powerful tool for many purposes, including recruitment. It appeared in first draft a month after the announcement of the launch, and was used to find people who 'also passionately believed in the quality process'. So a would-be chief actuary who believed only in managing by numbers wouldn't fit and wouldn't be recruited. Early on, a vision conference was held off site to develop further the concept and rationale. But the statement, deliberately, wasn't finalised until September 1992, when all the senior executives were in place.

This wasn't the idea of some enthused visitor from another industrial planet. Churchill comes from a deep background in financial services, having spent his career largely with Allied Dunbar, one of the highly successful players in equity-linked life assurance whose common bond is the business genius of Sir Mark Weinberg, the South African who revolutionised the marketing of insurance in Britain. Some of that revolution's results, in terms of sales ethics in particular, were less than splendid. Churchill wanted a vision which would transcend all previous standards and transform industry practice.

To that end, every member of the seven-man team had to agree every word of the statement. It took long discussions for them to reach unanimity, but by the time they did the new company's leaders were committed to a vision in which they wholly believed. It may sound like a somewhat academic exercise, but the start-up succeeded brilliantly. After only fifteen months, all the necessary systems were in place on time; all the insurance products had been designed and implemented. Success in the offices was matched in the market: so much business had been transacted within the first three months that a company with a market value of £1 billion had been created on total initial capital of £300 million.

By the end of 1994, the start-up had won an amazing tenth position among Britain's life-insurers. Visions are no use unless they likewise embody effective strategies and lead to efficient execution. Churchill's task was to exploit the strong sales foundation laid by the parent National Westminster Bank in many years of insurance-broking. The bank also supplied a massive database from which the fledgling company discovered an unsurprising fact: a dozen of the sixty insurance products offered by the bank accounted for over 90 per cent of sales. NatWest Life could therefore start up with a streamlined roster of products known to appeal to the customer.

In modern business, this is the starting point for most vision statements, whether or not the company concerned is practising TQM. The aim is the same: to satisfy or, far better, delight the customer. The highly renowned American retail group Nordstrom consequently enjoins its people to 'respond to unreasonable customer requests'. If the request is unreasonable, the customer doesn't fully expect it to be met, and doing more than the customer expects is the key to delight. That could even mean changing a customer's flat tyre in the car park.

Delight in turn is the key to customer retention, or loyalty. The delighted customer who thinks your service excellent is six times more likely than the merely satisfied customer, according to research by Xerox, to buy from you again. That's why Rank Xerox's quality aims lead off with: 'Be number one in customer satisfaction in reprographics and printing and make significant progress towards the goal of 100 per cent satisfaction.' It's also why NatWest Life affirms in its vision statement that: 'Our customers are the focus of everything we do,' and adds: 'We value our customers, and will:

(1) Enable them to achieve a more secure future for themselves and their dependants.
(2) Build lasting relationships with them.
(3) Deliver outstanding service and heed their feedback.
(4) Provide simple, easy to understand products and above-average investment returns.

This is all stirring and excellent stuff, but you won't find much different in other life-insurance companies that have composed vision statements, and before long you won't find many such companies that haven't. Anybody can write fine words, though. The question isn't even whether top management has agreed to and under-written every word, as at NatWest Life. It isn't even a matter of whether an executive team like Churchill's, seven strong in all, is 'living the vision' or 'walking the talk'. The crunch question is whether everybody in the company is equally enthused with the vision – and, above all, with turning it into action.

One NatWest executive, recruited from the parent bank, plainly felt that this had been achieved. 'I was sold by the passion for living the vision – it doesn't give anyone else the chance not to believe. I've never seen anything like this before in the bank.' This kind of indoctrination doesn't come easily. Churchill isn't exaggerating when he says that the fifteen-month timetable 'was colossal'. That would have been true even if the launch had gone unbelievably smoothly. In the last five launch months, however, executives were 'up to our armpits in alligators'. Yet, crucially, top managers kept 10 per cent of their time free for the vision and the culture.

Getting right the 'hard' things, like insurance technicalities, was vital, of course. But the team accepted that the 'soft' beliefs and values were just as critical. Nobody, least of all Churchill, denies that keeping up the quality momentum was 'a strain': it would have been 'easier to stop. But I'm very glad that we didn't.' Like a great sports team, the vision-driven company can't halt the drive without losing both impetus and vision. The evidence that they've been preserved lies on the field of play: 'The behaviour of staff tells you whether the vision is living or not.'

We saw one piece of behaviour that told a great deal. As a total quality exercise, a group of new finance department recruits – green employees in a green-field company – had been asked to look at the accounts payable operation to see if it could be improved. They had come up with a better system, but one which offered no savings. So they sent themselves back to the drawing board and came up with a far superior, truly radical idea. Why have an accounts payable function at all?

The reasoning was that all invoices are preceded by a purchasing order. Why not rebuild the system round the orders? Then, as soon as correct delivery is confirmed, the system would automatically issue the cheque. We were doubly impressed. First, this young, inexperienced team had, completely independently, reached the same conclusion as seasoned managers at Ford Motor in the US. Second, they had been trusted to review not some minor detail of administration, but a major area of corporate concern. The vision was being lived – and empowerers and empowered alike were quite visibly tickled pink.

The similar reform at Ford was part of changes which, during the 1980s, according to Goss, Pascale and Athos (*Harvard Business Review*, November–December 1993), created 'an entirely different company' – or so Ford's employees say. 'Ford had left behind its past as a rigidly hierarchical company driven by financial considerations to pursue a future in which a concern for quality and new products became the overriding priority.' A new and radically different vision, in other words, can 'reinvent' a company so powerfully that it can come near to the green-field standards of a Nissan UK or a NatWest Life.

But there's a catch. As the three authors continue: 'Unfortunately, the company's leaders at the time were not similarly reinvented, as their failure to invest sufficiently in the core business revealed. Sustaining the company's momentum in the 1990s, therefore, has become a challenging task.' In fact, Ford's performance in Europe slipped back badly into losses:

in contrast, General Motors' business flourished, even though
Ford's American operations were showing GM a clean pair of
heels. The total quality ethos is right: you can never afford to
let up, anywhere, anyhow, or for any length of time.

That's why all the successful TQM efforts we visited were
distinguished, not by the words in the statements, but by the
personal commitment of the leaders to the vision. Their styles
differed markedly, but men as disparate as Churchill, Sir Iain
Vallance of British Telecom, Dennis Kennedy of Honeywell UK
and Bernard Fournier of Rank Xerox share the ability to keep
their sights on the long-range vision while mastering the detailed
work that alone turns vision into action. Measurement, meetings,
training, tools, techniques, etc. make the total quality life total
indeed.

Staying number one

The sporting analogy is obvious. The vision is lofty and
inspiring and long-range – like making the final of a rugby World
Cup years ahead, or winning gold at the next Olympics but two.
But achieving the vision rests on long hours of arduous training
and practice, on the effort to achieve continuous improvement,
on surviving challenge and difficulty, on being prepared to
endure and respond to criticism. That doesn't sound much
fun, but neither does losing. Strong vision statements are about
winning, about becoming and staying number one; significantly,
Honeywell was that, in nearly all its markets, when Kennedy
launched his total quality drive – with the object of staying
on top.

In other words, the vision has to be focused on results – not
just any results, but those which will take a particular company
forward into a better and brighter future. Many vision statements
fall at this hurdle. They are interchangeable, not only between
companies in the same industry, but between industries. We
have even come across major companies whose vision statements
were entrusted to their public-relations advisers. The ideal vision

should be short, sharp, to the point – something (like fast-food chain Taco Bell's aim 'to be number one in share of stomach') that everybody in the business can grasp.

Moreover, the object of the vision is to set the scene for changes in behaviour that will achieve the mission. At NatWest Life, a top insider claims that 'people don't walk away from difficult issues': that 'the flat structure' – only three layers, compared to a dozen in the parent bank – means that 'you can cut across more easily from function to function'; that 'jobs are larger – you are empowered, no doubt about it'. People are aware that 'it's very important to correct glitches quickly' and to get rapid answers to 'whether it's OK to do XYZ'.

All that doesn't make jobs less onerous. On the contrary, people whose jobs have genuinely been enlarged, and who now have total responsibility for a whole process instead of only part of it, may well feel a heavier weight on their shoulders. That was the case in another life-insurance company. Yet when staff were asked whether they wanted to return to the previous method of working, the answer was an unequivocal no. 'Living the vision' is thus not something confined to managers: indeed, the vision won't be realised unless people right down the organisation feel that they are part of turning dream into reality.

It would be easy to dismiss NatWest Life as a one-off, operating in a special set of circumstances, adopting unusual ideas to confound the critics who thought 'we couldn't do it'. But Churchill goes on to stress that the quality processes which his managers put in place were 'all things they had to have anyway'. All companies have at least some vague, unarticulated idea of purpose and role, and all these organisations consist of systems and processes. The total quality companies choose articulation and ambition and they adapt their processes in order to realise their expressed, understood and shared aims.

It isn't an easy option, and it doesn't guarantee victory. Of the dozen TQM companies we studied in depth, two have serious business problems, and a couple more are plainly under-performing by their own standards. Sometimes, failures of ownership contribute to disappointments (for instance, when companies are under obstructive state control); often, leadership is at fault. But the principles of the start-up that started right can't be gainsaid. More than that, realising visions keeps you in start-up mode all your life.

3

Closing the Management Gap

For every business and every manager, there is nearly always a distance between 'where we are' and 'where we want to be'. It's the crucial divide in management, and you won't cross it without closing the management gap between what needs to be done and actually doing it. It's a more complex process than it sounds. You must first be sure where you are. Then you choose your destination – your vision. Then you must work out the route, and how to check progress all the way. Then comes the really difficult part: doing it.

The ambitious athlete holds obvious advantages over the manager at every stage. For a start, the athlete's ambitions, and thus the performance gap, are much easier to define. When Brian Lara asserted his claim to be the world's most successful batsman, clear targets were involved: among them, the largest Test innings and the first first-class innings to pass 500. But when British Petroleum announced its intention to be 'the world's most successful oil company in the 1990s and beyond', what did that vision mean? In many fields outside sports, success is an elusive concept at the best of times. It is especially hard to pin down in business management.

True, business generates more statistics even than American football, where every move in a fast-moving game is calibrated.

Just as the ultimate statistic on the gridiron is that of touchdowns
and goal-kicks, so in business the ultimate measure is money.
That sounds simple enough: the more money you make, in
relation to the opposition, the more successful you are – just
like the team that scores more points. Unfortunately, this doesn't
resolve the business issue. What's the right measure of money?

How should ambition be scored? Is it the absolute amount
of profit, the percentage return on assets or sales, or growth
in turnover, or the increase in earnings per share, or the
rise in the shares themselves, or the advance in shareholders'
equity? Or what? Whatever the choice, it's clear that financial
numbers alone are neither the be-all nor the end-all. 'Best',
as in sport, refers to quality as well as quantity: the quality of
corporate performance outranks quantity, just as the long term
must outweigh the short.

When a company has been losing money for five consecutive
years (averaging about a billion dollars a year), you would expect
financial considerations to dominate its strategy. Making a return
to profits was indeed very important to Digital Equipment in
January 1994, when Vincenzo Damiani arrived to head its
European operations after twenty-nine years with IBM, where
he ended up as general manager of marketing and services for
Europe. He was hailed by the *Wall Street Journal* as someone who
'spurns vision'. The new man, however, instantly drew up 'the
Damiani agenda', a succinct one-pager which wasn't financially
oriented at all. It stated baldly that:

(1) The overall goal is SATISFIED CUSTOMERS.
(2) The focus is on leadership and management actions.
(3) Three objectives and ten action points form the nucleus.

The three objectives were to create sustainable growth, 'increase
efficiency and optimise customer-focused management systems
and processes'. To reach Objective One, Digital would:

(1) Focus on small to medium-sized customers.

  (2) Team up with partners and develop alliances.
  (3) Optimise new opportunities for services and consulting.
  (4) Develop specific industry and product markets.
  (5) Improve distribution capability and market coverage.
  (6) Increase marketing and selling competence.

Objective Two would require:

  (7) Optimum sizing of organisation and reduction of organisational structures.
  (8) Consolidation of support activities.

Finally, to satisfy Objective Three, Digital would:

  (9) Focus on processes and process ownership.
  (10) Show leadership, communicate more, and more efficiently.

To us, that agenda fits all the criteria for a vision statement. Damiani chose the destination, mapped out the route, and left nobody in any doubt over what was required. Most of that requirement was practical and measurable. But note that the words 'money' and 'profit' don't occur anywhere in the agenda.

Those words are, of course, implicit. Satisfy the customers, sustain growth, increase efficiency and optimise your processes, and if you don't make profits, you must be in the wrong business. One of Britain's most 'successful' managers, monetarily speaking, once rightly told us that profit wasn't his corporate objective: profit was the reward for doing the right things in the right way. More recently, the same super-manager had changed his mind, or at least his tune: now profit was the aim. It may be a coincidence, but his group's financial performance has deteriorated since he correctly saw profit as the reward for success, not as the proper ambition in itself.

'Profit is a result rather than a goal'

The great Konosuke Matsushita, founder of the world's largest electrical group, never changed his mind: he maintained a famous corporate philosophy around the earlier concept that 'profit is a result rather than a goal':

Profit comes in compensation for contribution to society. Profit is a yardstick with which to measure the degree of social contribution made by an enterprise ... If the enterprise tries to earn a reasonable profit but fails to do so, the reason is because the degree of social contribution is still insufficient.

That quote introduces two other notions of success: social contribution and 'reasonable profit'. Many businessmen will deny that profit can ever be 'unreasonable'. Their reaction was once epitomised by a *New Yorker* cartoon character, shown telling an equally hard-jawed manager: 'I've been in this company man and boy for forty years, and I've yet to see an excess return on capital.' But plainly excess can exist: and excess may well not mean success. Overcharge for a monopoly product, for example, and the competition attracted may well reduce the excess profit to rubble.

Not only is profit alone inadequate as an objective: many companies don't pursue it anyway. Some years back, a comprehensive study of printing companies divided them into successes and failures, using every possible criterion to separate the sheep from the goats. The differences between the two were stark on every issue of strategy and tactics, none more so than on the central matter of ambition. Asked if they aimed at continuity, profit or growth, 53 per cent of the failures plumped for the first, only 4 per cent for profit, and just 14 per cent for growth. The successes plumped equally for profit and growth at 46 per cent apiece. Note that the figures of the failures fall far short of 100: 19 per cent of the relative flops had no objectives at all. You succeed in winning continuity by driving for and achieving profitable growth. But that achievement rests, in the spirit of Matsushita, on aiming to do the right things in the right way.

This simple formula has become enshrined in what can appear to be a complex business: the total quality discussed in the previous section. This measures success, not in financial terms (although the financial consequences are formidable), but in many ways, led by customer satisfaction and absence of defects. Quality is about unceasing improvement on these and other scores. Leading quality companies devote enormous energy to achieving tiny gains in figures that are already highly impressive.

Thus Motorola's five-year programme for reducing defects in its electronics business by 90 per cent by 1986 was followed by seeking the same 90 per cent improvement by 1989 and again by 1991, with a 'six-sigma' target for 1992 (that means at most 3.4 failures per million parts). Getting to 99.9997 per cent of perfection is assuredly another measure of success, more accurate and more specific than most money measures, but also truly lucrative. The difference between that and 99 per cent quality, or 10 defectives out of 1,000 products, may sound very little: but eliminating nine of the faulty fellows, if the profit margin is 10 per cent, will increase profits by a tenth.

Ambition is doing the right things better

What is more, achieving this success will demand a whole chain of other successes, leading all the way back to design. The 'total' in total quality takes this driving idea through to every activity in a company, from technical manuals and answering phones to internal audits and innovation. Ambition is thus defined as doing the right things better, and then improving all over again. It's a concept with which all players in all sports are deeply familiar. However good you are, the PB (personal best) can always be improved, and only as a result of a chain of progress in technique and application.

Total quality management can be seen as a series of PBs, specific and measurable ambitions for every process and department in the company, which continuously saves time and money by reaching consistently higher standards. This is essentially project-based work, and success in projects need have no financial dimension (other than keeping within budget). Finding a new oilfield, bringing it on-stream, getting the oil to market – these are technical and logistic operations of the highest order, whose completion to plan is unquestionably 'success' and fulfilment of high ambition.

The crucial words are 'to plan'. In life as a whole, some successes are essentially unplanned, or at least unpredictable: a gambling win, buying a grimy old engraving that proves to be a Rembrandt, backing a friend whose company becomes a Klondike. But in both sport and business management, while luck plays its part, it comes most often, as the French philosopher Pascal wrote, to the 'prepared mind'. Being dropped, like Lara, at 19 is luck: going on to score a quintuple century is not. The perfect bounce of an elliptical rugby ball into your hands in the perfect scoring position is luck, but what took you into that position?

In oil and mining, outstanding exploration records are created not just by good fortune, but by experience, expertise and that essential concentration of mind to which Pascal referred. Planned success, though, doesn't mean the exact fulfilment of a predetermined strategic ambition. That rarely happens, in life, sport or business. It means the achievement of predetermined objectives along lines decided in advance, but modified, along with the aims if necessary, as events dictate.

In any good business, at all times, multitudinous lesser aims are being pursued in this methodical way in all of its thousands of operations. That's the essence of TQM, as noted. But the lesson of great success is that these subordinate aims are much more likely to be realised in the context of an overall, unifying thrust:

that vision which is the theme of this chapter. You can call this an ambition, or the focal point of a value system, or whatever you wish. But without this guiding light, companies more easily get lost in the dark.

When the sceptical, or often the neutral, observer looks at the usual business terminology – like that used in the vision statements mentioned previously – the reaction is to query the worth of mere words. It's easy to talk about being 'best', or to specify responsibilities to employees, customers, suppliers, the community and shareholders. Credos, written statements of values, differ from company to company, but they mostly strike the same note: and it's plainly a 'soft' note as opposed to the 'hard' language of profits or defects per million parts.

Thus BP believes 'in continually developing a style and climate which liberates the talents and enthusiasm of all our people'. That is in complete harmony with jeans-maker Levi Strauss, whose 'aspirations statement' says: 'We all want a company that our people are proud of and committed to, where all employees have an opportunity to contribute, learn, grow and advance . . .' What do such qualitative sentiments have to do with the crucial matter of quantified ambitions and results? A great deal, according to facts reported in the *Harvard Business Review*. It found that US companies which had lived by written value statements for a generation had grown thirty-two times faster than the gross domestic product.

The Levi Strauss record stresses the point: from 1985 to 1989, profits rose fivefold. More importantly, however, the company, which had gone astray in a brief period under public ownership, had recaptured its sense of purpose; it had redefined its ambitions and had turned the new words into successful deeds. Public ownership need be no obstacle to such success. Value-driven companies as different as Marks & Spencer in British retailing and Hewlett-Packard in American electronics have satisfied both shareholders and the corporate conscience for many years.

The quality process known as 'benchmarking' holds the secret:

if each aspect of its operations equals or betters the standards of the best competitor, a company is well on the way to an objective which all organisations can share – to lead its competitors or counterparts on economic return to shareholders or their equivalent and on everything else. In fact, the evidence indicates that those companies which rank the interests of shareholders no higher than those of employees and customers far outdo others – from the *shareholders'* viewpoint.

Sportsmen know the same phenomenon, best expressed in the Zen approach to sports, which emphasises total relaxation as well as total concentration. By the same token, 'trying too hard' is a sure way to drop the ball or miss the pot – remember the great Steve Davis missing the simple black that would have won his World Snooker final against Dennis Taylor, certainly a lesser player. Staying on top is always tough, even for a champion of champions. It's a tremendous challenge, that vision: 'to lead competitors on economic return to shareholders and on everything else'.

Completing so ambitious a journey, though, depends on something else: not only doing things right, but doing the right things. The strategic platform is necessarily decisive: choices like where to invest, or where to disinvest, determine the possibility of ultimate success or failure. Thus Vincenzo Damiani's agenda for Digital in Europe, powerful though it is, can succeed only if the company has chosen the right strategic stance – switching from being a supplier of mini-computers to a company whose future revolves around networking micro-processors.

There's a direct analogy with individuals. Chris Brasher was an ordinary middle-distance runner. Switching to the steeplechase, he won Olympic gold. Companies whose vision is focused on the wrong strategic objectives – like the insurance companies and building societies which weirdly believed that part of their futures lay in estate agency – won't win any gold. Likewise, individual managers who choose the wrong career in the wrong company are most unlikely to succeed by any standards, no matter how much effort goes into their work.

Success means working more effectively

Successful, ambitious companies with clear visions need successful, ambitious people who can live the vision for both the business and themselves and who can see that the two go hand in hand. That principle was enshrined for forty years in the teaching of the late American management expert W. Edwards Deming. From his brilliant work in statistical quality control, he observed that successful operations result not from working harder, but from working more effectively. That in turn was primarily the result not of individual efforts, but of the system in which the individuals worked. Group success won by raising the performance of the system automatically increased the success of the group's members.

The analogy with sports teams is self-evident. Buying an expensive star won't make a bad soccer team good, but a good side which has a shared vision of excellent performance, and knows how to achieve it, turns mediocre players into star performers. This importance of group vision doesn't diminish the role of the individual, but enhances it. A system in which individuals can correct defects and suggest improvements in everything – including the vision and its fulfilment – will have higher performance and more satisfied, better-motivated people, than one in which they are confined to obeying orders from on high.

The Deming philosophy hinges on releasing the initiative and ability of individuals to perform better, and to go on raising their game – in short, to make progress, a word which conveys the essence of true success and the power of true vision. The most successful company is the one that has made the most progress along the most ambitiously chosen paths. And the same definition applies to the most successful individual.

Not everyone can come first, but anyone can advance closer and closer to important goals and, having reached them, can pitch their vision higher still. Again, total quality provides a telling metaphor. For companies and individuals, success can never be total, for progress can always be made. There will always be a gap between the vision and realisation, as between potential and performance. This concept of the management gap is basic, but the process of closing it is equally fundamental.

The fact that the gap never closes entirely, and that execution seldom, if ever, reaches perfection, only sets the stage for new ambitions. Vision not only always looks ahead, but moves ahead as circumstances change and landmarks are passed. The higher the aim, however, the greater progress and success are likely to be – and that applies on any measure.

II

Self-Belief – How to Believe in Yourself

4

Daley Thompson's Tenfold Triumphs

'I always thought I was going to be the best at something one day,' says Daley Thompson.

I've even asked people I used to go to school with, and they would say, 'God, you used to go on about yourself and tell us how good you were and how good you were going to be.' So I always thought I was going to be really good at something, but I just never really knew what it was, until I was about nine or ten, and then I started wanting to be a footballer.

Then for some reason I went to my local athletics club, basically to get fit to go on tour to play football in Holland for a couple of weeks. I had a really good time and when we came back from the tour I went back to my athletics club. After about a month it never occurred to me that I ever wanted to play football again. So after five or six years of wanting to be a footballer, the next day all I ever wanted to be was an athlete.

Thompson adds wrily: 'I've only ever wanted to be two things in my life, but I've done them backwards, because I'm nearly a footballer now!' He is without doubt the most successful all-round athlete the world has ever seen and also one of the most confident people you could ever meet. But it soon becomes apparent that Thompson approaches life from an angle that differs completely from the typical human attitude.

His *raison d'être*, as he says, was to be the best at something; the best in the world. He believed that he could achieve this end because of the crucial difference in his whole thought process. Even among all the famous people he has met in sport, none, Thompson maintains, has quite matched his own self-belief. There was nothing he held to be beyond his capabilities, given a bit of practice. As he says, 'Obviously I'm never going to be the fastest runner in the world, but I'll have a very good go at it.'

The difference in his mental approach comes down to the viewpoint 'that I'm good at it until proved otherwise'. Most people, he believes, approach things from the opposite end, feeling that they're probably not going to be very good and hoping for a lucky surprise. That fundamental difference in mind-set has been with Thompson as long as he can remember. Approaching everything you take on in the confident belief that you will excel is very different from the way in which most people face challenges.

The majority feel trepidation: they are uncertain about how they are going to cope, and almost certainly they have very little confidence in their ability relative to the opposition. Most people can recall lining up for an athletics event when young, or taking the field with a team, already convinced that the opposition was either bigger, or stronger, or faster, and most certainly better. Very few youngsters take the field in any competitive event believing that they will convincingly beat all comers.

Success reinforces success

Daley's great innate ability, of course, made it easy for him to best the competition in his younger years. He remembers all his successes, and how success reinforced success. Probably more importantly, if he was beaten – and he concedes that he may well have lost sometimes – he doesn't remember the defeats. He recalls only the positive experiences; always, a failure or a defeat would have been registered, learned from and then forgotten. Defeat never preyed on his mind, as happens with many people, inside and outside sport.

Thompson recognises his abnormal talent, of course, but contends that he has competed against and beaten people who possessed greater natural gifts. True, he is also fanatically determined: but again, he thinks there are people (though it isn't easy to believe him) who are more determined still. But Thompson is adamant that nobody he has ever met beats him on both counts. It is the *combination* of ability and determination that creates unbeatable self-belief.

Daley Thompson fell into his event, the decathlon, as casually as he entered athletics. He was already one of Britain's best junior sprinters when his club went to a competition in Wales and found itself one short for a decathlon. One of Thompson's coaches asked if he would make up the numbers. Thompson had done the high jump that morning, and the long jump, he'd run the 100 metres, so that was half the first day gone. Did he fancy having a go at the other seven events?

Thompson is one of those who will always say, 'Yes, I'll have a go at anything.' He was then sixteen years old. He and his coach in those days, Bob Morton, still meet and talk about football, in much the same way as they used to talk about athletics. Having stumbled into the decathlon, Thompson realised almost immediately that the event was what he'd always been looking for. His astonishing record of success thereafter proves abundantly that he made the right choice. But was his confidence always so supreme?

We were convinced that, somewhere along the line, he must have faced self-doubt, however briefly. Daley, though, is adamant that, even the night before a crucial competition, he never had any doubts. But there was always a point, he confesses, usually a couple of weeks or maybe a couple of months before, when one day his training would go badly awry; when nothing would seem to go right; when for one reason or another he just wasn't in the mood.

Those are the moments which, for many people, lead to panic or self-doubt. Not for Thompson. He says that he merely walked away, knowing that, the next day or the one after, he would return to training and everything would come right again. He would be back into his winning frame of mind. And he never had sleepless nights. What he did have, always, was the anticipation – 'I couldn't wait to get out there; it couldn't come quickly enough for me. I just loved it. I loved the moment where you had to put it on the line.'

He is emphatic that this is 'the best thing in the world for me. If you told me to get ready to do some sit-ups in a year's time, I couldn't wait for the day to come and give it a go, just to see.' He didn't 'care about winning or losing'. He only wanted to know if he could achieve what was asked of him. 'That was

Daley Thompson takes off towards another Gold Medal –
Los Angeles Olympics, 1984.

it – I loved the moment. The moment is the thing for me.' As he discusses the subject, in a T-shirt, over lunch, his arms develop goose-bumps. 'There, you see,' he says, pointing at the arms, 'even the thought of it still brings me out in goose-bumps; even the thought of competition fills me with adrenaline!'

The recurring theme with Thompson, as with all great achievers, is preparation. His training programmes are legendary. Frank Dick, the former British athletics team coach, and Bruce Longdon (who now coaches Sally Gunnell, the 400-metre hurdles gold-medallist) put together Thompson's training. As he remembers, it was very well constructed, but enormous in sheer volume. He used to train for five or six hours a day. Not that he minded – as he says, he had nothing else to do.

What he enjoyed, though, was the challenge: doing all the work one day, coming back exhausted the next, but giving it another go all over again. He wanted to ensure that he trained more than anyone else. As he says, athletes will never give away their training secrets, and nobody would expect them to. But one stimulus that spurred on Thompson to train three times a day was his belief that everyone else would train only twice, or even just once. He aimed to get in at least half an hour more work than everybody else. Daley even used to train on Christmas Day, but not for a single session – he trained twice, just in case one of his competitors had also decided to train on that holiday. 'If I trained twice, I would still know that I was up on them.' His main competitor, the German Jürgen Hingsen, was so close to Thompson in ability that only three points separated their best decathlon scores – the equivalent of a hundredth of a second in the 100 metres. Yet even though there was so little between them, Thompson always won, and he asserts that it was purely for mental reasons.

Mind-power applied in two ways. First, he always trained harder: that was the basis for believing that he would be mentally stronger, secure in the knowledge that he was better prepared, fitter, and physically stronger, if only fractionally. Second, Hingsen would know that the Briton was always in the best possible shape on the day of competition – and Thompson always reckoned that this placed immense pressure on his opponent. Hingsen would realise that he had to perform to his absolute best simply to stand a chance.

So surely Hingsen would feel the same way? Wouldn't he have been training as hard as he could? Wouldn't he have thought likewise – that Thompson would have to be in the best possible shape even to have a chance? The questions produce a slow smile across Thompson's face. 'I've always come from the positive side, and his best was still not good enough for me.' You might read this self-belief as sheer loudmouthed arrogance, but when we looked behind the bravado at the training, the mental logic became apparent.

Thompson maintains that he trained too hard to get things wrong. Training those two or three times a day, he might be getting in 2,000 javelin throws a month. Basically, he would go through exactly the same routine with his throwing, which is why he trained so much. He wanted to ingrain everything into his training, so that 'I could do it almost with my eyes closed, and it would always get to an acceptable level' – so that his worst performance would always be good enough.

The target in Thompson's training was higher still: to make his worst better than anyone else's best – and he believed that it nearly always was. On all his ten events, hours and hours were spent to make sure that, even under the most intense pressure, his performance would remain almost instinctive. The programme was highly structured so that he could peak at the moment that meant the most to him – the Olympic Games. World records, he maintains, were almost irrelevant, but not quite. The Olympics were the spur. It's almost a level playing field – everyone knows that, in four years' time to the exact day, he or she has to produce his or her best. To structure your training and your life, to overcome all the barriers and the problems that present themselves along the way, and then to prove yourself the best in the world, is to Daley Thompson the ultimate challenge.

Thompson won his first gold medal at the 1980 Olympics, but carried on in the belief that he had barely scratched the surface of his potential, and could do very much better. Even now, in retirement, that's his frustration: in his total self-confidence, he feels that he never realised his full potential, never performed as well as possible. Having to carry injuries was the big disappointment that stopped him from achieving the supreme decathlon performance, the best of which he was capable.

He competed in his first Olympics in 1976, at seventeen, only a year after that first chance entry in the event. He came eighteenth. On the day he returned home, Thompson wrote in his diary that in 1980 he would get an Olympic medal – possibly gold; in 1984 and 1988, however, he would definitely win. The man who thus reckoned to achieve up to three Olympic decathlons won only two, and for Thompson that isn't enough. He still maintains that he could have done better.

Like all great champions, Thompson competed above all with himself. He knew that, with his basic capability, he would always be among the first four. Performing reasonably well, he was certain of a place in the first two. But 99 times out of 100, he knew, he would be first. He was obsessed with striving for perfection. Competitors became almost irrelevant compared to this effort to achieve the perfect decathlon. 'Perfect' is the man's own honest analysis of his true potential.

Compared to that, even the crowd was unimportant. As Daley says, the people watching couldn't make him try any harder. 'I only have one gear, and that's 100 per cent – that's all I've got. What you see is what I have. It was too important for me to worry about a crowd.' So what would have happened if he had lost the Olympics? 'It wouldn't have happened.' He came only fourth in 1988: 'I got hurt and I had a bad leg, and I came in fourth. But for me it was no big deal, because I was only 150 points off winning, which is nothing. I could have done that.'

The philosophy of confidence

Thompson therefore 'never had any problem' with the 1988 defeat. It didn't disturb his overall philosophy of confidence. 'It never occurred to me that I would ever lose anything. I had come from the other way round' – from total confidence in victory – 'I had lost because I was injured.' By 1992, circumstances had changed irrevocably: 'I was an old man.' The confidence, however, was irrepressible: he still thought he might have won it.

That may chime oddly with his statement that: 'I have always been really positive, or mostly realistic, about whether or not I can win things.' For right to the end, there was no 'whether or not': Thompson always thought he could win. Part of the reason is that throughout his athletic career, 'I hardly ever messed up a competition.' As noted earlier, that didn't apply to training, which he 'messed up loads of times, because you have down days and off days'. Down or off, though, 'you've still got to put in some time and still try to do it well'.

Thompson remembers: 'There were just days when I couldn't throw, and things just weren't happening. Then you just cut your losses and hope that it's going to be better the next day. I always knew it would be.' That encapsulates a vital truth about self-belief. It isn't just conceit: beneath all the confidence lay Thompson's crucial ability to analyse, with total honesty, exactly what he could do. His normal standard was best in the world. On the rare occasions when he did lose, he knew why. There were no excuses, just cold, hard facts which had to be understood and accepted.

His self-belief was unaffected because, in the final analysis, he only set himself achievable goals: they tested him to the very limit, but never exceeded the bounds of a capability which he always knew exactly. To Thompson, athletes who are full of doubt – and he has come across them all the time – are a puzzle. To his mind, provided that you have a certain level of talent and put in the requisite work, your performance will match your ability. You have to be realistic about whether the best of your ability is good enough for a medal or some lower ranking. If you are honest, and achieve that level – the best of your ability – you should never lose confidence.

Another puzzle to Thompson is why athletes get so wound up over their performance on the day of competition. That, he believes, should be the easiest day. 'Because if you're doing 5,000 throws in training, three during the competition should be easy. You should look forward to doing three, because you should be able to do three good ones, instead of having to go through the repeat, repeat, repeat of training.'

As he recalls, 'That was so boring – but, importantly, it enabled me not to have to worry on the day.' He could enjoy the competition, 'because I knew I had put the work in'. Unlike most competitors, Thompson couldn't wait to get out on the field. He loved playing, loved the competition, loved the tests which showed whether he could 'push the envelope' a little bit further. The vital point is that they were tests, not of his self-belief, but of his capability. Confidence helps you to make the most of your talents. Self-doubt causes you to under-perform – and that Daley Thompson never did.

5

The Transformation of Glaxo

There aren't many candidates for the title of Britain's greatest post-war corporate success, but Glaxo would certainly figure on everybody's short-list – almost entirely because of the explosive change in its performance from the start of the 1980s. Nothing in Glaxo's earlier record prepared outsiders for the surge in profits and growth. Although the company was reasonably well positioned in the world's most profitable industry, pharmaceuticals, it seemed, along with the great majority of large UK manufacturers, to lack the vision and self-belief required to make the world its oyster.

As the architect of Glaxo's transformation, Sir Paul Girolami, has observed: 'What was missing through the greater part of Glaxo's history was a global strategy.' Oriented, like its peers, to the narrow British market, Glaxo started its wonderful eighties with pre-tax profits, at £87 million, that were unchanged from four years previously, even though sales had risen by nearly half. In the next five years, amazingly, sales doubled to £1.4 billion while profits multiplied seven times to £612 million.

Both the rate of expansion and the profitability (55 per cent on net capital employed) were probably without any parallel for a large British company – and the surge continued. By 1993–4 Glaxo was turning over £5.6 billion, on which it made a stunning

£1.84 billion of profit, a return on sales of a truly remarkable 32 per cent. The key to this magnificent performance was a single product: the drug ranitidine, marketed under the name Zantac, an extraordinarily effective treatment for ulcers and other gastro-intestinal disorders.

Zantac is a triumph of research and marketing. But Girolami, the chairman from 1985 and before that chief executive from 1980, is neither pharmaceutical expert nor marketing man. An LSE graduate born in 1926, he qualified as an accountant in 1953 and joined Cooper Brothers when it was just setting up in management consultancy. Girolami was a founder member, becoming a director when the consultancy was turned into a separate company. As a consultant, he worked in many industries and companies, including heavy engineering, oil exploration and textiles.

His first role on joining Glaxo in 1965, however, was that of financial controller. This involved introducing electronic data-processing and initiating and developing systems for financial and budgetary control, planning and management information which were still current many years later. In 1968, appointed as Glaxo's first financial director, Girolami began to widen his sphere of operation outside finance, getting deeply involved in the crucial defence of Glaxo against a bid from Beechams in 1972.

He also played a key role in developing many of the overseas interests. In the late 1970s, Girolami bought Meyer Laboratories in the US, and turned it into Glaxo, Inc. In what turned out to be a master-stroke, however, Glaxo entrusted the initial American marketing of Zantac to a joint operation with a rival whose presence in the marketplace was far larger – the US subsidiary of the Swiss giant Hoffmann La Roche. Zantac could thus be promoted immediately by a sales force matching the US majors in size at a time when Glaxo, Inc. was still in the early stages of development.

A great strategic shift meant that virtually all of Glaxo's sales would come from pharmaceuticals. Previously, if wholesaling is

included, the proportion had been only half. Half the sales had
been made in the UK, too; in ten years, the ratio fell to 15
per cent. Research spending over the same decade quadrupled.
The most vital statistic, though, is that for anti-ulcerants. From
contributing nothing to sales, they rose in the eighties to a
stunning 43 per cent.

Girolami emphasises that Glaxo's underlying strengths have
long existed: a fundamental commitment to research and development, and also a vague yearning for international expansion.
But 'that aspect was very much within blinkers'. When he first
joined the group, the blinkers meant that managers saw only
the Commonwealth. 'The rest were "foreigners" whom you
had to treat rather carefully before you ventured – and there
was a positive hostility shown towards the States and Japan.
However, the germs of internationalism were there, and so was
this commitment to technology.'

Girolami's ambition was to inject two or three additional

Sir Paul Girolami, architect of Glaxo's transformation.

constituents 'which would turn this basic element into a very dynamic force'. The first element follows from deciding, as you must in true internationalism, to engage in all major markets, despite their differences, difficulties and risks; you have to have the self-confidence to do it yourself, not just through agents or exports. That meant 'setting ourselves up as a company taking on local colours and tackling that market as a national. Very difficult, but that's what we did.'

The second element also requires great self-confidence – answering the question, what are we trying to do? What is Glaxo? The management asked, was it milk, or babies, or surgical instruments, or genetics? Or all these? 'We emerged from this, rightly or wrongly (and I think very much rightly), saying: no, we want a specific objective, we address all our resources to a high-quality business.' That was pharmaceuticals. Girolami was backing Glaxo's ability to compete in one of the most competitive markets against some of the world's most competitive companies.

The third important element was the organisation of the group around a single purpose. Geographically, Glaxo covers the whole world. 'We've developed by trial and error into a flexible organisation which somehow combines local initiative, local control and good local management with a central leadership and direction.' Girolami thinks it was this combination of two latent forces – research strength and internationalism – with the new, concentrated strategic direction that gave the group its dynamic impetus.

Zantac, which transformed Glaxo's fortunes, was a result of the first latent force, 'our continuing commitment' to R&D. But Zantac wouldn't have had its sensational effect without the simultaneous self-belief in terms of international expansion. 'If we hadn't, before Zantac was taken in, decided to go hell-for-leather into the American market and to tackle the Japanese market and to put all the strength behind the European market, that product would have been a flop.' American companies would have taken out licences, and Glaxo would have earned only slim royalties.

Products don't sell themselves

Billion-dollar products like Zantac aren't given their commercial success 'by just producing a good product in the laboratory'.
That's the starting point. 'But many starting points finish where
they start. Any good product which makes money doesn't sell
itself' – a vital principle which nobody at Glaxo was allowed to
forget. Girolami's people were told that they had to sell and sell
hard, because otherwise the product would not meet its targets,
however good it was.

Glaxo had always been 'a very good marketing company'.
Its origins, unusually enough, lay in New Zealand, where the
original firm made and marketed baby food. The marketing
tradition survived all the subsequent expansion and change.
Although that didn't make all Glaxo companies equally good in
the marketplace, Glaxo has always, Girolami believes, 'produced
examples of the very best marketing in this pharmaceutical area.
We've known how to market products for a long, long time. The
answer is team-work and a sense of direction and a determination
to make the most of what you've got.'

As Girolami has pointed out, there's a national message in
that analysis, and the message for other managements is also
very clear. 'I don't think we are any different from any other
industry, really. Though we strive to get a better product, the
fact of life is that we are not the only clever people in this world.
In fact, there are a hell of a lot of clever people.' While Zantac
was a cleverer product than the rival Tagamet from SmithKline,
which began the revolution in ulcer treatment, and profited
enormously thereby, Glaxo marketed the drug on its traditional
formula: 'You tend to rely on the fact that it is only marginally
better.'

If that's the case, 'this is where the whole process of marketing
comes in. You've got to price it right; you've got to use all the
management techniques employed by Glaxo, as by any other
successful company, to beat the competition.' In marketing,
self-confidence is pivotal, so that belief in the product can

be transferred from supplier to customer. With Zantac, Glaxo took a bold – and much-criticised – step. It priced the product significantly *above* the established leader – an act of faith in the superiority of the product.

The competition in pharmaceuticals, according to Girolami, 'isn't as nakedly in terms of price as in some industries, but price comes into it'. The Zantac strategy was thus doubly bold, and required heavy support from other elements in the marketing mix: 'quality and design and persuasion and team-work and meeting deliveries'. As Girolami once told *Management Today*, 'Innovation means introducing new products successfully in the marketplace,' and for that to happen, a 'flash of imagination' is required.

In the pharmaceutical industry, however, a flash of inspiration is required first: 'Scientific discovery is the condition precedent.' The discovery of ranitidine, though, wasn't of the same order of inspired breakthrough as Sir James Black's research, which produced cimetidine (Tagamet). As Dr David Jack, then Glaxo's research director, explained: 'Ranitidine was the result of a simple piece of applied medical chemistry. It's not necessary to shake the earth on its axis to make money in this industry. We simply improved on James Black's product by choosing a substance with a cleaner reaction.'

This 'simple' competitive thrust was made possible only by the expertise which Glaxo had developed in treating bronchial asthma. That all sounds perfectly straightforward, but concentrating on high-quality ethical drugs is necessarily a high-risk strategy. As Girolami noted, 'They are *sui generis*. They don't really have synergy with anything else.' All the eggs thus go in one strategic basket: the company is betting on the ability of its researchers to produce compounds that will provide more effective treatment without intolerable side-effects.

The bets, moreover, are gigantic, and mounting gigantically. In 1975, Glaxo spent only £12 million on research and development. By 1983, the spend had multiplied fivefold. But that £60 million, too, looks tiny compared with what was to come.

By 1990, spending had increased another seven times to £420 million. It has doubled since, to 15 per cent of turnover. Nor does this huge amount of money guarantee disproportionate success: as Dr Richard Sykes explained when he was research director, 'There is no straight correlation between the money spent and the number of products: it's not like sending a man to the moon.'

Girolami and Glaxo's self-belief was ultimately founded on people like Sykes, now chief executive, who took charge of research in 1988, having returned to Glaxo after a long spell with the Squibb Institute for Medical Research at Princeton. 'A good organisation, with good people and good science, attracts more: it's autocatalytic,' he told *Management Today*. That creates what's now called 'intellectual capital.' It's the only kind that truly counts for a pharmaceutical company, according to Girolami: 'The degree of profit is not a function of the capital put in.'

Rather, 'to a peculiarly high degree, profit is a return on people, intelligence, specialised knowledge'. As Zantac demonstrated so spectacularly, the return can be huge – for every 1 per cent rise in turnover, Glaxo at the peak was achieving a 2 per cent increase in profit, thanks to its thumping victory in the anti-ulcer wars. Its chief opponent, Henry Wendt, ex-chairman of SmithKline Beecham, blames this victory, and his defeat, on the battle of scientific intellect, not that of the marketeers:

Though I knew SmithKline could have improved many aspects of the marketing programme for Tagamet, it really lost the advantage to Glaxo in development. Glaxo won regulatory approval for a twice-daily dose of Zantac, in contrast to Tagamet's four-times-a-day dose, and at a lower overall total dose in milligrams. Physicians drew the obvious inference: Zantac appeared to be a more potent and longer-acting agent.'

In addition, the official labelling listed fewer side-effects for Zantac. However, in emphasising that 'Glaxo won the battle in development, long before its product appeared on the market', Wendt ('someone who was deeply involved in the struggle') was shifting the onus from the marketing and general management. It wasn't only that SmithKline 'could have improved many aspects of the marketing programme': generally, Wendt's management had simply crossed the narrow line between self-belief and complacency.

At the launch of Tagamet, the management had boldly taken huge risks, building a factory in Cork and a worldwide marketing programme before it could have any certainty of winning big. With the world's first billion-dollar drug under its belt, however, SmithKline reacted too slowly to threat. Apart from the small daily dosage, 'all Zantac's initial comparative advantages', wrote Wendt later, 'have largely disappeared as a result of the continuing clinical development.' But by that time, Zantac was outselling Tagamet by 2–1.

Lack of self-belief is doing too little, too late

Doing too little, too late is practically a definition of lack of self-belief. It was, alas, a characteristic of Britain in the days of what Girolami has called 'the old classical industrial establishments', which 'were brought up in the time when the markets were there, and they were theirs for the taking. The older generation lacks the element of competitiveness which is essential today.' However, 'the young people are much better', and part of Girolami's philosophy was to provide the younger Glaxo managers with the right environment:

> The manager of any business enterprise has to have a clear set of values which guides appropriate business action. He has to know the business, and to understand the direction in which he has to lead it. He has, moreover, to have a profound sense of commitment, loyalty to the enterprise, and a capacity for hard work. Finally, he has to be able to act

decisively whenever the occasion demands it – even if, as is
so often the case, the elements for rational decision-making
are absent.

This philosophy was reflected at Glaxo by what looks like a
looser system than the American model, with its tight controls
and dominating financial ratios. Investment, management and
product-marketing aren't placed in a straitjacket at Glaxo, which,
for all that, a rival told *Management Today*, 'is one of the best
organised in the world'. It takes a powerful and self-confident
organisation at the top to allow powerful and self-confident
action lower down.

The emphasis, to quote Girolami, has to lie 'on leadership
and quality of management rather than central authority and
command'. It is 'trust and partnership', not 'bureaucratic control', that allow self-belief to flourish in a company. The logic of
this approach is even stronger in an international operation like
Glaxo's than in a purely national business because 'the ability to
apply management qualities to two or more different national
markets . . . calls for a style of management which is at least one
stage removed from direct control . . . which demands an ability
to combine command with delegation'.

In the transformation of Glaxo, the switch to true multi-
nationalism was crucial, especially the decision to become a
major player in the great American market for ethical pharmaceuticals. A few other companies had pointed the way, notably
Beechams in toiletries, under the leadership of Leslie Lazell
(ironically, having merged with SmithKline, Beechams is now
the owner of Tagamet). Like Lazell, Girolami saw that to compete
with the Americans in your domestic market, you had to match
them on their home ground. 'In the pharmaceutical industry I
would fear American competition more than any other, because
they have a very dynamic, scientific approach to life.' Glaxo's
record, though, has amply supported Girolami's belief that 'our
managers are as knowledgeable as the Americans'. The latter's
different management style – 'tough, rough, used to competition'

– poses a greater challenge than their know-how, but the challenge isn't what matters: it's rising to it that counts. 'In the end, we have to measure ourselves against the Americans.'

By any measure, Girolami's company had passed all its tests when he retired as chairman – except for that of achieving an untroubled succession: a messy process of trial and error preceded Sykes' appointment. He faced tough tasks: Glaxo, like all pharmaceutical companies, is now operating in a harsher, intrinsically less profitable climate. But the Girolami legacy consists of enormous resources, both tangible and intangible. That doesn't just mean patents and the scientific brain-power that created them. 'It demands a hell of a lot more than brains to run a company. Brains is one element, sometimes not even a necessary element.' What is truly necessary is what, perhaps above all, Girolami brought to the feast: self-belief.

6

If At First You Do Succeed . . .

What gives people the confidence to get things right? Getting things right does that. It sounds like a tautology, but mastering all elements of the system and self-mastery go hand in hand. What achieves mastery, though? According to one forthright prediction, 'The most successful corporation of the 1990s will be something called a learning organisation, a consummately adaptive enterprise.' That quotation comes from a magazine, *Fortune*, but it's based on the preachings of management gurus who are now demanding that business organisations join them in education itself.

The concept is nothing new. It's the foundation of success in sport. The great champion is at once master and pupil, giving lessons to others and learning himself from both experience and coaches. That applies to individual sports like golf or tennis, where Stefan Edberg, for example, was coached to two Wimbledon titles by his British coach, Tony Pickard. It's equally important in a team sport like rugby of both codes, where the top players of the day – like the massed superstars of Bath or Wigan – will take instruction and instructions from coaches whose own playing careers have been far less distinguished.

Most managers will pay tribute to a mentor or mentors who helped develop their skills and their self-belief. But it's a far cry from that to the learning organisation, in which managers are expected to coach as well as play. As usual, the trend was first signalled by Peter Drucker, who spotted that information had replaced physical assets as the backbone of business. In today's competition, what you know determines what you can provide and sell, and how: therefore, the competitor who knows most, and who uses that knowledge most effectively, must win.

There are three stages in achieving victory. (1) Knowing what to do; (2) knowing how to do it; and (3) doing it – without which, of course, the knowledge of 'what' and 'how' is useless. Each of the stages hinges on self-belief: belief that you can master the subject or the sport, belief that you can apply that mastery in real-life situations, belief that you will succeed in its execution. Moreover, all three stages are informed by the belief that you can continuously improve, forever raising your game or your management performance.

Today information is constantly becoming outdated, so winners will update their knowledge continuously. Otherwise, the lead will be lost. This general truth is illustrated very specifically by the ups and downs of information technology, where knowledge differentials have precipitated rapid changes of leader in fields ranging all the way from spreadsheets to super-computers. This isn't just a question of technology: the power of learning affects every activity inside the company, and dominates its ability to succeed outside, in the marketplace, where the customers live.

The learning organisation

'Today leading firms seek to understand and meet the "latent need" of the customer – what customers might truly value but have never experienced and would never think to ask for.' Those words come from Peter Senge, the MIT professor who has become heavily identified with the concept of the learning organisation. However, he takes issue with the *Fortune* writer quoted earlier on one key word. Companies, says Senge, don't only need to be 'adaptive'. They must above all become 'generative'.

To illustrate the difference, he cites the comment of one Detroit executive on Mazda's fun sports car: 'You could never produce the Mazda Miata solely from market research. It required a leap of imagination to see what the customer *might* want.' That's an example of generative learning, in which the learner 'acquires new ways of looking at the world, whether in understanding customers or in understanding how to better manage a business'. Senge might have added that the learner must also acquire the self-belief needed to form and back an imaginative judgement.

By contrast, the adaptive learner essentially reacts to changing circumstances. Rather than strike out into new territory, the self-doubting adapter follows the crowd – often over the edge of the cliff. Many companies have flopped on that score, like the car-makers which utterly failed to compete with Japanese rivals who produced new models faster, cheaper and to far higher standards of quality, both in production and use. Now, of course, everybody left in car manufacture has adapted or is adapting: it's do or die. But the stable door is being shut well after the horse has bolted.

Manfred Perlitz of the University of Mannheim points out that Western adapters – and not just in cars – are busy winning the last war. The competitive race will now go not to the most efficient user of just-in-time, with the lowest rate of defects and the highest output per man-hour, but to the leaders in creativity. It is the same distinction that Senge makes – and so do the Japanese. They've even invented a perfectly awful word, 'creagement', to describe the creative management processes needed.

Why do managers and generals so often fight the old battles rather than the new? It happens in sports as well. When the British Lions faced the All Blacks in Auckland in 1993, a week after humiliating the opposition, they made no changes in their approach, even though it was certain that the New Zealanders, having been so badly beaten, would play differently. The mixture as before, though, always looks safer. Change involves risk: but sometimes (as in the comprehensive defeat at Auckland) not changing is the riskier course.

In most situations, there's only one risk: that of being wrong. It attends every decision in life, big or small. Managers or players with self-belief are confident in the knowledge of 'what' and 'how' and never hesitate in putting that knowledge to the practical test. He who hesitates is sometimes saved, but far more often the fear of being wrong, which is the opposite of self-belief, leads to delay and error. Fear in any form is a bad manager. In this most common of manifestations it is literally self-defeating.

The self-believer doesn't maximise only the present. Without self-belief you cannot create the future. In shaping that future, the old targets expressed purely in financial terms have become even more inadequate. Perlitz advises that the necessary high rate of innovation won't be achieved unless companies set specific goals for, say, the annual earnings and sales to be generated by new products. It follows that reward systems must recognise future needs, partly by becoming less systematic. What carefully calibrated yardstick can you put on creating the future of the company?

Alan Kay, a great pioneer of personal computing, put the issue (and the power of self-belief) in a nutshell: 'The best way to predict the future is to invent it.' The learning organisation seeks to generate the future it wants. This philosophy is the opposite of 'that's the way we've always done things round here', 'sticking to the knitting', 'not invented here' and other outworn defences of the status quo. Senge calls rather for 'creative tension', which means 'seeing clearly where we want to be . . . and telling the truth about where we are'. This establishes the gap between 'vision' and 'reality', and is precisely the exercise to which corporate strategists and total quality companies have long been accustomed. The difference is that Senge challenges the realism of most ideas on reality. Managers, like everybody else, focus on isolated events rather than on patterns of behaviour. Even if they look at the latter (which is how you spot trends), they rarely look

behind patterns to the 'systemic structure'. That's where you find
the ultimate reality and the ultimate test of objectivity about your
strengths and weaknesses.

The car industry again serves as an excellent – and chilling
– illustration. The event that everybody spotted was the rise in
Japanese car sales. Nobody had the self-confidence to face the
truth: that the Japanese were manufacturing and even marketing
cars more effectively on every score. Rather than make this
self-damaging admission, all kinds of irrelevant explanations
were offered, from cheating to unfair cultural attributes. Then
attention turned to the patterns of behaviour, the common
characteristics of the way the Japanese produced and marketed
cars, and the great wave of imitation began.

But what really was the defect in the Western methods? They
flowed from rigid corporate systems in which design, marketing,
production and finance were separate, warring camps. Cor-
rection required overturning the whole stable framework to
which insecure executives had clung for years. Not surprisingly,
the Western giants, from General Motors and Ford to Fiat
and Mercedes–Benz, experienced even more difficulty in re-
engineering their cultures than in changing their engineering.

New methods, however, modify cultures. For its new Omega
executive range, GM Europe, for the first time in its history,
formed thirteen teams for each part of the car, each manned
by all ten functions. By working together, people learn from
each other. That's one way in which the learning organisation is becoming reality. More and more, managers, and
other employees, for that matter, are forming self-directed,
self-believing teams in which know-how and information are
pooled. More and more, too, management development itself is
founded on team-working, tackling real-life corporate problems,
from strategy downwards.

Many such problems, on analysis, tend to be of the type
that Senge calls 'shifting the burden'. An agonising symptom
shows up, say, falling sales. You can treat the symptom in two
ways: by attacking the sales shortfall directly, or by finding the

underlying cause and treating that. Human nature being what it is, most managements take the route least likely to damage their self-esteem: they go for the symptom, the obvious event that comes to view. So they launch a marketing promotion drive to boost the sales. Even if that succeeds, the problem will recur, possibly in more virulent form.

In a real case cited by Senge, a management team looked beneath the symptom to find the underlying cause of just such sales difficulties. Curing the symptom by intensive promotion had indeed worsened the disease. The fundamental defect was lagging introduction of new products – the company had never heard the Perlitz message or the Kay clarion-call: it wasn't inventing its future. As a side-effect, the reliance on marketing expenditure to save the day had inevitably promoted the saviours to high positions in the company. They knew masses about marketing, but nothing of new product development, which had languished accordingly in a vicious circle.

Three chief executives in succession had come from advertising. The remedy for the firm's decline turned out to lie as far from the consumer as possible – in the boardroom. Even if the side-effects don't worsen the problem directly, as they did in this case, they always exacerbate it indirectly by delaying the truly necessary action. All this is evidently true, but what does it have to do with learning? Shouldn't common sense alone have spotted the new product lag, or the advantages of Japanese car-makers?

In fact, common sense alone wouldn't have been enough: *informed* common sense is the catalyst for effective change. What shocked Xerox into a massive effort to change all its ways was *learning* that Japanese photocopiers, like Japanese cars, were winning not by skulduggery, but by superior methods of production and management. A further crucial point, though, is that the findings were made by a team of line managers. Outsiders wouldn't have been believed, and line managers wouldn't have believed staff experts.

The ultimate test of athletes or managers, however, is how they react on hearing the bad news about their performance – being dropped from a national side, say, or getting a message like the one Xerox's team brought back from Japan. The individual with weak self-esteem has it weakened further by the bad news. For stronger people, the setback serves as a spur to renewed and better-focused effort. The person who has self-belief bounces back again and again, always in the conviction that the next time will be the best time.

This ability to take and learn from criticism is the acid test of self-belief. This was brought home to us by the remarkable case of a defence contractor which had one advantage over most businesses: a single customer, the military. The advantage lies in the fact that, with only one buyer, you can obtain perfect knowledge of customer satisfaction (or dissatisfaction). Other companies rely on conducting expensive surveys which, unless very carefully constructed, yield imperfect and even misleading information.

This particular contractor had a brave managing director who invited the chief purchasing official to give a full and frank assessment of the company's performance. The official did an excellent job. He consulted his people, who worked intimately with the contractor day to day, and reported their findings, many of them close to damning, without pulling a single punch. The chairman, who had been managing director previously, reddened with every blow, and could barely control his anger. He accused the customer of misrepresenting the facts, but his most passionate attack was based on the damage the customer had done to the morale of managers who had been doing their utmost to deliver performance and quality. As we found in conversation afterwards, his managers were indeed angry – not with the customer, but with their chairman. The customer, they said, had given them benchmarks, targets at which they could aim. They knew precisely where, in his eyes, they were going wrong and what outcomes they had to achieve to get it right. Furthermore, they firmly believed in their ability to perform, and they were not deceived in this belief. A few months after this incident, the company won a desperately needed order from its single customer. Likewise, the managers at Xerox reacted to the bad news from Japan by accomplishing vital changes which reversed its calamitous loss of market share. That involved resorting to coaching and learning on a massive scale.

At Rank Xerox, every one of 28,000 employees has been trained in the principles and practice of total quality. Work on 'continuous improvement', or 'business process re-engineering', or any other approach to radical reform of specific activities, is a double education. First, the participants have to learn the tools and techniques required to tackle the process and its improvement. Secondly, they learn from the experience of undertaking the project as a team and driving it to a successful conclusion. Both processes build self-belief, and ultimately depend on it. Total quality rests on the conviction that everybody, from the summit of management to the shop floor, can be involved in learning and improvement by acting with confidence on his or her own initiative. Like the application of an athlete to his or her sport, the work never ends. The defence contractor and Xerox exemplified Robert Bruce's famous maxim, learned from the persistent spider: if at first you don't succeed, try, try again.

But that isn't enough. Analyse the collapse of companies like those which once formed the British Leyland Motor Corporation, now reduced to the German-owned rump named Rover, and you will more than likely find a sorry tale of winning positions weakly surrendered by failure to build on success. Steffi Graf's opponent at Wimbledon in 1993, suffering a fatal last-set loss of self-belief, exemplified the same failure. The champion not only comes from behind, but, like Pete Sampras a year later, tightens his or her game inexorably when on top. This has been one of the winning Japanese traits in world markets – in other words, if at first you *do* succeed, try, try again.

Be conscious of strengths *and* weaknesses

This is the opposite of arrogance. The arrogant company

imitates the British Leyland bosses and basks in a false sense of security. Self-believers are always deeply conscious of the strengths which generate superiority and of the weaknesses which threaten it, and work hard to reinforce the former and eradicate the latter. That means learning. In the learning organisation, everybody learns, which means that everyone is taught – and that's an idea which many senior managers find personally uncomfortable.

Entering anything that looks like a classroom damages their fragile self-esteem. But if they don't learn, the discomfort will eventually prove much greater for them and for the organisation. The organisation *per se* can't learn: it's amorphous and inhuman. But the humans who animate it, if they only believe in themselves and everybody else, can create an environment which is both adaptive and generative. Without that environment, and without that self-belief, managers who seek successful change are wasting their time – and their greatest, human, assets.

III

Results – How to Focus on Outcomes

7

Adrian Moorhouse's Gold

Swimming, even more than athletics, is a sport in which competitors can and must focus on precise results. Weather conditions don't affect the issue, the 'track' doesn't vary significantly, and the odds are overwhelming that each successive competition will be won at faster times. Adrian Moorhouse, Britain's gold-medal-winning Olympic swimmer, likes to quote the case of one American competitor who worked out that in four years his Olympic event would be won in a certain time, and then calculated his preparation over that period to take off the necessary seconds from his own performance, year by year.

The intense concentration on times dovetails with focus on winning, which is often measured, as in Moorhouse's Olympic win in the 100-metres breaststroke, in tiny fractions of a second. As he admits, he was 'pretty lucky – in fact very lucky' to win by even that margin: 'It was the worst-paced swim I've ever done.' His consolation, though, is that it was also 'the best race I've ever had'. As often happens in sport and business, the true competitor wins in spite of tactical error: and this was Moorhouse's worst piece of tactics.

'You don't go flat out for a 61-second race,' he explains. 'You've actually got to go about 97 per cent for the first length.' After a 'terrible dive', Moorhouse 'took it too slow, and from that moment on I almost threw it away'. He knew that he should have been ahead, not trailing behind. But he wouldn't give in. Above all, Moorhouse kept himself 'just focusing on the end'. He wasn't actually ahead until the final, winning stroke. As tense, nail-biting viewers round the world will bear witness, 'in terms of racing other people, in terms of a pure race, it was actually a great race', and he won.

But here the voice of the true, analytical champion intervenes: 'It was organised chaos, not organised racing. It was totally random, which shouldn't happen.' Nothing in Moorhouse's preparation for that one event had been random or disorganised, and the preparation had in effect begun eleven years before. His life was transformed when, at the age of twelve, he watched the Olympic swimming covertly upstairs in his Leeds home: it was the first thing he'd seen of the Olympics, and 'the first memory I have of the Olympic Games is seeing David Wilkie win a gold medal'.

'Seeing his emotion on the podium, and then the playing of the national anthem, I thought, this looks really good. But I had no real idea what it meant.' Moorhouse was already a promising swimmer, having begun at five in the local swimming pool. To start with, he wasn't at all keen on the sport. Nevertheless he went to Aireborough pool in the heart of Leeds, where he joined the Aireborough Dolphins. He was racing by the age of eight, which is when he won his first medal, gold in the Under-9s backstroke, followed by silvers for breaststroke and freestyle.

Plainly the talent was there: now, so was the ambition. The day after Wilkie's win, 'I got on the coach, where we all met to go to a competition, and I was really excited. I had no idea of the gap between where I was and Olympic level. It just seemed like an interesting target, and it all looked so special on TV.' In fact, Moorhouse lost his race that day, though he 'wasn't that bothered, because I still wanted to win the Olympics'. This wide-eyed dreaming child still had to learn what it took to be a champion.

His evolution into an organised competitor who had targets

and a clear focus for realising his dream was excitingly sudden. In April 1979 he joined Leeds, one of Britain's top swimming centres. People kept asking if he had entered various competitions for his age group, competitions that he knew nothing about. But his coach saw that Moorhouse was capable of times that would place him among the best in England, and encouraged him to train hard. A few months later, he was entered in the age-group championship at 200-metres breaststroke. It was only the fourth time he had ever swum this distance, and he won.

That first results focus at the age of fourteen was on targets that Moorhouse found unbelievable. His coach actually thought he could win the national age groups, which he had never entered before. Between April and August, Moorhouse went from nowhere to national champion in an event for which he had little experience or liking. 'I'd only been swimming 100s and only ever done one or two 200s, and they were hell – too long and too hard.' Moorhouse was told to do two or three more and keep training, 'which I did, and I got better each time'.

Stretching targets

The importance of setting 'stretching targets' is well known in management, but not necessarily well understood. The target shouldn't exceed the manager's abilities, but should exploit them to the full, closing the gap between potential and performance. That raises the sights, not only in the sense of making the specific task more worthwhile, but in giving managers a better realisation of their own powers. In Moorhouse's case: 'All of a sudden I was beating these kids from London, Manchester, Newcastle, and I'd never swum against them, or even heard of them, and they all knew each other.' But he liked that level of competition, and he liked experiencing the real 'feeling of winning' for the first time.

That was stage one in the advance from daydream to golden reality. Stage two required focusing on a new target: a record time. As Moorhouse's coach kept pushing him past new boundaries, the swimmer closed on the British junior record. The pair set themselves the target of training to beat this under-16 time. The focus was very precise: 'This is the time you need to beat, and this is your current best time. We have a year in which to beat it.' Moorhouse needed only three months. That was in January. Another three months and he was competing in his first senior championship, coming second to Duncan Goodhew, who went on to win the Olympics. Between August and April, the youngster who had never entered a national age-group competition had become a record-breaker and a senior competitor. Coming second to an Olympic gold-medallist stimulated his own ambitions still further: 'The guy I was swimming with everybody knew as this bald swimmer who was going to go on and win the Olympics for Britain, and he did – and then it was real.'

Moorhouse's picture got into the papers, and not only the local ones. He was targeted, aged fifteen, as a future Olympic champion: Wilkie in 1976, Goodhew in 1980 – it could be Moorhouse in 1984. To the ordinary person, it would all have seemed too good to be true. But top achievers typically ride their successes and don't much remember their failures; or, if they do, look at them positively. Managers, too, don't like to dwell on failure, but too often for different and less satisfactory reasons: because they are averse to confronting the realities of error.

Unless you do learn from your mistakes and failures, though, you're liable to repeat them. Losing to Goodhew in that first senior outing was what Moorhouse regarded as his first encounter with failure: other, lesser defeats didn't count. 'When I swam against Goodhew, it was only six months after I'd entered the first age groups in that April competition. I thought I was going to beat him. When I didn't, I was gutted. I got out thinking, I've failed, this is the end of the line.' Losing to a twenty-four-year old who was heading for Olympic gold was no disgrace for a lad of fifteen. But Moorhouse went sadly to see his coach, who was on the British team, convinced that he'd 'blown it', that he was 'no good, because I hadn't beaten him'. The constant focus on higher and higher results, faster and faster times, had backfired – and when Goodhew also beat him by about one and a half seconds in the 100 metres, 'I got out really disappointed': he had finished only fifth.

The coach sat him down and administered the perfect antidote: 'Listen, you've actually broken your own junior record.' Moorhouse recalls that sitting down and realising that he was still improving was what really drove him on. Like the pursuit of continuous improvement in total quality management, 'breaking those junior records and getting on that ladder and starting to move up it' kept the swimmer focused: 'That's what kept me going.'

In February 1980 Moorhouse swam with four other youngsters in the national junior team. They all broke records, and, sitting around afterwards, the others talked about how they were going to win senior team places in April. For the first time the thought dawned on Moorhouse that he might be good enough for the seniors. His selection is a vivid memory: 'We were picked on time. So you swam out of your skull, and they selected you no matter what your age.'

The selection letter, however, warned Moorhouse that he might have to swim in an outside lane, because Goodhew was number one, adding that the selectors weren't sure whether to give him an England tracksuit. That provided Moorhouse with another focus: to earn his tracksuit and depose Goodhew. He concentrated on new targets, times and records. Thereby hangs a management lesson. Much business success rests on long hours of detailed, dogged, uninspiring work, but clear focus on truly worthwhile results provides the missing inspiration.

Nothing in management, though, is quite as dull as swimming ('having my face in the water') for four hours every day, and for Moorhouse the results focus likewise gave him the inspiration to carry on. Passing strict targets at set points along the way, he broke Goodhew's records in 1981 and 1982 and won the Commonwealth Games in his build-up for the 1984 Olympics. First, though, came the 1982 World Championships, in which

Moorhouse finished fourth. That didn't rule out the possibility of an Olympic win, but deep down, though he desperately wanted to win, he didn't truly believe he was ready.

The media and the swimming fraternity didn't share these inner doubts, and wrongly thought Moorhouse mentally and physically strong enough to be a contender for gold. He was only nineteen, though, and physically still somewhat slight. In early 1984, however, Moorhouse did swim a very fast time which put him top of the world rankings. This naturally heightened the expectations of the press and everybody involved with British swimming. Moorhouse alone was aware that his main opponents hadn't yet swum seriously: the rankings didn't reflect true strengths in the sport worldwide.

For the first time in his career, Moorhouse suffered from muddled focus. He aimed to win the Olympics, but didn't really believe that he could. In hindsight, he might have done better to concentrate on winning any medal he could. In the event, 'I was actually afraid of not getting a gold medal, rather than targeting getting it. So huge chunks of my time were spent worrying about what would happen if I didn't.' Concerning himself about how family, friends, the media and his swimming colleagues would react, he 'wasn't focusing on what it required to win the gold'.

His self-esteem entering the race wasn't positive. It became downright negative when he lost – and was told he was a flop. Big black headlines recorded his failure to come any higher than fourth, and one newspaper actually advised: 'Adrian Moorhouse should do himself and the sport of swimming a favour and quit.' That's heavy stuff to bear at any age, but being told to retire when you're only nineteen is unbelievably harsh. The ability to ride rough criticism and injustice, though, is a necessity for champions in any activity. The right response is to prove the critics wrong by going back and doing better.

Moorhouse went back – but he did worse. Still the best in Britain, he was picked for the European Cup, where he'd won a year before. This time he came eighteenth and didn't even make the B final. Something was obviously and seriously wrong.

Tests showed that he had suffered from German measles for six months. 'I thought,' he recalls, 'that eighteenth is really bad, and it makes fourth in the Olympics look pretty good. And then I started to realise how good that actually was. I was fourth in the world.'

On New Year's Eve 1984, Moorhouse spent the evening on his own in his parents' house. For the rest of his swimming career, he spent New Year's Eve in the same solitary way, 'and around midnight I sat down and set my goals for the whole year'. In 1984, the issue was how to get out of his problem. Fourth in the world, now eighteenth in Europe. 'What can I do and where can I start?' The first answer was the National Championships, just four months away. They became his focus.

Finding the right focus

Training as hard as he could, Moorhouse aimed to knock half a second off each of his best times. His muddled focus cleared as the times become his sole objectives. With his coach, Moorhouse planned exactly what would happen in the four months before the championships. His training sessions – when, how, where – were all written down in his diary and checked off when completed. It all worked: he got all the records, restored his confidence and enjoyed a very definite surge of renewed vigour. The Olympics again became his focus, but he was also rebuilding a self-belief that had become fragile.

He started to move up the world rankings. The year 1986, which included the World Championships, suddenly seemed wide open. Somebody had to be the best in the world. 'We're all pretty similar, so why not me? That's what I swam for in 1986.' Winning the World Championships would establish the mental state required for the Olympics. Moorhouse did win, but was disqualified, to his intense disappointment. But this time there was a huge difference – he had seen people finish behind him; he had touched the wall, looked both ways and seen clear water.

Adrian Moorhouse celebrates Gold in the Olympic Men's 100m Breaststroke – Seoul, 1988.

He had led by nearly a second, which in Olympic terms is a huge winning margin.

Seeing that clear water was the moment when he began to believe in Olympic victory. That New Year's Eve, his solitary re-analysis was positive. He had made it. The only way now was upwards. No longer the scared nineteen-year old, now he could scare others – for instance, by being the first man, in 1987, to break a minute in his event. That summer, he won gold, silver and bronze in the European Championships. Other wins included the US Open, the American Nationals and the European Cups. New Year's Eve 1987 thus gave an encouraging vista on to the coming Olympic year.

Moorhouse could remember exactly how he had felt in the build-up to 1984: half scared, half childlike, wanting to win, but not knowing how. He realised that the external pressures he had experienced four years before would again well up. His strategy was to anticipate the media speculation and interest, and to seek to dissipate the impact in advance, so that nothing would disturb his concentration and planning. The gold medal was his reward – not only for the four hours of daily training for four years, but for the mental strength displayed after the 1984 débâcle.

Moorhouse had refocused his mind and his training to produce short-term goals whose achievement would carry him on to the long-term prize. Looking back, he doesn't believe he would have won without those short-term targets. If he hadn't given himself a focus, celebrating every achievement along the way, he wouldn't have stood on the podium in 1988 – like his hero, David Wilkie, eight years before – to receive the gold medal on behalf of Britain. He couldn't go to sleep that night. 'I just lay there with my eyes wide open, wearing my medal. I just didn't want to take it off.' He wore it all the next day, too.

8

The Reinvention of ICI

'During the last twenty years at the beginning of each year I have taken a few hours out to write down on a pad which I keep in my desk drawer the hopes and aspirations that I had for achievement in the coming year.' This is a classic example of personal focus on results. The writer, Sir John Harvey-Jones, used his own focus to transform the results of the company he chaired – Imperial Chemical Industries. One of his predecessors had remarked, 'You can't turn a large company like this round every eighteen months.' This blinkered attitude goes a long way towards explaining why, in 1981, ICI ran into a crisis that required a massive turnaround – which Harvey-Jones achieved decisively, and well within eighteen months.

He threw aside the negative and accentuated the positive in his determination to make ICI 'the best chemical company in the world'. It was not a necessary part of that ambition to concentrate on one specific result: the target of earning a British-record profit of a billion pounds in 1984. But the number, which Harvey-Jones knew was feasible, gave a tangible expression to his ambitions for the group, and helped to focus attention, inside and outside ICI, on its transformation.

Naming objectives

Quantifying a qualitative ambition – focusing on a real, large result – has the same concentrating effect on individual minds. But there is yet another solid reason for naming an objective in hard, financial terms. It provides a benchmark, a measure of progress, proof that you've done what you set out to do. When ICI made that billion it was proof of its success and, for that matter, its chairman's. He had made things happen at ICI, as he had promised. Hence the title of his management book, *Making It Happen*, subtitled *Reflections on Leadership*.

That billion-pound result, of course, was the outcome of many decisions, starting with redefining ICI as 'a chemical service company', taking it away from production, round which the group had always been centred, and towards the customer, from whom profits now had to be won. That clear and rational decision about what ICI's business truly was, where its true core lay, was the start of the chairman's drive to turn the company's lumbering bureaucracies into faster-moving, more profit-conscious commercial organisations. The turnaround rested on an eight-point programme:

(1) *Leadership is the fulcrum*: either that of a single leader (the most likely) or of a tightly knit group of like-minded people, or better still, both – which is what Harvey-Jones sought to achieve at ICI.

(2) *Nothing is sacred*: crisis gave Harvey-Jones the licence to kill any aspect of the organisation that gets in the way of its restoration. This included exiting from two businesses, bulk polyester and polythene, which ICI had actually pioneered.

(3) *Decisions are taken firmly* when and where they must be made: at ICI, that started with the top management, which Harvey-Jones forced into a decisive, proactive mode.

(4) *Necessary action is taken* equally decisively and fast: again, emergency acts as a forceful spur, and Harvey-Jones thus instituted sweeping changes at the top of the company as soon as he gained power.

(5) *What is being done, why, and with what results, must be clearly communicated* – inside and outside the organisation. Here the ICI chairman was aided by the natural gifts that made his TV

appearances in *The Troubleshooter* and other programmes so effective.

(6) *Change must be facilitated and strongly symbolised by unmistakable actions*: Harvey-Jones was frustrated in his symbolic wish to close down ICI's monumental HQ at Millbank, but he did use lesser, still powerful symbols, such as abandoning the old Imperial boardroom (and personally sporting loud ties and flowing locks).

(7) *The basics of the business* (starting with the management of its cash) must be as efficient as human beings can make them: they always deteriorate over time unless somebody deliberately tightens them up, and ICI was no exception.

(8) *The future lies ahead.* Management must look beyond present objectives, indispensable though they are, to future aims (like that billion-pound profit), no matter how hopeless the present abyss may seem. At the nadir of Britain's military history, ringed by defeat and despair, with nightly bombardment threatening collapse, Winston Churchill was already planning the post-war settlement to follow victory, which American entry (then not even secured) would, he knew, make inevitable.

Without the heroic element injected by a charismatic leader like Harvey-Jones, the eight-point programme may seem bloodless. But it is universally effective. Moreover, study it carefully and a compelling truth emerges. This isn't just a programme for corporate renaissance or turnaround: it's the essence of creating and sustaining a company which never needs turning, whatever the starting point, whatever the core.

(1) Leadership.
(2) Challenge.
(3) Decisiveness.
(4) Speed.
(5) Clarity.
(6) Change.

(7) Basics.
(8) Objectives.

They describe a sequence. The new leadership takes charge, defines the challenge, moves decisively and fast to meet it, communicates clearly what is happening, and then institutes sweeping change in all operations – including the basics – as the organisation moves towards the new objectives. Within that overall results focus, the whole organisation is guided by the drive for measurable and measured outcomes.

What did drive ICI so rapidly and decisively from a quarterly loss to annual profits of over a billion pounds? Nobody could doubt, after meeting him, that much of the answer lay with the chairman himself – not least with a frank, warm, forceful personality. Bottle Harvey-Jones and you could make a fortune from seekers of distilled management effectiveness. Hear Harvey-Jones the orator describe to a conference how he revitalised ICI, the processes by which he cured ICI's version of the English disease, and the impact of this iconoclast on a habit-ridden corporate bureaucracy comes vividly alive.

The charismatic communicator

In a long, late-starting career with the multinational giant, Harvey-Jones had made no secret of his iconoclasm, even as he followed the standard success pattern: progressively more important posts leading to the top of a major division, followed by elevation to the main board, and, in his late fifties, to the summit for the usual limited period. The uniqueness of his tenure lies elsewhere: not only in the radical change that he injected into ICI, but in his emergence as a charismatic communicator who, more than anyone before, could make industry and management come vividly alive.

Yet his autobiography, introspective in a most uncommon way, describes an apparently different ideal: a sort of *Boy's Own* composite, the archetypal British gentleman – simultaneously strong and compassionate, stiff upper-lipped yet emotional, courageous both physically and morally, doing incessantly to others as you would be done by yourself. Leading ICI and helping to try to arrest Britain's industrial decline were crucial in this pilgrim's progress, but they were not the ultimate results on which the pilgrim focused.

In fact, he found his 'years as chairman, despite their apparent success, and the excess of praise which I received, one of the hardest and least enjoyable periods of my life'. That's an odd contrast with his emergence as management superstar, a rare breed in any country – especially since Harvey-Jones's stardom wasn't thrust upon him: he deliberately used a high profile to further the sorely needed regeneration of ICI and its image. But while the heroic role suited his needs and talents, Harvey-Jones was uncomfortable wearing the purple: just like his *Boy's Own* ideal, no doubt.

His autobiography continually refers to the Jekyll and Hyde

Sir John Harvey-Jones, the chairman who reinvented ICI.

tension between the outwardly bluff and successful leader and the cowering small boy who lurks within, painfully aware of his inadequacies and longing for the respect of his own father. This human sensitivity must have contributed powerfully to Harvey-Jones's first successes – as a professional naval officer at sea; as an operator in the secret world of naval intelligence; and later as the man who welded ICI's huge, incoherent Wilton site into a harmonious whole.

Yet for all the personal insecurity, for all the slightly tortured feeling that life (including an adored family) is more important than work, Harvey-Jones never refused a challenge, never took his foot off the ladder, and never, on his own account, hesitated to act vigorously, even when starting from positions of serious ignorance. A superbly self-taught manager, he was well prepared for the chair by his own critical observations. Many of his 'heresies' were formed when he was a main board director and found himself under-loaded for the first time in his career.

He entitled that phase 'The Bored Years'. The board, by no means untypically, combined great theoretical power with strange weakness. How many other companies would allow divisional heads, led by Harvey-Jones in his pre-board days, to form their own committee, an act which some directors understandably thought 'subversive and even insubordinate'? The truth is that Harvey-Jones is subversive by nature and mind. The *Boy's Own* ideal doesn't include the humorous, troubleshooting irreverence that piloted its possessor through the convoluted coils of ICI's workings to a position where he could and did straighten some of them out.

Harvey-Jones thus genuinely gave ICI, the largest manufacturer in Britain, the chance for greatness. His successors, unable to maintain the momentum, settled for another solution, partly under the pressure of a predatory share purchase by Lord Hanson's empire: they split ICI into two halves – the basic chemicals businesses, and the higher-technology lines, led by pharmaceuticals. Harvey-Jones had probably been given too short a time (five years) in which to apply his rare quality of being the anti-bureaucrat in the bureaucracy, the individual grit in the collective oyster.

In normal circumstances the oyster spits out the gritty executive well before he or she reaches the top. The circumstances at ICI, however, were abnormal, as they were for most of its major contemporaries in British industry. The recession of 1979–80 had exposed horrible weaknesses not only in ICI, but in great companies like Courtaulds, Vickers and Thorn-EMI. The sufferers had sometimes been led towards their difficulties by managers who failed to build management structures or develop business strategies that could cope with a quarter-century of rapid change.

Whether these leaders survived personally or left the scene, their companies needed to find new people, new ideas and a new professionalism, and it's now only too well known that many didn't. Too many replacement managers – successors, but not successful – showed inability or disinclination to take their companies onwards and upwards. Bureaucratic 'success' for them personally was accompanied or followed by failure for their businesses at a time of acute challenge – not just from recession, but also from the accelerating threat of international competition.

At ICI, the mounting business difficulties, culminating in financial loss, led the board to turn to Harvey-Jones for rescue. He repaid the compliment by promptly halving the board's numbers and dispensing with its two deputy chairmen. Whether he would have been elevated (doubtless not) without the urgent stimulus of crisis isn't an academic question. Cometh the moment, cometh the man – or woman. Margaret Thatcher's genius for leadership would likewise have lain unused but for the failures (like losing the 1974 election) of her predecessor, Edward Heath.

Disgruntled Conservative MPs, intending to administer a mere rebuke, did so in such numbers that they accidentally brought Heath down. The matching of moment and man is always accidental. But only a Thatcher could have exploited that chance regicide so ruthlessly; just as, at ICI, only somebody able to match Harvey-Jones's powers (including ex-naval bluntness, a keen and far from naval business sense, and a natural genius for public relations) could have turned the corporate supertanker through so many degrees.

It proved less easy to turn the wardroom or boardroom. 'Very upset' by the news that Harvey-Jones was to write his memoirs, his former board colleagues insisted that they should not be mentioned by name, 'or in any way that any of them could be identified as individuals'. What made these men so afraid? Five years, as noted, may not be long enough to change a corporate culture – even at main-board level. After his retirement, more-over, former colleagues were heard to disparage his contribution. Yet it can hardly be ignored.

He had successfully treated symptoms that were truly alarming: nobody was looking after the interests of the company as a whole; the cash was being controlled, but not managed; new business wasn't being generated fast enough; creeping centralisation was following in the wake of bureaucratic swelling; managers were simply not profit-conscious. But Harvey-Jones had made no secret of his iconoclastic remedies, and he took the unanimous vote that elected him chairman as a mandate for action on precisely those lines.

The 'federation of free men'

That in itself was a sweeping innovation, given ICI's previous strange shyness about having a single chief executive. Not only did many board members feel personally the immediate consequences of their vote: the remaining directors were taken away for a week to reconsider the entire basis of the company. From that strategy session (whose repetition became a regular event) flowed many critical decisions. Among them were the removal of all layers of management which were not making a unique contribution, the treatment of the redefined 'chemical services' company as individual businesses and not as 'divisions', and the placing of a tightly knit executive octet at the summit of 'a federation of free men co-ordinating themselves'.

The philosophy is difficult to separate from the personality of its architect. That ex-naval bluntness was brought to bear on the business as a deliberate hallmark of his style – 'blunt to the point of painfulness', he likes to say. The executive octet was to discuss everthing as a group, with no holds barred and nothing sacrosanct, including their own performances. The business heads received simple, one-sentence objectives such as 'stay in the colours business', 'improve your performance', 'make a specified contribution to the centre and live off your retained cash flow'. Moreover, they were expected to meet their objectives and, if they failed, to explain themselves in front of their peers.

It sounds like a breath of fresh air, and it blew through ICI as a hurricane of change. It also sounds like a textbook example of results-focused management. Interestingly, though, the ICI salvationist has no entries under 'management' in *Making It Happen*. Here, Harvey-Jones makes a curious bedfellow to another iconoclast, H. Ross Perot, the computer-services king who made life miserable for the General Motors directors after they purchased his company, and who then badly bothered George Bush as a presidential candidate. In a *Fortune* critique, Perot unrolled a hypothetical action programme for GM which included, 'Starting today, the word "management" will no longer be used.' It was to be replaced by 'leadership'.

Yet Harvey-Jones surely doesn't mean to convey any disapproval of management science, technique and theory. On the contrary, he calls management 'an absorbing interest. Industrial management, perhaps above all, has depths of fascination which few other callings can enjoy.' He stresses, however, that there is no real management without action, without 'making things happen', without focusing on results. Action, of course, must be preceded by careful thinking that establishes the focus:

Before the ICI main board goes away for one of its regular

strategy discussions 'off campus', an enormous amount of time is spent working out the balance of the meeting, and how it should be carried out. It is essential that the time is used to best effect, and this means structuring the meetings so that there is an adequate input of fact.

But it's equally important to understand that 'small actions have a tremendous catalytic and change effect'. That's why the day that Harvey-Jones assumed responsibility as chairman, instead of meeting 'as we always had done, in the ICI boardroom, an imposing but somewhat impractical room, we met in what had been my office'; there he could better organise 'free and uninhibited' discussion. What worked for ICI from that day on will work for any company, great or small, as the *Troubleshooter* TV series demonstrated.

It's fashionable to argue that Harvey-Jones got most of the *Troubleshooter* cases wrong. In fact, his diagnoses and prognoses were largely correct because, unlike his subjects, the trouble-shooter sought to focus the businesses on results and to put in place solutions that would achieve those outcomes. The assorted and troubled British companies which he held up to the light, though, neither focused on results, nor, unsurprisingly, achieved good ones. The end doesn't justify the means, but without having an end in view, preferably a highly ambitious one, you won't even know what means to adopt.

9

What You Want
is What You Get

The difference between winners and losers often doesn't lie in innate abilities, or even individual effort, but in the choice of objectives and measures which chart progress towards the goal. But can anything so complex as a company, even what the jargonists call an 'SME' (small or medium-sized enterprise), have a single goal?

In terms of overall aim, the answer is yes. Taco Bell's afore-mentioned desire to be 'number one in share of stomach' is exactly the right clarion call for a fast-food business, better than ICI's wish to be the 'best chemical company' in the world. Such broad objectives are fine and grand as far as they go, but they need breaking down into clear, defined, measurable tasks before anybody can respond to the call. You must ask the really hard questions: what does 'best' mean? On which criteria? In whose eyes?

We believe strongly that, while business results are the *sine qua non*, the equivalent of the final score when the whistle blows, their achievement depends on two other counts: the satisfaction of customers and that of all employees. Actually, 'satisfaction' is an unsatisfying word in this context. The issue is the totality of thoughts and emotions about the organisation as experienced by everybody who buys from it, works for it, supplies it. If you think of this totality as vague and beyond measure, you will fail, for the measures available provide the focus which produces the winning results.

The first deeply considered US attempt to provide a general answer, useful to all businesses rather than one, is now enshrined in the criteria for the Baldrige Prize, America's top quality award. The European Quality Award's list is very similar, and now widely used by companies internally, as a way of measuring divisional performance. It contains nine criteria.

The first of the EQA elements is leadership. This is one of five 'enablers' and carries 10 per cent of the weight of the final assessment. The others are people management (9 per cent), policy and strategy (8 per cent), resources (9 per cent) and processes (14 per cent). The enablers make it possible for companies to achieve results, in which there are four elements: people satisfaction (9 per cent), customer satisfaction (20 per cent), impact on society (6 per cent) and finally – the objective of the entire process – business results.

In most companies, of course, business results are the be-all and end-all. Some companies boil it down to a single number: net income, the famous 'bottom line'. But the EQA model awards business results just 15 per cent of the total weight – a quarter less than customer satisfaction. The logic behind this is clear enough. Since you can't achieve optimum business results from dissatisfied customers, putting results above satisfaction is putting the cart before the horse.

Measuring their satisfaction by product alone, moreover, won't get either cart or horse very far. That's obviously true of a service business. But all businesses are service businesses now, whether or not their managers know it. Within 'manufacturing' companies, more and more staff are in service functions. More important still, service has become a competitive weapon, possibly the crucial means of differentiating one supplier from another.

Very few firms, though, measure their service performance with the same interest and effort that their accountants bring to the financial results, even though the latter are heavily influenced by service outcomes. Service includes the finance function itself: how effective – and cost-effective – are the bean-counters? In total quality companies, the principle is that everybody has a customer, including the finance people, and that everybody can therefore be judged by their customers, external or internal, and must be. That's what lies behind the following catechism:

> Customer satisfaction is vital to our strategy; the business enjoys a strong quality image with our target customers; our marketing and operations people couldn't co-operate any better; all departments are as customer-driven as we would like.

That's the right (but rare) answer to 'right questions' on service posed by experts John Bateson and Paul Tiffany. They postulate a perfect business which is oriented towards the front line – the place where customers make contact with a company which is dedicated to their satisfaction. To hear managers talk, this is the focus they all have: customer satisfaction is at once sovereign objective and ultimate measure, guiding value and operational mechanism, strategic kingpin and tactical trigger. Today, Bradley T. Gale observes, 'most companies employ some kind of customer-satisfaction measurement system'. So why aren't customers more satisfied?

Asking the right questions

The answer is simple. If you're employing the wrong yardstick, your measurements will be useless. Some systems, Gale reports, 'are rudimentary surveys that actually discourage people from working on quality improvement'. Anybody who has answered a typical questionnaire knows why. What does it mean when you're 'very satisfied, satisfied, neutral, dissatisfied, or very dissatisfied' with this or that aspect of service or product quality? And do other respondents mean the same thing?

More serious still, what do the replies say about the relative strength or weakness of the competition, or the relative importance of the aspects considered? The answer is little or nothing. In contrast, the 'customer-value analysis' advocated by Gale tells managers everything they should want to know. The information, however, doesn't come easily. The 'market-perceived quality profile' takes careful construction. It demands establishing 'the company's position relative to competitors in each key business segment, showing the key quality attributes, relative importance weights and performance scores'.

Even with that big task completed, Gale's prescription has far to go. The full analysis requires six other tools. Some are transparently valuable, like an 'orders won/lost analysis, showing recent sales efforts won or lost against the competition, with an explanation of why each was won or lost'. Others, like a 'head-to-head area chart' or a 'key-events time line', take more explanation. And even the seven tools aren't enough: you also need to chart progress on 'managing customer value', or 'the internal view of quality', and much else besides.

The prizes on offer, though, are glittering indeed. If your quality as perceived by the market (and as measured by Gale's meticulous methods) is rated 24 per cent or more above the competition's, you can expect to earn 12 per cent on sales – three times as much as benighted competitors whose quality is perceived as worse by 24 per cent or more. Customer service tells the same tale. If you're rated equal to the competition, return on investment is 20 per cent: worse, and it's 12 per cent: 'better' service, though, is rewarded with a 28 per cent return. You can't ask for a better guide to better business results.

Everywhere the story is the same. Superior quality drives profitability; improving quality over the opposition boosts market share and builds market leadership; inferior quality cripples cash generation; superior quality boosts stockmarket valuations. Nor need the prizes come at higher cost. Nearly a third of 2,746 surveyed companies which were perceived as offering better quality actually had operating costs equal to or lower than those of inferior-quality competitors. If you hit both cost targets (low) and quality targets (high), market share will be larger and profitability greater.

That's only to be expected. But one of Gale's most valuable and high-powered points does look surprising. 'Good' isn't good enough. Quality experts rightly prefer 'Would you buy from us again?' to the standard satisfaction queries – and 60 per cent of the respondents will declare themselves 'very willing to repurchase' if they think your total quality is good. But if it's 'excellent', the repurchasers leap to 90 per cent. Nobody can afford to ignore customer retention or loyalty, a hard measure with direct and quantifiable impact on profits, for losing customers is expensive and so is replacing them.

The pursuit of quality excellence is thus mandatory on every count, and Gale's procedures can't be dodged. First, ask people in the market – not just your own customers – to list the important factors in their purchasing decisions. Second, ask the customers to weight the factors they've cited, taking 100 points in all, and dividing them between the factors by relative importance (in the customers' eyes, of course). Third, ask them to score the competing firms on a 1 to 10 basis on each factor. Now you're in a position to find out where you really stand.

The crucial person in registering this properly measured customer satisfaction can only be the customer. But who delivers that satisfaction? Only the people working in the firm. Author Jeffrey Pfeffer believes that better people-management is the single greatest source of competitive advantage. He notes that America's five top stockmarket winners in 1972–92 operated not in wonder sectors, but in retailing, airlines, publishing and food-processing, which all featured 'massive competition and horrendous losses, widespread bankruptcy, virtually no barriers to entry . . . little unique or proprietary technology, and many substitute products or services'.

His clear conclusion is that the super-performers gained their superior results from focusing on their people, a source of advantage which is widely and sadly neglected by most managements, and for unacceptable reasons. A contract manufacturer named Solectron took a different attitude: it couldn't get its overall customer satisfaction index above the low 90s (out of 100). Trying to reach the high 90s proved counter-productive, until 'the company looked to more fundamental changes in its structure and its ways of managing people'.

So customers are not the only vital parties who need satisfying. But neither do employees complete the list. What about suppliers? And, speaking of employees, what about the higher-paid ones, the managers who commission all the surveys? Do employees and management share the same values? Are human resources strategies compatible with service-quality focus? Is your company aware of how staff morale can impact on customer satisfaction? Dissatisfied employees won't satisfy anybody else, including their managers.

Quality companies, again, may well judge managers' performance, for pay purposes, on a basket of results that include employee satisfaction. But only a minority of managements have reasonably accurate measures of how employees feel about their work. Yet one measure, available to all managements, is as concrete and telling as customer retention: people retention, or labour turnover. We have even found high-tech consultancies, whose manpower is their only asset, paying no attention to this key, hard indicator of employee loyalty; and yet employee disloyalty costs them money just as surely as losing customers, and indeed may well cause that loss.

Other indicators, like the results of employee-attitude surveys, take longer, are costlier and need careful interpretation. For instance, when International Survey Research looked at firms in eight European countries, it discovered significant variations between both businesses and nations. While 70 per cent of Swiss workers gave a 'favourable response', that fell to only 54 per cent for the bottom marker – Britain. According to ISR, fewer than half of British workers 'believe they are well managed, are well communicated to, or have good career development opportunities'.

Compared to other Europeans, UK workers feel that 'they are badly organised, inefficient, poorly supervised, badly trained, produce low quality work, have less job security and have low levels of company identification'. Some of these complaints (for example, on training) match objective reports from other sources. But managers who feel that the subjective views exaggerate the UK reality are probably right. National characteristics influence results, and British workers are simply harder to satisfy than the Swiss or the Dutch.

But this is irrelevant, because perceptions, justified or not, are facts. If that's how workers feel about their companies, the attitude will affect their performance and, as noted, the perceived levels of customer service, and thus profitability. By the same token, improving their perceptions on the vital dimensions – led by job satisfaction, working relationships and operating efficiency – will demand real and valuable advances. You can, moreover, kill all those three birds with one stone.

There's only one way to find out how employees feel about the company. Ask them. It also happens to be the best way of improving their performance. Ask them. People on that mythical front line know full well how customer service and satisfaction can be improved, and self-managed teams are the best and quickest way of exploiting that front-line knowledge. The same is vitally true on the factory floor. Going to everybody, from the customer contacts to the backroom boys like the accountants, and asking for advice on improvements and their implementation has revolutionary implications.

Both this approach and, very likely, the proposals flowing from the working parties will affect not only business results, but the way in which managers manage. So be it: for all managers are in the service business, too. And their front-line customers are the managed, who, on all the evidence, are served none too well. When the progressive Redbridge Council asked staff about their work, MORI found some impressive scores on matters like 'interesting work' (77 per cent) and 'serving the public' (71 per cent), but some less encouraging results on 'becoming less bureaucratic' (62 per cent) and 'having efficient working practices' (58 per cent).

Those findings have obvious implications for the quality of managers. So does a parallel survey undertaken by Investors in People. It found that under half of those polled could explain Redbridge's aims to outsiders: 'Many people feel confused by the lack of corporate identity and purpose.' Nearly 60 per cent of staff never discussed training and development needs with their bosses (who, almost certainly, would give themselves a much higher score on this count). In general, management direction, support and encouragement were less than people wanted, and no doubt needed, in order to achieve the desired results.

Where direction, support and encouragement are lacking, so is focus – and the reason is often that managers themselves lack the same three necessities. Consultant Peter Zentner of Strategic Retail Identity uses interview techniques instead of polling to construct profiles of the complete business system. Auditing one large organisation, Zentner got responses from managers like this: 'The head office is completely hierarchical. We should push responsibility down the line.' Or, even worse, 'We don't know how to manage risk. People are frightened to make mistakes.'

Not surprisingly, these failings feed into the front line. Customers observed: 'The staff are not unfriendly. But they're not actually friendly either. They won't waste time on a customer.' Or 'They are understaffed. Always so busy. Everybody gets irate. You have to wait for ages.' Or 'Managers gathered in the aisles. Lengthy discussion about where to display new products. They wouldn't move for anyone.'

Listening to external views

As for suppliers, Zentner found them making these comments. 'They could save themselves a fortune if they used us properly.' Or, worse again, 'Pedestrian response time. An organisation where everybody can say no, but nobody can say yes.' Note how that last comment dovetails with remarks made by employees: 'Senior management doesn't speak to the staff. We're invisible,' or 'Our strength is we're customer-focused. Our weakness is our customer service.'

This, surely, isn't the picture top management wanted to see. Nor will it achieve either focus on the results or the right results. But it's the reality. To see yourself as others see you is difficult, but essential, which explains why researching into those external views justifiably takes up more corporate time and money than ever before. But even obeying Gale's instructions doesn't complete the picture of the truly customer-oriented, results-focused company. That's because the customer-leading company will win over that which is merely led. Leadership isn't required only inside the firm: it's vital outside, in the marketplace.

The Quality Award criteria miss a vital trick here. They call for evidence 'of the company's success in satisfying the needs and expectations of customers'. True market leadership calls for focus on *creating* customer expectations by innovation and imagination. Success in this ultimate success zone, though, will be captured by another EQA criterion: 'What the perception of external customers is of the company and of its products and services.'

This brings us back to our starting point. Winning companies focus on the hard facts of customer retention and labour turnover, learn why people stop buying or quit, and act on policies that will retain and motivate the customers and colleagues they want to keep. They also focus very seriously on the results of properly constructed surveys which show how the company is perceived by the people who create its results, because improving these perceptions improves those results. Moreover, the high regard of customers and employees enables continued and continuous success.

In business as in sport, the score when that whistle blows is what matters – at that moment. But other games, other seasons, other financial years and other business cycles lie ahead. The great management doesn't focus just on winning the game in hand. It looks beyond to discover the next game, and to make sure, to the fullest extent of human powers, of winning again – and again.

IV

Courage – How to Take Risks

10

Coe's Comeback

Nobody will ever forget the marvellous moment at the Los Angeles Olympics when Sebastian Coe, after a year plagued with injury and disappointing performances, came home with gold in the 1500 metres for the second time. Arms aloft, he pointed aggressively skywards with both hands: he had proved that he was number one. It was the toughest challenge, met in the most courageous way. But those who remembered the Moscow Olympics of 1980 shouldn't have been surprised by that courage. Coe's running was a thing of beauty, but it's character that makes a champion.

Moscow was the arena for the much-celebrated, much-anticipated 'confrontation' between Coe and Steve Ovett. Widely regarded as two of the greatest middle-distance runners of all time, the two Britons had been winning medals and breaking world records from the mid-seventies. But they had not, as yet, faced each other on the track. The experts had it all worked out. There could be no doubt of the results. Coe would win the 800 metres and Ovett the 1500. But the experts had it all wrong.

The reality was that Ovett won the 800 metres, in which Coe ran one of the worst, most lethargic races of his career. Why? And how in two and a half days could he have hoped to return to the track and challenge successfully for a 1500-metre gold medal when his

conqueror was clear favourite? The question misunderstands both
the nature of athletic competition, which is fought out in mind as
well as body, and the character of the true competitor, who aims
to conquer himself as well as the opposition.

Enjoy what you do

Coe will explain to you that he has loved running for as long as
he can remember. He acutely enjoys the actual physical sensation
of his sport. This, he believes, is one of the keys to success in any
field. You should truly enjoy what you do; you should hunger to
go out and repeat what you enjoy again and again. As a small child
Seb lived with his parents just outside Stratford-on-Avon. Instead
of riding a bicycle, as most children did at his age, he used to insist
on running in and out of town, some two to three miles every day,
without a second thought.

Coe ran his first serious race at the age of thirteen in the
1969–70 season. Before long he was running thirty to forty
cross-country races each year. This impressed his father, a racing
cyclist of no mean quality. Peter Coe decided to start coaching his
offspring and to take a serious interest in Seb's athletic ability.
By 1975 Seb had earned a junior vest running at Burghley
against France and Spain, where he won the 1500 metres. At
the end of that year he ran the same distance in Athens for the
European Junior Championships, coming in well down the field
in twenty-third place.

His first senior season was 1976. The next year he gained his
first senior title, winning the European Indoor Championships in
San Sebastián, Spain, again at 1500 metres. Coe had started his
competitive career well in a sport that, like all major sports, was
changing dramatically. The golden stream of television revenue
has played a key role in many of these changes, which often, as in
athletics, has involved moving from fairly pure amateurism into
the very grey area of semi-professionalism.

These changes might have blurred an athlete's horizons, but
Coe's focus was always clear, and always directed at winning

medals, especially in the major international competitions. He remembers lining up with other members of his club one evening to see and touch the silver medal of Trevor Wright, runner-up in the cross-country event in San Sebastián. He was, he remembers, in awe at this achievement – not surprisingly, since medals won by Britons in top-class athletics had been few and far between in the post-war years, dominated by the Americans and the state-subsidised athletes of the Soviet bloc.

Coe never ran for money. He based his whole training and preparation on winning the major competitions. His most intense focus was on the Olympics. His whole desire, his great dream, was to win an Olympic gold medal. Many people, no doubt, dream of this prize, and a dream is how it stays. Without courage it can never be realised. It takes courage, for a start, actually to commit your whole life to achieving a dream of such difficulty. You have just one chance every four years, and even then only one of the many dreamers will succeed.

For every minute he's been seen on the track running in a race, says Coe, there was sixty hours' worth of training; amazingly intense and arduous training. It was overseen by his father, who would often follow Seb in the car. Timing his son's repetitions of 800 metres, acting as guide and mentor, Peter Coe made sure that the runner's schedules and speed were always on track, heading towards that golden goal.

Looking back, Coe remembers what he calls his 'bread-and-butter' months, the period from October to April/May, the long and lonely weeks of hard training through the winter, going out in all weathers, splashing through the rain, doing endurance training in the snow, running around the Midlands through the cold, bleak nights, with no company except the image in his mind's eye of a gold medal. Those months built up the bank of fitness on which he would draw to compete in the gruelling season, itself probably only three to four months long.

If his commitment ever wavered in the bread-and-butter months, he knew, performance would be affected in that brief period of peak competition. His commitment was, of course, sustained by the coach–athlete relationship, which is often regarded as the most crucial in sport. Coe's situation was unusually sensitive in that his coach was also his father. Seb remembers that early on the relationship was almost entirely one-way, with all the advice coming from his father and Seb obediently doing the work on road and track.

Crucially, however, Coe had the courage to develop the relationship in his early twenties. It took emotional strength to become more involved, to challenge his father on training techniques and to develop the path forward to the top as a genuine two-man team. This shifting of the balance, Coe's deepening involvement in planning his own progress and his increasingly assured ability to adapt his training programme to the requirements, is what enabled him to be consistently one of the greatest runners in world athletics.

That was the background which enabled the athlete to build up his strength, speed and experience, breaking world records along the way, in preparation for the Moscow Olympics of 1980. It's that build-up which underpins the athlete's courage under pressure. To non-athletes, the pressure of the putt that will win or lose the Open, the penalty that will win or lose the Grand Slam, the serve on which the vital Wimbledon tie-break depends, seems impossibly severe. To the champion it is just one more test of skill, concentration and preparation.

Grace under pressure

Managers need the same mental conditioning to generate the courage to make their decisions and take the actions they know to be right. Once doubt creeps in, for athletes and managers alike, the courage falters: the kick, the serve, the putt, the business opportunity are missed. 'Grace under pressure' is almost a definition of courage. It doesn't mean having nerves of steel. The greatest sportsman can suffer extreme nervousness before the event. That's part of the adrenaline build-up that produces peak performance, and is in no way a sign of weakness.

Yet no pressure can be greater or more sustained than that of the Olympics – especially for first-time competitors. For Coe, it was intensified in Moscow by the hype over the 800-metres confrontation with Ovett. The British media, even the world media, seemed to comment on little else. Not only was this Coe's first experience of life in an Olympic village, it was his first encounter with pressure and press coverage of this intensity – and he failed, running, as he freely acknowledges, one of the worst races of his career.

He is still somewhat unsure about exactly why he failed. Any athlete can remember days when, for little or no apparent reason, there was no desire, no edge in the competitive thrust. Coe tragically experienced that lack of impetus in his first Olympic final. He remembers the gun, taking off in an alarmingly lethargic manner, running as if in a dream. He felt as though his senses were numb, as if he were on the outside looking in. The shock realisation, with 200 metres to go, that his race position was far from ideal did produce an electric reaction, but it came far too late for Coe to challenge for his dream of Olympic gold.

In the aftermath of defeat, Coe was in shock, and so too was his father and coach. How could a man who was at his peak of physical condition, acknowledged as the world's best over that distance, fail so dramatically? Peter Coe kept asking himself what he had done wrong. How had he let his son down? What crucial part of the preparation had been mishandled? A devastated Seb, for his part, found it hard to explain his mental state to the people around him. He remembers almost a lack of understanding, a lack of sympathy.

The significant point is that, although Seb Coe had won an Olympic silver medal in the event, it made no difference to his desolation. The vast majority of people can only daydream about even competing in the Olympics, let alone a silver medal. This man had done both, and yet he was shattered. As he said, he hadn't lain awake at night hoping for a silver medal, and he certainly hadn't committed so many years of his life to coming second. Settle for second-best in any competition, and that's what you're overwhelmingly likely to get: champions want and know better.

Fortunately, Coe had two and a half days between losing the 800 and qualifying for the 1500 metres. He had, he remembers, the luxury of getting out of bed the following morning and saying, 'OK, I ran like a complete idiot, but I don't have to repeat it.' The next day he forced himself to go out and train. He ran hard, for close on twelve miles. He had to refocus and kept telling himself that he needed to restore his pride. He took a realistic approach to the longer distance. He might not win the race, but he was certainly going to win back his pride as an athlete.

Whatever his position, Coe determined, he would walk off the track knowing that he had competed to his maximum, that he had fulfilled his potential; that if he didn't win, whoever did would have proved himself the better athlete. This hard-edged realism was a kind of growing up, for Coe was actually very inexperienced in terms of major competitions. He only got into the British team in 1977 and this was his first taste of Olympic competition. He hadn't, he agrees, accepted how nervous he was, but now he got back into training with a vengeance, ensuring that his physical condition couldn't be bettered.

Moreover, Coe told himself, he hadn't become a bad athlete overnight. The key to achieving peak performance lies in having the courage to believe in your own ability. You can tell yourself many things about your talents, but you will not turn them into achievement until you believe in yourself. Coe spent those sixty hours reminding himself how good he was. He went over all the races he had won in the previous few years, the times that he had set, the world records he had broken. He recollected all the training he had been through. Now he had to get himself into the best mental, as well as physical, shape of his life. He had to maintain a strong focus on the positive experiences of building up to the Olympics. Everyone and anyone can fail once. The great achievers, though, do not make the same mistakes twice. They have the courage to learn from those mistakes, to digest the reasons why they happened, and to make sure that those particular scenarios of failure never recur.

Number One again – Seb Coe celebrates his Olympic Men's 1500m victory – Los Angeles, 1984.

For his part, Coe's father was convinced that Seb would win the 1500 metres. Seb himself was not so sure. Ovett, he conceded, was by a very long way the best opponent he had ever run against. Over this distance, Ovett had won forty-two consecutive races, and few could see that sequence being broken. But Coe knew not only that he was at his physical peak, not only that he was a great athlete, but that he had an acute hunger for gold. Ovett had won his gold medal, though at the less expected distance. Would that achievement take the ultimate edge off Ovett's will to win?

For Coe that edge was provided by the desperation he felt in the build-up to the race; his mind was focused not so much on winning, but on restoring his pride by doing so. The result was that he ran a far more intelligent and tactical race. Alert both mentally and physically, he didn't allow himself to fall out of contention at any point along the 1500 metres. With victory, Coe achieved his dream – and showed his mettle. He had turned defeat and disaster into exhilaration and success.

Coping with failure

It took great courage to absorb and learn from that first failure. It took mental strength over those two and a half days for Coe to refocus on his abilities and strengths and then produce a great victory. But in management and sport alike, the one-off success is not what separates the top performers from the rest. Every success carries within it the seeds of its own decay – a truth which has particular poignancy for athletes, who know that at some point their physical prowess will decline. That's inevitable: the failure of once-excellent businesses is not.

Athletes can wane long before their physical powers. Companies can start to founder while still possessed of excellent strengths. In both case, mind-sets are to blame. The athlete, perhaps, doesn't have the mental courage of a Seb Coe, the strength to see that one lost race doesn't spell total failure, the readiness to take the blame entirely rather than find excuses for under-achievement. The company, very likely, doesn't have the courage to recognise incipient failure, to challenge the practices and precepts of a successful past and transform itself internally to fit the forces of external change.

For Coe the true test of his courage was to succeed consistently, to win gold medals consistently, to be consistently one of the best among the greatest runners in the world. The true test of management is no different, but just as tough, which is why so few companies have long records of uninterrupted growth and profitability. As those raised arms at Los Angeles indicated to the world, Coe went out as number one, leaving his sport of athletics after making a lasting impression on the way middle-distance races are run. He also left a legacy of unmatched physical grace – and invincible grace under pressure.

11

What Packard Gave Hewlett

No subject is more fashionable than the management of change. Mostly, those following the fashion are major companies left stranded, at least temporarily, by external change, and striving to get back into the water. Very few leviathans simply surge onwards from decade to decade. By the common consent of the gurus, the American company Hewlett–Packard is among these few. Where the beached whales have lost the secret of their dynamic pasts, which changed them from small to middling to large to mighty, HP has managed, and been managed, to keep moving from mighty to mightier still.

It's probably no coincidence that the two founding partners survived right into the nineties. Entrepreneurs often come in pairs, one partner complementing the other's strengths and compensating for his weaknesses. Bill Hewlett provided the technological skills to which Stanford classmate David Packard applied business acumen and administrative ability. Together they built a great West Coast high-tech business, long before the birth of Silicon Valley. They started in a one-car garage in 1939, armed with capital of only $538 and a single drill press, to provide the archetype for the electronics start-up.

At that point, there was little, apart from their talent, to distinguish the pair from countless other struggling entrepreneurs.

Even to launch such enterprises you need courage, risking what
little money you have to back your own judgement of your abilities,
your own instincts on what the market will want, your own qualities of persistence in the face of almost certain adversity. What
Hewlett gave Packard, and vice versa, was sustained courageously
through all stages of growth – and that's where many of their
contemporaries faltered.

Hewlett's key invention was the audio oscillator to measure
sound. The first customer was Walt Disney, who bought seven
of the devices for his studios. The company did well enough
to achieve incorporated status in 1947, but there was nothing
inevitable about the progress which made HP a world leader
in precision electronic equipment of all kinds (it's still the
largest producer of its original speciality, test and measurement
instruments). Under Hewlett's direction, HP added leadership
in scientific calculators and a powerful position in computers
– minis, PCs, work stations, printers, etc. The founders left
their executive posts in 1983, both with immense fortunes,
but continued to play a crucial behind-the-scenes role in the
corporation. In 1991 Packard (who in 1969–71 was absent in
Washington, working in the Defence Department) was especially
active in planning and pushing through a major reorganisation
designed to cut bureaucracy and reinvent the corporation's
ability to generate new products.

After that injection of new impetus, Hewlett–Packard cut its
operating expense ratio by 19 per cent in three years (with no
job losses) while still growing fast: by 24 per cent in 1992 and
another 24 per cent in 1993, which meant adding $3.9 billion
– an amount larger than the total sales of the 131st biggest
industrial company in the US. To help accomplish the 1992
surge, 5,000 employees had to change businesses. They moved,
across the US if necessary, from low value-added enterprises to
high. CEO Lewis Platt thus lived up to his words: 'My strategy
is to make sure that we're doing the things that can assure us
some top-line growth.'

Clearly, there's no inherent reason why the growing has to

stop, although there are inherent barriers before which the faint-hearted often fail. Corporate metamorphoses like HP's, however, display a well-established pattern of crossing these obstacles. The first hurdle, the make-or-break point, is the transition from personal, proprietorial domination to professional management. It's the most difficult and bravest transition because it involves some surrender of personal power. The entrepreneur who has driven his business to riches has to hand over elements of control to administrators and bean-counters.

Some would-be tycoons never dare to cross the divide: others condemn the transition to failure by appointing the wrong professionals, or by giving the professionals (rightly or wrongly chosen) only enough rope with which to hang themselves. Bill Hewlett and Dave Packard neatly dodged this problem; as noted, Packard himself had all the talent required to become a top-class professional manager, leaving Hewlett to mind, and gloriously expand, the technological store.

Bill Hewlett (left) and David Packard built Hewlett–Packard from garage to giant.

Effective partnership is a marvellous agent of change. Two minds and two willpowers are always better than one. The partnering presence, moreover, protects the business from the potentially lethal vice of personal domination, but without losing the priceless dynamic of personal, entrepreneurial drive. When one partner's courage weakens, the other's may restore the balance. It follows that true partnering – deploying the ability to work with others productively – is a key element in managing change.

What is 'professional' about Packard's kind of management, though? It rests on control, organisation and process. Control means that authority (especially spending power) is specifically allocated and its exercise monitored by efficient reporting systems. Organisation creates structures that channel responsibility in an orderly fashion to enable the achievement of desired results. Process sets up the business systems that achieve these ends.

The catch is that control, organisation and process breed bureaucracy. In the initial stages of professionalisation, the bureaucratic threat doesn't matter: substituting order for chaos establishes tremendous momentum. As that impetus exhausts itself, though, the second break-point arrives. Does the business reach a plateau from which it can't generate new and vigorous growth? Or does it metamorphose again into a third stage of dynamism?

The engine of HP's growth has been the founders' bold willingness to take the company into new sectors, despite the formidable risks associated with high technology. Where they failed, it was through defects of vision rather than lack of courage. Shortsightedness explains how even Hewlett missed some great opportunities: Stephen Wozniak, the breakaway who created the personal computer boom by founding Apple with Steve Jobs, couldn't get his idea accepted by HP. But the 8 to 10 per cent of sales spent on R&D has generated a formidable roster of several thousand products, including very successful PCs, despite the false start.

Taking calculated risks

The quality of courage in business needs to be carefully defined. It isn't a matter of just taking risks: risk is always there, but it should be carefully calculated and moderate. In other words, the risk-taker should be sure that he's right, and certain that, while betting money, he's not betting the whole corporation. Hewlett followed the principle of safety in numbers: 'We've simply got more bonfires burning at one time.' Equally important, he had the courage to allow others to start the fires.

The much rewritten corporate credo, 'The HP Way', laid great emphasis, throughout all the rewrites, on the individual freedom and enthusiasm from which innovative thinking comes. It emphasised that people were to be given 'a chance to learn by making mistakes'. The culture was carefully designed to encourage risk-taking and discourage top-down direction: 'If I have to tell a guy to do something,' said Hewlett, 'I consider myself a failure as a manager.' That attitude shouldn't be misconstrued: Hewlett led the innovative effort very much from the front.

In the excellent Arthur D. Little book *Breakthroughs!*, there's a sobering account of how Hewlett, disapproving of one product dear to the heart of some young engineers, said he didn't want to see the wretched thing next time he toured the labs. They decided to take him at his word and rushed through the work, completing the product (a very successful one, as it turned out) before the great man returned. As the story shows, Hewlett often decided personally which products were to continue and which to be abandoned.

As late as 1986, when he was in his seventies, Hewlett was actively involved in promoting work on the coming genera-tion of much faster RISC (reduced-instruction set computing) micro-processors. The risk in RISC lay far more in missing the technology than in developing the capacity to exploit it. While Hewlett thus found the areas where the risks were worth taking, Packard ensured that they were not only moderate, but carefully calculated. As an HP executive once said, 'We like to sneak up on things.'

That strategy long ago took HP past another crucial break-point, from monolithic form to multiplicity. The single-product business typically becomes multi-product and multi-market, crossing into new businesses and new geographical areas. Basic professional management no longer suffices: managing diversity has become the prime necessity. The centre can't manage the businesses; instead, it must create the conditions in which they can manage themselves – and that transition is just as difficult as the progress from proprietorship.

Once again, it involves a courageous surrender of power: this time, from head office to the business units. Once again, too, crucial issues of control, organisation and process must be tackled. How do you ensure that subsidiaries are performing as you want without riding herd on the managements in ways that impede their performance? How do you build an orderly organisation without loading too much structure on top of local initiative? How do you both win the benefits of shared processes and keep the virtues of distinct enterprises?

The paradox is that professional administration, which pro-vides the right answers at the first break-point, gives the wrong ones at the second. The smoothly running machine has to become more anarchic as its markets multiply. That ICI chairman who remarked (see Chapter 8), 'You can't turn a large company like this round every eighteen months,' was your died-in-the-wool professional speaking. The true change-manager thinks quite differently. If change is demanded, you change – even if, this time, it means substituting chaos for order.

A remarkable exponent of this principle was Ken Olsen, founder of Digital Equipment Corporation. He twice turned his creation upside-down. First, to cope with and generate multiplicity, he created 'product champions' who turned DEC into a collection of entrepreneurial businesses. In his own words, the system was a 'miracle'. DEC, growing by 30 per cent annually for nineteen years, became the second-biggest computer company in the world while managing to steer well clear of IBM.

But the development of the VAX line of mini-computers took DEC into direct competition with the giant, whereupon Olsen decided to disband his miracle, substituting a centralised organisation that could win over the big-business customers. The turnabout caused tremendous pain, both personal and financial, but DEC emerged from five years of turmoil so strongly that Olsen earned a *Fortune* accolade as America's Most Successful Entrepreneur.

Changing for growth

That enormous success makes the same point as DEC's more recent collapse into billion-dollar losses. Growth demands brave readiness to change anything and everything, including the procedures nearest and dearest to your heart. At this later stage Olsen wasn't ready to accept the decline of the mini-computer market that built his company's billions. Too old to remake the organisation radically a third time, he was forced to quit, leaving behind a company in dire trouble.

Olsen's difficulties arose in part from staying too close to the action. It's a common trap which Hewlett and Packard (like typical Japanese super-managers) avoided by leaving appointed top managers to manage. As noted, though, Packard was still excellently placed to intervene when HP ran into bureaucratic blockage in the eighties. Control, organisation and process had become so over-developed that HP suffered a severe case of corporate constipation. Packard reappeared to help the chief executive dismantle the committees and other procedures which had dangerously slowed decisions and actions at a time when market changes were accelerating.

That speed-up is especially marked in electronics, and one result has been to shorten the gestation period for major businesses. Most mighty companies took a generation to reach their full stature. Thus, from Tom Watson's arrival to IBM reaching

$100-million status took thirty years; HP, too, took the typical three decades. But Compaq, like Apple before it, was a leading, worldwide, multi-billion-dollar company within a decade.

Yet the vital stages of, first, entrepreneurial drive, then professionalism, and next devolution aren't short-circuited by high technology. The same break-points must be passed. As in a Mack Sennett comedy, the chase has been speeded up, but the motions of managing growth are much the same. To keep on the growth track, an element of anarchy may be essential to cut across regular controls, organisational patterns and established processes. The high-tech examples magnify (because of the scale and speed of technological change) what must happen to all businesses which want to sustain modern success.

Peter McColough, one of two men primarily responsible for the phenomenal growth of Xerox, once asked: 'Is it inevitable that such organisations as Xerox should have their periods of emergence, full flower of growth and prestige, and then, later, stagnation and death?' The answer is a resounding no. The irony, though, is that, as he spoke, Xerox was itself about to stagnate – most remarkably, through never launching the first PC, a working miracle created at its Palo Alto Research Center. Then management allowed its copier business to degenerate to the point where Japanese machines *sold* for less than Xerox's manufacturing costs. In the last decade, recouping some of its lost market share, Xerox has engaged in a massive effort to change the company from top to bottom (see Chapter 17). The longer you leave reaction, though, the more painful it is to change the corporation, and the more pressing – and threatening – the need for change becomes.

The nearby presence of a detached change-agent (like Packard) is obviously helpful, but it shouldn't be required. Change is most easily managed when it's anticipated, as in the very first stages of growth. In those heady, hard-working days, companies are automatically geared by their ambitions to the expectation of change, and they gain in flexibility what they lose in tidiness. The middle phase, when they become more orderly, but also more rigid, is the most dangerous, because the habit and expectation of change may disappear.

In the third phase (if they get that far), companies replay the second-phase crisis as organisations seeking stability collide with markets that demand volatility. That's when managers start talking about managing change and 'reinventing the corporation'. But reinvention, funnily enough, often turns out to resemble the original corporate invention. Today's great growth businesses require the same bold attributes that won the chance of greatness in the beginning: partnerships of talented individuals focused on clear business purposes who change the processes and personnel as these purposes demand.

That can happen in the most unpromising circumstances, such as those of British engineering in the mid-1950s. The industry contained one middling-sized firm exhibiting the faults that killed off many of its breed and which still plague many small- to medium-sized businesses: restricted product range, over-dependence on the UK market, low reputation, inadequate management. Three young managers saw that not only the company, but also their careers, were on the line, and moved with decisive courage to correct all four faults. By the seventies, the firm had already soared from obscurity, having multiplied profits thirty times on a fivefold rise in turnover. A determined drive had transformed a narrow-based business: it now had two strong legs in North America and Western Europe (the UK was absorbed into the latter in the trio's eminently correct thinking). A third leg was waiting to develop in the Pacific Basin. With that leg now also strong, the group has powered on to world-class scale (£10 billion-plus of sales) and fame. Its name is BTR.

The highly effective management principles of BTR's leader, Sir Owen Green, became the basis of Robert Heller's book, *The Business of Winning*. They formed an acronym – IT BECAME FAST:

(1) Improve basic efficiency – all the time.
(2) Think as simply and directly as possible about what you're doing and why.

(3) Behave towards others as you wish them to behave towards you.

(4) Evaluate each business and business opportunity with all the objective facts and logic you can muster.

(5) Concentrate on what you do well.

(6) Ask questions ceaselessly about your performance, your markets, your objectives.

(7) Make money: if you don't, you can't do anything else.

(8) Economise, because doing the most with the least is the name of the game.

(9) Flatten the company, so authority is spread over many people.

(10) Admit to your failings and shortcomings, because only then will you be able to improve on them.

(11) Share the benefits of success widely among those who helped to achieve it.

(12) Tighten up the organisation whenever you can – because success tends to breed slackness.

The dozen points are equally applicable to the growth saga of Hewlett and Packard, and to that of any company whose managers have the courage to renew constantly, raising their sights to higher and higher targets, and never forgetting that the courageous pasts of their own companies may well provide the main lessons required in the present and the future.

12

From Dinosaurs to Dolphins

The key to innovative risk-taking is to match the organisation to the characteristics of free-thinking, original, courageous minds – and then keep judiciously out of their way. It sounds a very tall order, but the principles are no different from those of managing anybody who you respect and trust. And if you neither respect or trust them, why are they employed at all? The courage to back others is part of the courage required to manage in the new environment.

This environment has changed the managerial career to marked degree. Most managers, however, haven't come to terms with the change. The ideals of the traditional system persist, with its job-for-life, hierarchical promotion and safe stability, but the many redundant middle managers can testify that old ideal and new reality are far apart. Safety used to lie in not taking risks. Now avoiding risks can be positively dangerous: it's the courageous, creative, risk-taking manager who gets promoted, and the time-server who can be severed without pain – except to him.

The gap between the old corporate world and the new can only widen as companies seek shorter lines of communication and move towards horizontal organisation in the drive for faster and more innovative response. As the new boss of a high-tech multinational told his senior colleagues at one Insights seminar, their jobs are no longer permanent. Their security lies not in their roles within the collective scheme, but in their individual skills. So long as these stay strong and relevant, their pay and prospects will remain excellent. Otherwise . . .

The new manager's position thus resembles that of a top sportsman, who keeps his place only as long as he displays superior form and fits the strategy. Only a few players in any sport are world-class, absolutely certain of selection until they decide to retire. Only a few managers – and those are mostly proprietorial entrepreneurs – are in the same superstar category. The others have to prove themselves again and again, striving to achieve peak performance by exploiting the always under-used personal potential. Like the sportsman, the manager has to work to overcome the internal barriers, which include lack of courage, to reach for peak performance.

The Insights sessions invariably reveal that organisations themselves heavily reinforce internal inhibitions, often in self-defeating and eminently curable ways – say, by advocating long-term creative contributions while insisting, above all, on short-term, bottom-line results. Managers know this only too well: they customarily rate their own attributes significantly above those of the organisation. That, however, doesn't absolve individual managers from the need to exploit their own potential to the full. Indeed, the new management career makes this imperative.

High performance in each role (leading a project, running a subsidiary, reorganising a department, etc.) is the field-marshal's baton in the manager's knapsack. But the successful development of individual skills depends very heavily on helping others to develop and exploit their own talents. As stated at the start of this section, managing creatively is the key to unleashing creativity. This is made admirably clear by Gerald Kushel, the American psychologist and management lecturer, in his book, *Reaching the Peak Performance Zone.*

He recommends a three-part system:

(1) Take total self-responsibility for all your own job performances. Then model that quality and teach your direct reports how to do the same thing.

(2) Make available to each of your direct reports some very good reasons for wanting to perform at peak.

(3) Mentor (which includes counselling and coaching) your direct reports to the point where they are clearly performing at peak. After that, *stay out of their way.*

We've italicised that injunction in its second appearance in this section because of its sovereign importance at all levels, from shop floor to top management. It places responsibility where it belongs, and demands courage on both sides of the relationship. Good managers don't, to quote Kushel, 'blame others or external events' for their performance. That's not because they're wonderfully unselfish. On the contrary, WIIFM – what's in it for me? – always applies. The self-interest of your direct reports is also where you find the 'very good reasons' for them to perform at peak.

Kushel's three-stage process fits perfectly with the way in which Geoff Cooke turned the England XV from also-rans to double Grand Slam-winners and World Cup finalists. It fits far less well with the traditional management career, in which seniority and status count for more than achievement and ability, and playing safe for far more than taking risks. Unfortunately, too many companies are organised in much the same way as they were in the past. That explains many of their difficulties, which are only intensifying as the pace of competition accelerates.

There's an interesting analogy from the US car industry in its prime. All the 'big three' manufacturers concentrated on the so-called 'dominant design' – the rear-wheel drive, separate chassis, engine-in-front machine. The dominance didn't spring from customer preference, as was shown by the soaring rise of the rear-engined VW Beetle to fourth-largest-selling brand in the US. Rather, it suited the economics of Detroit to continue with the dominant design until long after competitors and, more importantly, the public had turned to other approaches.

The dominant organisational design, with its safety-first centralisation of decision-making and its hierarchical relationships, can't generate fast or bold enough reactions to cope with – let alone anticipate – rapid external change by swift internal initiatives. The centre is too far from the market or the factory floor, separated from both by too many layers, which in turn are reproduced in the over-dependent subsidiaries. If the latter also embody brands, the lack of independence jeopardises the vital brand identity.

Twenty-first century management

The difference between the dominant design and twenty-first century management is charted exactly by a questionnaire which the English psychologist Mark Brown uses to differentiate between 'dolphins' and 'dinosaurs'. Score your organisation from 0 to 6 along the distance between the two extremes:

(1) Those around me 'yes, but' new ideas to death/ Those around me encourage new ideas.

(2) We are geared to providing what we want to provide/We provide what the customer wants.

(3) My organisation is focused on solving problems/ My organisation is focused on opportunities.

(4) Many of our people are mentally retired/ Our people are highly motivated.

(5) The match between individual values and those of the organisation is poor/ The match between them is good.

(6) People feel disempowered/ Individuals show high levels of initiative.

(7) People's minds are fairly set/ People are very good at 'thinking afresh'.

A score of 21 marks the dividing line between dolphins and

dinosaurs. Brown also adapts the questions for personal grading ('*I* feel disempowered', '*I* take a lot of initiatives', etc.). He points out that you can be a dinosaur in a dolphin organisation, or a dolphin living within a dinosaur. The latter situation, a very uncomfortable one, must relate to the best managers in many organisations: it's doubtful whether most corporate denizens would award their companies a half-best score of 21.

In any event, nothing less than an all-dolphin score of 42 can be praised. Look again at the seven opposed extremes: the ideals all embody 'natural' and rewarding ways of behaving, while the zero scores result from unnatural, cramped conduct. The ideals, too, all involve courage, the willingness to take chances; their opposites all embody self-defeating attempts to play safe.

Emphasise opportunities

Brown's advice to his dolphins is very different: emphasise opportunities, not problems. Solving problems creates opportunities – provided that the problems *are* actually solved. According to one industry consultant, that didn't happen at General Motors: 'They have programmes that are going to solve every problem, but they never get solved.' He describes the 'biggest problem' as 'to get the organisation actually to do something'. But taking the risk of doing something, of course, is only half the battle: doing it right wins the war.

Such big company errors have a common theme: an instinctive preference for taking action at the centre rather than on the periphery. The conventionally wise centre can order massive investments, buy other companies, reshuffle entities, close plants, but it can't increase efficiency, delight customers, raise morale or beat the competition by bold and unconventional means. Those essential ends can be achieved only by penetrating to the true nature of the organisation and giving it the systemic treatment it requires.

The heart of the matter is that organisation provides a

framework of discipline. The discipline gives creative cour-age its direction and its constraints. For example, the great comedy director Preston Sturges, after an unbroken run of money-making hits, broke with Paramount over his increasing irritation at front-office imposition of its authority. This was enshrined in strict rules, like shooting three pages of script a day, which Sturges found irksome. But after his bid for freedom, Sturges made nothing but costly flops.

By throwing money at its problems, confident that it would never run out, GM not only spent itself into the biggest loss ever made by any company, it also took away a vital constraint. The constraints usually applied, though, are not helpful; they're more likely to be totally obstructive. Gifford Pinchot III points out that 300 large corporations account for 85 per cent of all R&D spending in the US (a pattern which is probably typical of other countries, too). Yet the big outfits produce less than half the major innovations.

This isn't because they lack inventive power – they have that in abundance. Rather, they fall down on the implementation. This is readily avoided if you have the courage (and it needs plenty) to accept this advice:

(1) Don't focus on the short term.
(2) Don't have multi-level approvals.
(3) Don't cut discretionary time to useless amounts.
(4) Don't expect big wins every time.
(5) Don't operate rigid planning systems.
(6) Don't allow turf battles over who does what.
(7) Don't become fearful of making mistakes.
(8) Don't oppose individual initiative.
(9) Don't allow authoritarian traditions to rule.

As with Mark Brown's dolphin qualities, the positive attributes are far more attractive and natural than the negative: exploiting constraints rather than succumbing to them. The instinctive reaction to setback in the bad manager or sportsman is to give up: the good executive or player has the courage, like Seb Coe, to regard defeat as a challenge, a spur to raise his game and to plunge back into the arena. In fact, that's how many great businesses achieved greatness.

An intriguing book entitled *Getting It Right the Second Time* by Michael Gershman recounts some of the uphill struggles survived by some of today's bestselling brands. Clarence Birdseye launched his first frozen-food company in 1923. It promptly went bust. After further vicissitudes, General Foods, set up to exploit Birdseye's inspiration in June 1929, finally made a profit in 1937. How? By facing up to a seemingly fatal constraint – housewives wouldn't buy frozen food.

The answer was to tackle the institutional market – hotels, restaurants, hospitals, etc. Success there filtered back into the retail market. The Second World War, which sharply boosted the demand for convenience foods, did the rest. Another example is Hoover. From 1910 to 1917 sales rose from 2,140 cleaners to 48,878, but the major constraint was that busy retailers couldn't demonstrate the machines. After Hoover put its own demonstrators into stores, sales quintupled. The big breakthrough came with door-to-door canvassing, which had a fantastic 31 per cent success rate.

More interesting, though, than such anecdotes are the conclusions that Gershman draws from his studies. He found it 'safe to say' that, as a group, the heroes:

– took total responsibility for their products, because only by controlling the variables that had tripped up their predecessors could they improve them
– were committed to doing the job right – no matter how long it took or what it entailed
– looked on failures as part of the process and learned something from each one.

On that last point, the author quotes Thomas Watson, Sr, the founder of IBM: 'Remember, that's where you'll find success.

On the far side of failure.' For that to happen, however, you must have the courage to face up to the reality of failure and its true causes. At many companies that have 'downsized', the *causes* of their problems were not too many plants and workers – these were merely severe symptoms. The roots sprang from plants and workers making the wrong things in the wrong ways because of bosses managing the wrong things in the wrong ways.

Unless you have the courage to remedy that condition, a strategy which is far less expensive and painful than closures and redundancies, all other 'cures' will merely lead to a recurrence of the disease. What CEO Jack Smith has already accomplished at GM shows how sick large organisations can become. There are now 2,500 corporate staff where once 13,500 earned large salaries. That's an astounding 81.5 per cent cutback – or, viewed from the opposite perspective, a previous bloat of 5.4 times more people than were actually required.

Decisions on car prices 'used to wend their way through five committees over weeks or even months'. They now take 'a matter of days'. Again, that's an improvement. But should pricing decisions rise that high? Shouldn't the people responsible for making and marketing cars be competent to decide their prices? And shouldn't top management have the courage to let them do precisely that? In the dinosaur days GM managers held pre-meetings and even pre-pre-meetings to ensure that the main meeting went smoothly. But even the present system is far removed from the dolphin culture.

His success at GM in Europe, where it came from far behind Ford to lead the continent in car profits, is an encouraging omen for the Smith regime at GM. But the most hopeful sign lies in words etched on a copper plate as part of a desk ornament of Smith's: 'A leader is best when people barely know he exists. Not so good when people obey and acclaim him. Worse when they despise him. But of a good leader who talks little, when his work is done and his aim fulfilled, they will say, "We did it ourselves".'

Those admirable sentiments come, not from the twentieth-century Mark Brown, but from the philosopher Lao-tze, who wrote six centuries before Christ. The dinosaurs, of course, lived many millenia before that. But without that brave philosophy – helping people to do it themselves -- the dolphins will never take over. With that help, organisations can swim anywhere, and as fast as they want, even into the uncharted waters of the future: for that's where courage meets its hardest test.

Man cannot predict the future, but he is continually forced to try. For companies, the issue is truly daunting: the winners and losers of 2005 are being determined by views formed this very day. The 'safe' way of forecasting an unknown future is extrapolation. But that's not only intellectually unsound, it also tends to lock companies and industries into existing, continuous patterns in a world of discontinuity. That's why bold outsiders, such as Intel and Microsoft in computers, coming at their industry from a totally different angle, inherit the future.

Gary Hamel and C.K. Prahalad, in *Competing for the Future*, argue that established managements must be brave enough to adopt the same angle of approach, forgetting where they have come from, and concentrating instead on where they want to go. 'In business . . . what distinguishes leaders from laggards, and greatness from mediocrity, is the ability to uniquely imagine what could be.' IBM, for example, couldn't imagine the prospect of great mainframe computers being elbowed aside by increasingly powerful, tiny micro-processors. Spotting such shifts, though, doesn't require crystal balls: just balls.

Time and again, the true cause of corporate failure isn't inability to read the future but gutless refusal to acknowledge what is already under executives' noses. The swing away from Detroit's large cars, for instance, couldn't have been signalled more loudly or clearly. To act on braver perceptions, as Hamel and Prahalad say, 'What is required is an ability to mobilise every ounce of emotional and creative energy in the company.' In the phrase of Kevin Kelly, author of *Out of Control*, you're seeking 'the incubations of something from nothing', which means following 'the nine laws of God':

(1) Distribute being.
(2) Control from the bottom up.
(3) Cultivate increasing returns.
(4) Grow by chunking.
(5) Maximise the fringes.
(6) Honour your errors.
(7) Pursue no optima – have multiple goals.
(8) Seek persistent disequilibrium.
(9) Change changes itself.

Kelly's language is obscure in places, but his drift is perfectly clear: have the courage to think and act freely. That doesn't mean plunging into the unknown. The future is not a blank sheet of paper. All ambitions start from somewhere: from what you have, in the widest definition. As individuals, and in concert, managers, no less than sportsmen, need courage to make the fullest use of their intellectual and physical assets; to base their own strategy on the foundation philosophy required for any business, which is to do whatever you're good at better and better, and on a broader and broader scale – and then to go beyond.

What matters above all is courageously to look for new opportunities and for new evidence that old opportunities and basic strengths are no longer providing the organisation with the necessary dynamism. If management isn't looking for a golden future, and taking the associated risks, it's most unlikely to find one. Ignoring that truth is the greatest risk – but this is one risk which takes no courage at all.

V

Integrity – How to Create Credibility

13

Reaching Gary Lineker's Goals

After an alleged gouging incident in a League rugby fixture in the 1994–5 season, the accused front-row forward waxed indignant, protesting that he was known to one and all as the 'Gary Lineker of rugby football'. While this provoked considerable hilarity, given the player's known proclivities, it said far less about him than it did about Gary Lineker. Few other players in soccer, perhaps in any sport, have had a higher reputation for sportsmanship; for true and blameless personal integrity.

It's hard, in fact, to think of any other sportsman whose clothes that rugby player might have tried to don. In essence, integrity like Lineker's is intensely personal. But it communicates itself to others in any kind of team and is an essential element in leadership. Without integrity, there's no trust and therefore you can't have credibility, the foundation on which all leadership skills are built. But integrity is also the foundation of individual achievement. The magic words come from Polonius in *Hamlet*: 'To thine own self be true.'

In Lineker's case that Shakespearean truth extends to admitting that, in terms of natural ability, he was not the most gifted footballer who ever played for England. He lacked the sublime touch of the great naturals; he lacked the flair and daring of those who struck their goals from afar. Yet his tally of forty-eight international goals (second only to Bobby Charlton) proved, beyond doubt, that Lineker was among the most clinical and efficient scorers in football history, at home or abroad.

Appreciating strengths and weaknesses

The origins of this prolific goal-scoring ability, according to Lineker, are a slight mystery even to him. As a youngster, he was superbly quick, an excellent sprinter who caught the eye of one or two athletics scouts. But only football attracted Lineker's own attention when at Leicester Boys Grammar School – and one aspect of the game in particular: scoring goals was what inspired and excited him, and drove him on to his achievements. The exterior stayed famously calm, but inside, 'even as a young lad it was scoring goals that excited me. I just had this hunger to score goals – that's all I wanted to do.'

Lineker's football apprenticeship began at Leicester City, cleaning boots, washing kit, helping out on the ground. Honest and unassuming, he never believed he would make it even to the City first team. His chance came at eighteen, when he played a handful of games out on the wing. That reflected the club's appreciation of the youngster's speed, but the position also spoke of his lack of touch and ball-control. Lineker had a clear appreciation of his own strengths and weaknesses, however, and that's the basis, in sports and management alike, of both integrity and success.

His great asset, of course, was sheer speed, reinforced by basic coaching in sprint training. But Lineker was also beginning to recognise his ability to anticipate correctly where space would appear in the penalty box. His major weakness was touch – striking the ball at the right time with the right degree of force. So in his early Leicester years (he played for the club between the ages of eighteen and twenty-five), Lineker devoted endless hours to developing this vital attribute. The pursuit of excellence became a theme of his footballing career.

At each training session he would concentrate on trying to improve his first-time touch on the ball, watching and analysing players with greater skills and seeking to imprint these on his own play. Lineker has never been one of the assiduous and obsessive trainers: it's another mark of integrity to prefer quality to quantity. Quality training duly paid off at Leicester: he broke into the side permanently and became a goal-scoring sensation, reaching a century of goals in only 215 appearances.

Not surprisingly, he was eventually snapped up by Everton, where his goal output was even more remarkable – fifty-seven matches, forty goals. After just one season with the Liverpool club, he became an international in 1984, winning the first of what was to become eighty caps before he retired from international football eight years later. Stardom came very early in this distinguished career. Going with England to the 1986 World Cup in Mexico as a relative unknown, the twenty-six-year-old Lineker returned from the tournament as its leading goal-scorer, world famous, an overnight sensation.

But there is nothing overnight about such achievements. In almost all cases (as business biographies usually confirm), big personal breakthroughs reflect long years of preparation – like the hard and thoughtful training at Leicester as Lineker the apprentice developed his skills, or the rapid absorption of new lessons in the first year at Everton. Typically, Lineker also credits chance: in the World Cup, he recalls, the ball ran for him. But you need more than the run of the ball to score a hat-trick in the world's premier tournament – and to add further goals in every match.

Lineker's relentless work on his touch was paying off. As always, his pace left defences floundering, too. But the ball service received from his colleagues in a side of very experienced and well-drilled players was also a decisive factor. Lineker was their spearhead, and he knew it. But he also knew (as many players would not have known) that leading all the world's players in scoring World Cup goals wasn't enough. Integrity takes in not only uprightness, but wholeness and honesty. Being honest about yourself is its foundation stone.

Retaining his objectivity wasn't made easy by the inevitable public adulation. Lineker, instantly recognisable and hugely popular, was fêted wherever he went. He moved from Everton to the cauldron of football-mad Barcelona. The new recruit arrived as a hero, carrying immense expectations – the fans naturally expected a stream of goals. Lineker, however, stayed honest and level-headed through all this attention and adoration: stardom hadn't made him any less aware of his shortcomings, or of how much his all-round game needed improvement.

Emulating the best of expatriate business managers, Lineker immersed himself in the language, culture and life of Barcelona. His time there with his wife, Michelle, widened the experience of life and football alike for these children of Leicester, where they had been born, bred and married. As a player, he believes, his learning curve reached its peak in the Catalan city. For the first time he experienced man-to-man marking and the sweeper system, techniques literally foreign to the English football of the day.

In the high-pressure and highly skilled environment of Spanish football, Lineker needed to learn new techniques of acquiring space: his touch had to improve dramatically as well. How does a superstar set about improving? He found a simple and straightforward answer. He studied the great players around him, above all Hugo Sanchez, a man for whom he had enormous admiration, not just as a goal-scorer but as a genius at making time for himself, creating space for both himself and other players.

Learning from others

Lineker also watched as much football as possible on TV, studying the movement, the lines of running and the use of speed adopted by successful forwards in this new playing environment. His open mind and honest appraisal of his own qualities left him free of arrogance and able to learn from others. That's a crucial ability in sport as in management: yet in both fields, and in most other walks of life, many people find it hard to accept their own limitations and to transcend them by learning improved skills from associates who are more adept.

By now, managers have mostly learned that they should be coaches, but they have been slower to accept that they also need coaching themselves. Without that acceptance, not only is your ability stuck like a fly in amber, but you cannot then urge others to train and learn without displaying an obvious lack of integrity. Lineker had the humility we all require to be great. Sheer pragmatism reinforced the internal drive for improvement. What he did was common sense: he wanted not simply to adjust to the new environment, but to extract the greatest possible personal benefit from the move to Barcelona.

That early, insatiable goal hunger demanded no less. To score more goals, he had to overcome his playing limitations and develop experience of the Spanish field formation. Intelligent business managers do an honest SWOT analysis on their firms – asking what are our Strengths, Weaknesses, Opportunities and Threats, and asking the same questions about themselves and the competition. Likewise, Lineker observed and digested the strengths of the players around him in the intense and claustro-phobic Spanish atmosphere, and also analysed their weaknesses.

His reward (and that of the Barcelona fans) was fifty-four goals from 140 matches between 1986 and 1989. Lineker returned to the World Cup stage in Italy in 1990, the year he became England's captain. In his own mind, he was a far better player than he had been in Mexico. His experience was much greater, combining the lessons of continental football with the hard physical patterns of the English League game. Now a universally feared striker, he again proved to be England's deadliest finisher. His equalising goals against Germany in the semi-finals gave hope to millions of English fans – hopes dashed by defeat in the penalty shoot-out.

An older and wiser footballer, Lineker returned to Britain and Tottenham Hotspur as a superstar, and consequently also a highly marked man. He had distilled all his lessons into the basic art of scoring goals. He was on the field to finish movements for his team, to put the ball into the net. That's a very elementary viewpoint, but this simple desire to score gave Lineker his focus and developed the end result he sought: 'I was on the field to score goals, so I saw no reason for running back and wasting my energy defending in our own half.'

Rather, he needed 'to save all my energy for making sharp, incisive runs around the box in order to score those goals'. Many strikers, he says, are less disciplined and squander valuable time and effort trying to defend, rather than finishing their side's moves by scoring. Lineker directed total mental and physical alertness towards seizing his scoring opportunities. He couldn't best serve his side by running up and down the field, alternating between defence and attack. All his attention was focused on attack, on the penalty area.

This intense focus played a part in building the image of a squeaky-clean player of deep personal integrity. Never sent off, never even booked for any offence on the field, Lineker simply saw no point in reacting to fouls or attacking his attacker. How would that help? Fierce reaction, lashing out at the player who fouled you, didn't serve your purpose in playing. On the contrary, it ruined your concentration. Forcing a free kick, on the other hand, was doing your job, creating an opportunity for the team. Lineker's best policy was to get off the floor and move to a position where he might capitalise on the opening.

Many people would see such restraint as unnatural. How can you not react angrily when some dangerous, illegal footballing thug cracks your legs from beneath you? Wouldn't you have to be some emotionless, unflappable robot to keep calm? Not according to the American psychologist Dr Wayne W. Dyer. He maintains that anger is a choice which you don't have to make – and shouldn't. 'Anger gets in the way. It is good for nothing . . . anger is a means of using things outside yourself to explain how you feel.'

In other words, abuse and retaliation won't stop the fouling player from fouling again, and it certainly can't prevent the foul that's already happened. What is more, it might well immobilise you, and the last thing you want in a game is an immobilised athlete. Would getting angry improve Lineker's ability to score goals? That was his only objective, and it required unbroken focus and concentration on his own game to draw defenders away from another striker, to dummy and feint to create space himself. Where would the next ball come from? Where might it be deflected?

Lineker wanted always to be half a yard ahead of the opposition, which meant that he couldn't let himself be distracted by foul play. Of course he felt like reacting at times. But luckily that only happened when he was injured. Then he couldn't get up anyway, and by the time he was back on his feet the flash of anger had passed. This helped to create and prolong the myth of the unflappable, saint-like Lineker. He does indeed have a very calm and even temperament, and it isn't easy to make him lose his temper. But his demeanour when provoked on the field was also totally logical.

Is breaking into aggressive fury behaviour compatible with integrity? As Dyer says, 'The expression of anger is indeed a healthier stance than suppressing it. But there is an even healthier stance – not having the anger at all.' Many players use the negative emotion of anger for wholly negative purposes. To quote Dyer again: 'You can excuse losing or poor performance with a simple fit of temper.' But that doesn't help you to win games.

The angry manager is a bad manager who has lost control of both means and ends. It was Lineker's ability to keep control of both what he was doing and why, to be a whole player at all times, that raised him above the norm of England strikers. He was no robot, no unthinking machine that managed to jab the ball over the line from a yard out, but a creative, deeply thoughtful sportsman. Nobody understood the penalty box better: which lines of approach to use, which angles to take, which areas to exploit to attain his goal (or rather, goals).

Few footballers have ever used the space available to such great effect, or made chances look so simple – though the simplicity actually arose through sharp awareness and great anticipation. Even fewer footballers have been able to conduct their careers with such dignity and poise, or to cope better with success, or to sustain their achievement over so long a career. In his 139-appearance service with Spurs (including victory in the FA Cup in 1991, and ending in 1992), Lineker's eighty goals represented a strike rate of 58 per cent.

That scoring was better than Lineker achieved in his years with Leicester City as a young player, and was bettered only in the phenomenal two years with Everton. When he left British football in 1992, aged thirty-two, Lineker went off to the Nagoya club in Japan. He left behind him a record that was remarkable in athletic terms and unblemished by any hint of foul play or misconduct. Maybe that should be regarded as the norm in professional sport. But career-long demonstrations of ethical conduct are uncommon in sport – and, for that matter, in business. They shouldn't be.

Integrity isn't a halo worn only by saints. It embraces practical

Gary Lineker raises the FA Cup after Spurs' win over
Nottingham Forest – Wembley, 1991.

necessities that managers require just as much as sports players. They include:

(1) Knowing at all times what is expected of you – and what you expect of yourself.

(2) Knowing what your true resources are – and how to enhance them.

(3) Being aware of the opposition – and outperforming competitors by superior quality of preparation and performance.

(4) Experimenting, innovating and analysing success – to keep ahead, not just for the present, but into the future.

(5) Being true to yourself – standing up for your beliefs and for your team fellows.

Above all, people with integrity set the standards and, because of that, are always respected. Whether they are captains or players, chief executives or second-tier managers, they can't manage well without that attribute. Gary Lineker had only a brief spell as appointed leader, and the captain of an English soccer side has limited influence compared to the team-manager. Throughout his career, though, he led by example. That can be done by anybody at any level, and integrity achieves goals. Not 322 of them, perhaps, but more than enough.

14

The Seminal Thoughts
of Semco

No doubt 60 per cent of the top management of Semco, a small Brazilian engineering company, thought none too highly of the integrity of Ricardo Semler. They were promptly fired when the new boss, aged only twenty-four, took over from his father. The firings, though, stemmed from the fact that the business was in deep trouble. Nobody could have guessed that they were the first stage in a process that was to make Semco world famous.

The company isn't famed for its sales, products or profits, but for the inventive, anarchic management Semler pioneered in the effort 'to make people look forward to coming to work in the morning'. In doing so, Semco has created an organisation which, more than any other in our experience, strives towards the ideal of integrity – 'entireness, wholeness', says the dictionary, adding for good measure, 'uprightness' and 'honesty'. A company with Semco's levels of integrity and credibility is amazingly different from a typical organisation – and there, no doubt, lies a lesson in itself.

Semler's father, an autocratic engineer, was middle-aged when his son was born, which explains Ricardo's youthful takeover.

The management style which created his fame wasn't in evidence at the start. Semler went through a fairly typical period of professionalising management and forcing a specialised manufacturer (marine pumps and centrifuges) into diversification: over-diversification, you might say, after looking at the present range. It still includes pumps along with commercial dishwashers, cooling units, mixers and whole biscuit plants – and that's after several other lines vanished as Semler adjusted to the hard, variable weather of the Brazilian economy. He'd thrown himself into acquisitions and other activities with frenzy and stress (personal and organisational). The growth was sensational, doubling every year, but it 'took us almost a decade to learn that our stress was internally generated, the result of an immature organisation and infantile goals'.

The 'infantile goals' were those still pursued by adult managers in every company with any ambition: what Semler calls the 'adolescent urge' for 'more people, more plants, more products, more revenue' – a compulsion which often explains (but doesn't excuse) gross lapses in integrity. At the price of 'money, time, and gastritis', Semler cured himself of the urge, and is now adamant: 'To want to grow just to be big is an idea that comes from the sandbox.'

The adult manager still seeks growth: to create new opportunities and wealth for people, to boost motivation and productivity, and to generate change. But not to please the sandbox minds of financiers. Sandbox management, moreover, is a prolific source of wasteful activity. In Semco's acquisitive phase, a hundred targets were studied. There were negotiations with fifteen of these and only four were actually purchased. Since 'buying small family firms is a certain way to skip the ulcers and go straight to bypass surgery', the buys were discarded subsidiaries of multinationals. 'The closets are typically full of skeletons,' but at least the books are accurate. These subsidiaries had suffered from the same kind of matured but 'immature' organisation that Semler was to abandon. The mature corpocratic system achieves splendid *results* – it goes through all the right motions. What it may not achieve is right *outcomes.*

After professional management had wrought its wonders, Semco could

> track with great precision virtually every aspect of our business, from sales quotations to the maintenance records of each of our innumerable welding machines. We could generate all sorts of new reports almost instantly, with dazzling charts and graphs . . . We thought we were more organised, more professional, more disciplined, more efficient. So, we asked ourselves with a shudder, how come we were constantly late on delivery?

The poor outcomes, Semler came to realise, were the consequence of processes that led to other objectives which, while inner-directed, caused both internal and external dissatisfaction. The quest for 'law, order, stability and predictability' becomes an end in itself. Because nobody trusts, or is trusted, the corporation makes 'rules for every conceivable contingency. Policy manuals are created with the idea that, if a company puts everything in writing, it will be more rational and objective.'

The consequent standardisation of methods and conduct, Semler writes, 'works fine for an army or prison system'. Actually, even that can be argued. Armies and prisons have contemporary problems, too. But you can't challenge Semler's contention that in business corpocracy doesn't work – certainly not for a business that wants people to 'think, innovate, and act as human beings'.

That realisation drove him to devise a new concept of the company. 'Looking back on it, I can't remember a single decision that I made in that period. Which was just as well, for I am at my best when I am doing nothing.' Ricardo Semler's new dispensation at Semco was built on a new dispensation for himself. While the company continued to revolve around him in an enabling sense, its processes stopped doing so. He lived by a new philosophy of management, not only for himself, but for other managers.

In a dozen years, an orthodox pyramidal hierarchy was transformed into a bazaar of unorthodox trust: of operatives trusted
to set their own production quotas and to have a say in product
redesign and marketing; of managers trusted to fix their own business strategies and their own salaries; of open, trusting revelation
of all financial facts (including those salaries); of major decisions,
including acquisitions and plant relocations, submitted to the vote
of all employees; of factories moved to multi-disciplinary working
in groups which were trusted to reorganise and innovate, doing it
their way.

Semler calls this last unorthodoxy the 'amoeba' treatment. At
one amoeba factory, set up to make electronic scales (which
had been money-losers), the 'kids' took only a few months to
create such excellence that their plant became Semco's flag-
ship operation. Its productivity doubled that of the food service
equipment plant, its inventories fell by 40 per cent, its defects
dropped to under 1 per cent. What caused the turnaround? 'The
kids innovated all over the place.'

Their actions recognised an important and much-neglected
management truth: that internal, non-technical innovation is just
as important as technological invention (and much cheaper).
Examples from the 'kids' are a short start-the-day meeting for
all employees and, instead of a time-clock, a peg on which
arriving employees placed a mood tag – green (good mood),
yellow (careful) or red (not today).

As Semler notes, the mood peg may be somewhat 'cute', but
it exemplified the new culture in which people made their own
rules, while top management abolished central ones (a particu-
larly easy and satisfying form of innovation). After concluding that
'some departments were better not created and some rules were
better not written', the management wisely decided to proceed
by stealth. Rule manuals were simply collected up over three
or four months. People gradually found that no new manuals
were forthcoming, and the rules (including control over travel
expenses) came tumbling down.

Perks were abolished, too, and so was power – much to the

distress of many managers: 'To be the boss is what counts to most bosses. They confuse authority with authoritarianism. They don't trust their subordinates.' Semler points out that in the pyramid structure, 'there is always a group of supervisors, department heads, and other professionals in the middle . . . It isn't unusual for these middle managers to be more zealous with authority . . . than those at the top.'

Semler doesn't gloss over the resistance he encountered, mostly from the middle, and not least because he insisted on doing business with the unions. Nor does he minimise the problems that Semco met as it grew and became 'too big for our own good', and too complex. Attempts to combat complexity by computerisation made the confusion worse (Semler believes this to be a general rule). A clinching discovery was that only 120 invoices were being issued monthly against 150. 'Two days later the unit was off the computer and back on the primitive, manual system.'

Simplifying systems

To Semler, everything now seemed clear: 'Either you can adopt sophisticated, complex systems, or you can simplify everything.' He simplified. For example, the mainframe was disconnected. 'Our worries about making one computer compatible with another are over. It's every micro-processor for itself and to hell with the economies of scale.' Semco may well regret this as networking becomes more important, but it will never regret the introduction of manufacturing cells or its simpler amoeba-like division into smaller, identifiable units.

With similar simplicity, Semler cut through the Gordian knot of profit-sharing. Instead of complicated schemes, each unit got a democratically agreed 23 per cent of any profit and was free to allocate the money as the members decided (they mostly opted for equal amounts for everybody). This principle – letting people decide on issues that most top managements keep to their troubled bosoms – cuts out forests of complication and bureaucracy.

Semler spills out other useful hints by the score. For instance, insist on one-page memos with newspaper-style headlines ('New Toaster Will Sell 20,000 Units for $2 Million Profit'); or set up a 'women's programme' to sweep away discrimination; or rotate managers between functions. Or subject managers to six-monthly appraisal by their subordinates with 'multiple choice questions designed to measure technical ability, competence, leadership and other aspects of being a boss'. There are three dozen of these questions, each with four possible answers, with a passing grade of 70 per cent: below that, a manager's job is in danger. Here, doubt begins to creep in. The procedure looks somewhat cumbersome. The suspicion of overkill arises at several points in Semler's account of his progress. Originally, Semco seems to have had a dozen hierarchical stages for a hundred-odd employees: the transformed business never had more than 850 people, but the number of managers and managerial posts mentioned by name in his book, *Maverick!*, makes the company sound strangely top heavy.

Today Semco has only 300 employees, averaging $92,000 of sales each – nearly nine times the 1980 figure. That high number, however, has been achieved largely by 'hollowing out' the corporation, subcontracting everything possible, often to small workshops established by ex-Semco workers with company assistance. In this respect, as in most others, Semco does little that's unique: it's the relentless combination of many advanced management ideas that is remarkable.

Can Semco's combination transfer to other, larger firms in other countries (whose big companies, especially in America, have shown flattering interest in Semco)? Can you emulate Semler in a pyramidal organisation, or do you have to demolish the pyramid and, like Semco, go 'circular', with directors becoming 'counsellors', unit heads 'partners', other managers 'co-ordinators', and everybody else 'associates'? All this is less important than the absolute integrity of management, the introduction of trust and delegation, the abolition of futile restraints and complications, and the wholehearted use of modern manufacturing methods

*Ricardo Semler's small engineering company became a big
management star.*

and people policies. Those principles should work anywhere.
But very few other companies have followed Semler's preaching
or practice. Nor does he actually want followers: he says there's
a 'fundamental difference' between himself and gurus who are
wedded to particular management theories.

'What we are doing is not the solution or the model – it's
one more laboratory experience of what can happen when you
remove some of the strictures'. For Semco, it's been a twenty- to
twenty-five-year process, which is no use for people 'looking for
a ninety-day solution'. He's not even sure that 'what we're doing
is a finished product, or ever will be'. While he's 'done a lot of
talking and sharing experience', he's done 'little to help others
follow our path' – and he won't.

Nothing can demonstrate the efficacy of Semco-style management one way or the other. But Semler knows that 'changes in
mentality do affect the numbers', and such changes are the
prime object of his philosophy. The Semco story is 'not about

empowerment and participation', which he dismisses as merely 'topical'. The experiment is 'more generic and comprehensive', an effort 'to shift the centre of gravity towards the middle'. The shift, moreover, is accompanied by the development of 'the most exciting thing': the 'boundary-less' company.

A BBC documentary team which filmed Semco in 1993 counted about two outsiders to every insider: the factory was filled with out-workers and 'consultants'. Some of the latter were accidentally recruited when 1,430 resumés arrived for a single engineering post: Semco took on forty-one of the applicants, one full-time for the actual job, and forty on a 'risk basis'. Experienced early retirees were given a day to find how they could help: one applicant, for example, had worked for the company that made Semco's gear-cutting machine. He reckoned he could raise its productivity, and his reward would be 20 per cent of the first two years' savings.

The core preserved for Semco itself is 'applications engineering and final assembly'. In these core activities, there's a 'distinct hierarchy and leadership'. On issues like what product to make, or the control of sales and distribution, the leaders have 'very clear responsibilities', even though, as noted above, 'people who are subordinates have a say and the capacity to interview and assess their bosses'. The capacity is used. In the marine products division, whose survival was in doubt, 120 out of 135 employees turned up to quiz its potential saviour.

Assessing the bosses

Despite its cumbersome appearance, Semler suspects that the recruitment cycle, from meeting potential executives to bringing them on-stream, is actually shorter at Semco. 'We take longer over the first decision', but the selection, by as many subordinates as care to attend the interview, is more effective – and more rigorous. The subordinates come armed with a list of tough, prepared questions. Moreover, the managers hired as a result appear to be performing well and contendedly: in a company with a tiny 1 per cent labour turnover, the proportion of managers who 'have left or bombed is negligible'.

Their self-set salaries and their gradings by their subordinates are published for all to see, and the average grading has steadily climbed two points every year. Some Semco managers have rated 90 to 98 per cent for three or four years, which sounds incredible – but, says Semler, 'the trend is what matters'. An uncorrected slump means that a manager is losing, or has lost, the 'capacity to lead'. In that case the solution is harsh but inevitable.

Whether or not Semco is over-managed is hard to tell because of the changed nomenclature. The 'co-ordinator' title applies to anybody with 'any kind of subordinate', which means everybody from foreman upwards. At its peak employment, Semco could have had one manager for only nine workers: however, if the visiting cards are anything to go by, the executives are fully employed. Free to use any title they wish, 80 per cent of them put only their names: 'they don't have time' for useless niceties.

The 'useless niceties' dismissal goes for other items, like where to park, or company car rules, which also cause 'a tremendous amount of grief' in traditional companies. In other respects, though, Semco's regime is stricter. In particular, it has a five-year plan, but only six-month budgets. The latter don't allow people to bunch 'all the ugly things, or the good things, in the second half'. If the orders aren't in the house, managers in other organisations may include hoped-for purchases in an over-optimistic one-year forecast. But you can't get away with that inside a six-month period – not in Semco's markets.

Most importantly, Semco compares the monthly numbers with expectations: that is, each executive makes 'an educated guess about the revenues, expenses and profits for his department at the end of each month'. Comparing that guess with actuals 'gives everyone a sense of how much each manager actually knows about his area'. That's yet another highly inventive simplification directed towards better outcomes.

Semler has no room for the 'macho culture' which worries

about results rather than outcomes and sets corporate achievement on a 'big scoreboard'. He asks, rhetorically, 'What are we
increasing?' and suggests that the general answer should be 'the
quality of life'. That's obviously a deeply felt personal view. But
when it comes to the specifics of Semco, its proprietor notes: 'I
can't talk for myself on any of these things.' Indeed, he uses the
word 'we' a great deal. Who are 'we'? The answer is never the
same. Semco's London lawyers were baffled to find themselves
dealing with a changing cast, all equally well informed about the
legal issue in hand. With the chief executive baton 'passing round
every six months', a weekly update 'on everything' is essential for
the counsellors. The baton won't pass to Semler, though. In 1993
he hadn't hired anybody, fired anybody or signed a cheque for
eight years and was planning to reduce his involvement – for good
reason.

'This myth-building thing goes on.' People think 'I must have
the Midas touch, but it's not true. But when I'm there, I have
undue influence. My opinions carry excess weight.' Semler wants
to 'remove this burden from the company so that self-confidence
grows'. When people are 'not interested in what I think', Semler
will have achieved an ultimate ambition, that of creating a 'self-
powered organisation'. Otherwise it's 'just personalistic'. That's
incompatible with total integrity. And if it isn't total, it isn't
integrity.

15

Denying the Deniers

The honesty that underpins credibility demands above all the willingness to face facts, however unpalatable, and to move away from denial to acceptance of reality and the actions it demands. Anything else is liable to be costly and even catastrophic in its results, for nothing prolongs business agonies more surely than denial, defined by one consultant as 'an unconscious coping mechanism to block out and not deal with major change that may have some pain associated with it'. The mechanism is highly effective – or, rather, ineffective.

Chief executives in trouble naturally deny to themselves and others that their own failings are causing the problems. Boards often not only accept the denials, but go one stage further, denying to themselves and the outside world that their support for the incumbent boss is mistaken. Eventually that support has to be withdrawn, but not before terrible damage has been done to the finances, in the market and to the morale of managers and managed alike.

Denial is much more comfortable psychologically than facing hard facts or taking hard action. A study led by Professor Jeffry Nutter of the University of Georgia provides resounding evidence on this point: all but 5 per cent of forty-six major companies, each with sales of over a billion dollars, blamed losses made in the eighties at least in part on 'poor economic conditions'. *Fortune* reports, however, that: 'Only 13 per cent said that bad management or mistakes may have had anything to do with it, and invariably these forthright types were new executive teams pinning the tail on their ousted predecessors.'

Any business journalist can tell the same story. New managements are perfectly prepared to confess to the dreadful failures of their forerunners. Managers who are still in place after presiding over awful setbacks are only slightly more likely than politicians to admit their mistakes. That's the antithesis of integrity. It took the new man, Louis V. Gerstner, to confess publicly in March 1994 to IBM's sins of sluggishness, internally and externally. Yet those sins had been evident to outsiders for at least a decade.

It isn't surprising, perhaps, that massive, long-term failings were missed by an IBM board whose business experience was either negligible or confined to other big battalions. But what about the managers further down? Many lower executives in troubled companies know full well how grave and grievous the problems are. At General Motors, for instance, David C. Munro was the car giant's chief economic forecaster for ten years. When he left, the company had already halved in size since his arrival – and he wasn't sure 'what will be left when it enters the next millenium'.

Munro diagnosed two main ailments: 'elephantine mass' and insularity. 'GM doesn't have a very good history of pulling in information and ideas from others, and at the top it has a history of resisting change from outside. There are an awful lot of people in that bureaucracy who only know what others are thinking down the hall.' We have heard similar painful observations inside many other companies. It isn't just a question of resisting change from outside, though: resistance to change proposed from inside can be even more deadly.

Consider Case 1. The chief executive of a major bank composes a mission statement for the company. It is to be 'the best retail bank' in the nation by 1997. Asked how they will know they are the best, executives down the line haven't the slightest idea. The boss hasn't attached any measures or targets to his ambitions, and the management cadre has played no part in the formation of the mission. What are the chances of said mission being successful? Significantly less than evens.

Case 2. A large financial services company sets up informal, separate sessions at which the top management and the stratum immediately below look at the composition and purpose of the board and the executive committee. The lower managers point out that the two bodies have five members in common, yet persist in the fiction that they are entirely separate. The juniors propose reforms that will greatly improve the effectiveness of both bodies and of the departments beneath them. What are the chances of the proposals being adopted?

The answer to that question – almost zero – is strongly suggested by another aspect of the same company. It had recently celebrated its 150th year of existence, and was proud of its past. Yet nobody had given any thought to the next 150 days. No business plan existed, even for the current year. A committee had once been formed to draw up a five-year corporate plan. In presenting the document, the committee argued for a small planning department to monitor the plan's implementation. The idea was rejected, and the plan was never enacted.

Those true-life stories may sound bizarre, but the situation they portray is common. Time and again, talking to managers at all levels, we're struck by their competence, knowledge of the business and its key people, and understanding of what modern, effective management requires – even if they've spent all their lives in one narrow industry and have very little knowledge of thought and action beyond its frontiers. Yet their cynicism is equally striking: they don't believe that what needs to be done will be done. In a word, top management lacks credibility.

That means it also lacks the ability to lead. 'What we found quite unexpectedly in our initial research and have reaffirmed ever since is that, above all else, people want leaders to be credible.' That statement from *Credibility: How Leaders Gain and Lose It, Why People Demand It*, by Jim Kouzes and Barry Posner, is credible to the point of truism. Who doesn't want to believe that their leaders' 'word can be trusted, that they have the knowledge and skill to lead, and that they are personally excited and enthusiastic about the direction' in which the led organisation is headed?

The two authors couldn't, however, find much research into credibility and leadership. No doubt there isn't too much research about motherhood and love, either. Credibility is something which people want to take for granted, although they are often disappointed. Integrity is its most important element: survey respondents said, when asked about the most important 'characteristics of admired leaders', that they should be honest (87 per cent), forward-looking (71 per cent), inspiring (68 per cent), and competent (58 per cent).

Intelligence, moreover, has only half the score of honesty, which surely demonstrates the emotional appeal of credibility and integrity rather than exercise of considered judgement. Trust absolutely in incompetent, unintelligent, but honest leaders and you're in the Charge of the Light Brigade, which is no place to be. Anyway, these data, for whatever they are worth, don't answer the vital question. How many people find what they seek? Kouzes and Posner quote another source – 1991 research into the statement: 'Management is honest, upright and ethical.' While that is 'very important' to 85 per cent of US office workers, only 40 per cent found it 'very true'.

That is far from encouraging. Once the importance of credibility has been asserted, however, what can be said that is specific? The authors have 'derived six practices' from their 'analysis of common themes in the cases we have collected'. These 'six disciplines of credibility' are discovering your self [*sic*], appreciating 'constituents' (subordinates, etc.), affirming shared values, developing capacity (i.e. capability), serving a purpose, and sustaining hope.

These qualities differ not at all from other recipes urged on managers by today's improvement literature. If managers want to achieve credibility, they have little choice but to engage in the collaborative, co-operative, bottom-up, consensual, value-driven, coaching, coaxing, self-aware and progressive management that is

enjoined by all the gurus – what a British company, Harvester Restaurants, calls 'servant leadership'. One Harvester 'team member'
self-avowedly 'gets up in the morning and you clean your teeth in
the values . . . and you know you're not going to screw up because
it fits with the values, it's going to be right'.

Credibility gaps

Don't get carried away by such warming anecdotes. In real-life
bossing, leadership skills are part of competence, not the other
way round. Top managers lose credibility by allowing huge gaps
to open up between their perception of their own management
excellence and the reality. That dangerous gap means that the
right questions often don't get asked, even by managers who
know perfectly well that they should be. The contrary behaviour,
however, enhances credibility – and vastly improves results.

For instance, SGS–Thomson's top managers, emulating the vast
majority of Nutter's sample, could have declined all blame for the
losses incurred when the semi-conductor cycle turned sharply
downwards in 1990. 'Poor economic conditions' undoubtedly
existed. But these managers dug down below the easy explanation
to ask why excessive numbers had been hired just in time for the
downturn. Better-quality management wouldn't have prevented
the decline, but it would have lessened its impact.

The company duly set about achieving that quality. Cutting
costs and firing people were still required, but the negative was
combined with a positive, bottom-to-top change in the targets
the organisation set out to achieve and the ways in which it
sought to achieve them. The phrase 'bottom-to-top' is crucial.
The Nutter study noted that, in its billion-dollar-plus subjects,
although average employment had fallen by about 5 per cent,
there was 'no evidence of abnormally high levels of forced
turnover in top managers'.

Coupled with abnormally high salaries for the latter, this creates
another dangerous credibility gap: between how top management
values itself and how it is valued by its internal customers – the

rest of the staff. You can extrapolate some tell-tale signs of this gap from *Fortune*'s exploration of companies in denial. They are:

(1) A higher energy level after meetings than beforehand. Do people talk about what wasn't said rather than what was?

(2) Managers who pass down top-level messages while stating that they don't agree.

(3) Aversion to taking risks, external or internal.

(4) Political jockeying for the favour of superiors.

(5) Failure (see above) to seek out and live by meaningful measures of performance.

(6) Excessive top-management interference in operations.

The sixth point often leads to the sudden adoption of fashionable techniques, like TQM or business process re-engineering. As one academic puts it, managers who 'deny the need for change' instead 'adopt an efficiency focus, pounding the same thing over and over rather than asking, "Are we doing the right thing?"'. This guarantees failure, for true TQM, like true re-engineering, demands radical reshaping of the organisation as a *sine qua non*.

Reshaping management

Another *sine qua non* is that management itself must be reshaped in order to be 'aligned' to the new processes. That's the word selected by James A. Champy, co-founder of the CSC Index consultancy, which specialises in re-engineering. His much-quoted book *Re-engineering the Corporation*, written with Michael Hammer, features an estimate that 50–70 per cent of all re-engineering efforts fail: that's since fallen to 30–40 per cent, Champy believes, but the failures are still attributable to the same fault: 'poor alignment of management'.

This will inevitably follow if managers believe that re-engineering is the same as downsizing. 'The latter doesn't change what you're doing,' says Champy. If people suspect that managers are using re-engineering as a smokescreen simply to cut jobs, credibility will be zero. We have seen the same damage done by boards which launch change programmes, but suddenly announce management redundancies without consultation – and with the promise (or threat) of more, unspecified dismissals to come.

Credibility starts with a credible plan. The true re-engineer, says Champy, begins with the 'business case for change', asking, 'How do we want to appear in the eyes of our customers?' Then you build the vision, and identify the core processes needed to deliver the vision. Next, teams are redesigned so that they can go straight into implementing. Management is not only personally involved but 'always driving'. As Champy tells his audiences, 'Never let up and always judge by progress against the objectives in the vision.'

It should go without saying that at all stages everybody has to be involved and informed. 'The team must have contact with senior management,' says Champy, who argues that 'a statement of culture is a statement of aspirations'. Unless managers have credibility, others will share neither their aspirations nor their belief that the aims can be accomplished, which means that they won't be. Unwilling soldiers fight badly. What Champy calls 'a culture of willingness' reads like a credo of credibility:

(1) Always perform up to the highest measure of competence.

(2) Take initiatives and risks.

(3) Adapt to change.

(4) Make decisions.

(5) Work co-operatively, as a team.

(6) Be open, especially with information, knowledge and news of forthcoming or actual problems.

(7) Trust and be trustworthy.

(8) Respect others (customers, suppliers and colleagues) and oneself.

(9) Answer for your actions, and accept responsibility.

(10) Judge and be judged, reward and be rewarded, on the basis of performance.

Those ten points set forth the ideals for team performance in any sport, any activity, any organisation. Managements and others in denial deny this credo. That's how boards of directors can stress the need for the business to become 'competitive' and 'world class' while simultaneously standing in the way of achieving those ends. This means they themselves are neither world class nor competitive. They also must lack credibility – which is one reason why the majority of 'restructurings', with their 'downsizing' and 'right-sizing', have failed to achieve corporate renaissance.

Such euphemistic therapies, moreover, have had terrible, counter-productive side-effects among the managerial ranks. There's a crucial trade-off between the potential gains of a reorganisation and the potential losses in credibility, morale and security. In companies in upheaval, the good people of all generations will tend to see better opportunities outside – better than those in a company undergoing continuous shake-ups against a background of deep uncertainty about its future and therefore their own. They are very unlikely to stay, or to join another company in the same mould.

Why the weak stay weak

The brightest and best of the younger generations will be first out of the door. Like top-class rugby players, they want to belong to winning organisations, and will shun losers, which is why strong clubs get stronger and weaker ones stay weak. This preference for winners was unearthed by the independent think-tank, Demos (*Generation X and the New Work Ethic*), from a study of the North American and European young. They're a demanding bunch who also want careers with open options. Moreover, they demand honest feedback from their bosses, which is a key aspect of credibility and a key test of character on both sides of the relationship. They seek project-based variety in their work: which means they need, and relish, skill-based ability to move from job to job and firm to firm. Their better elders won't be any different. As these professional men and women gravitate towards the best employment, the least credible employers will be trapped by the brain-drain.

Loss of the brightest and best virtually guarantees that the corporate accidents and the problems of bureaucracy, 'elephantine mass' and insularity will recur. Those characteristics are inimical to the new environment, in which opportunities have to be taken, to stand still is to fall behind, and the increasingly demanding customers call the tune. If you want the internal talent to respond to this challenge – and if it doesn't, the corporation is doomed – the recipe is obvious. In fact, it's the one which the relatively junior executives in that 150-year old financial services company worked out for themselves – and in a ninety-minute workshop, at that.

They wanted to divorce the board from the corpocracy, separate the most senior management from the operations, and devolve authority down the line to self-managed teams headed by effective leaders. On the other hand, they didn't believe that their seniors would accept any such solution. Lack of credibility, like some toxin, had infected a company whose top management sincerely wanted to take the organisation out of denial and into action.

In contrast, you can easily recognise the truly non-denying, credible company: its characteristics reverse the signs of denial. Meetings will have defined objectives and will always result in agreed action commitments. Top managers won't settle strategies and policies until they are supported by a fully informed consensus among the teams and their leaders. Balanced risk-taking is expected, encouraged and, if successful, rewarded. Internal politics are suppressed by insistence on promotion on merit and by instant, generous recognition of achievement at all levels.

Just like Champy's credo, this demands living by meaningful measures of performance and targets to which all managers subscribe. Most important of all, top management recognises that its own job is to add value, and that the board's function is to ensure this happens, not through mergers and acquisitions, but through building the businesses and the talents within them to create organic growth. That's the acid test. Managers in denial not only fail that test: they are incapable of providing outstanding leadership, credibility, or anything else.

VI

Team-Work – How to Build Effective Teams

16

Round the World with Tracy Edwards

No team bonds more closely than the crew of a racing yacht, and no team depends so vitally on its team-work. Rounding Cape Horn in winds of up to 50 knots, the crew members must be able to trust and rely upon each other. It's literally a matter of life and death. For Tracy Edwards and her *Maiden* team in the Whitbread Round the World race, there was an added and compelling dimension. They are all women – the first all-female crew ever to enter this competition.

They were also the first crew to *register* their entry, along with one other boat. Registering early and paying the fee gave the crew weekly updates on any rule changes and stop-over information. Their planning was always completely up to date, which kept their training and their mental vision one step ahead of the competition. They also developed an early relationship, even a rapport, with the race committee. As every sportsman or woman knows, a committee can make your life extremely difficult – or ease your voyage significantly, which, says Edwards, was the case with *Maiden*. The early start and its beneficial consequences bear out her belief that, when all is said and done, good team-work and effective team-building come down to organisation. Preparation and foresight are vital to team-work. To many, though, Edwards must have seemed like a whistler in the dark. When she contacted a top British yacht designer, and asked for immediate plans, she was not only far ahead of most other crews, but far ahead of her own finances. In fact, the necessary money was never raised.

The forethought, had however, left plenty of time to buy a second-hand and dilapidated boat, bring it back from South Africa and get it refitted. Moreover, the contact with the designer, including hundreds of pages of weather analysis, brought inno-vative ideas to *Maiden*. Finishing the refit in advance of her rivals, Edwards had a yacht ready for crew training and preparation before many other teams had even started boat-building. The disadvantage of having a boat that wasn't purpose-built was thus turned into an asset.

The value was especially obvious in the first stage of any team operation: selection. Edwards was inundated with applications from over 300 women all over the world, all eager to help her prove that an all-woman crew, not just women helping to crew a mostly male boat, could race successfully round the world. Once the hundreds had been reduced to a manageable short-list, Edwards was able to use *Maiden* to help in final selection, seeing how candidates reacted under pressure and starting the process of team learning. The eventual crew had already begun to learn about each other, about the boat, about mistakes and how to rectify them. Warm-up races could also be entered, although, amazingly, some crews in the Whitbread itself were racing together for the very first time. Team-work thrives on real-life, real-time experience. Knowing this, Edwards entered her raw crew members in as many races as possible, starting in December 1988 with the transatlantic Route of Discovery race from Cadiz in Spain to Santo Domingo.

Meticulous as ever, Edwards took a thoroughly prepared crew to Cadiz. Two days before the race, however, she started to worry. Every boat but her own seemed to be a hive of frantic activity. She felt that something must have been forgotten, that she had overlooked some very basic preparation. But then another skipper rushed over and asked to photocopy some of her charts. As a stream of others followed, Edwards relaxed: planning and foresight were again standing her team in good stead.

Maiden came first in its class on handicap and second overall, beating ten other Whitbread yachts in the process. The excellent result, however, counted for much less than the lessons learned while competing. Edwards had planned to enter another race, starting in Bermuda. Instead, the crew sailed back to England to correct the faults revealed in *Maiden.* They had met many situations which would recur in the Whitbread and they took time out to analyse these and evaluate their performance.

Team learning is psychological

As Edwards says, they had the luxury of being able to make mistakes and learn from them before the supreme test. Team learning is psychological as well as practical. The transatlantic race had strengthened not only the individual confidence of each crew member, but the collective confidence which each had in the others.

You can't just throw together a team of individuals, however talented, and expect mutual trust to ignite. A team must perform and learn together over time to develop real trust and confidence in one another.

Perfection of detail is essential to achieving general team confidence. Take safety, obviously a life-or-death factor in a round-the-world yacht race. First, Edwards recruited a doctor and taught her to sail (she actually saved the life of a man who went overboard from another, doctorless yacht). Second, careful research identified the best safety equipment. Third, the crew practised using the equipment until they were comfortable and confident with it, and all understood how it worked. Fourth, one of the crew members was appointed safety officer. She wrote an abandon-ship schedule, which, again, was rehearsed. For her pains, the safety officer was thrown overboard in the Channel again and again, to be rescued by the crew. They stopped

Skipper Tracy Edwards raced Maiden around the world.

dumping her in the sea only when they were fully satisfied with the routine. The net result was that *Maiden* had one of the best safety records in the Whitbread – and, of course, the team's confidence was boosted by their trust in the safety equipment and procedures.

If you don't allow enough time for training and team-building, which are inseparable, you won't be sure of putting the right people in the right positions. Until that's done, moreover, you can't start training for and tackling the team task itself. It's also important to bring outsiders into the team operations, a lesson which Western managers have been taught, after long and costly delays, by the Japanese. Like any business, *Maiden* had key suppliers. There was time for them to work with the crew and each other – the sailmaker had time to work with the sail-loft, the rigger with the spar-maker, and so on. One of the crew members had a mathematics degree and wanted to handle the boat's electronics. She became an apprentice with the company which installed all *Maiden*'s electrics and navigation equipment.

Edwards was beginning to assemble the equivalent of the basic unit of modern management: a team of specialists, covering every need, who can also work together as a highly efficient unit.

Another indispensable truth is that team-training, while it must always be relevant, must not be confined to the specific activities of the task. In addition to basic sailing, Edwards instituted a physical training programme put together by a sports instructor. Here, again, thought, planning and innovation paid off. Many of the male crews directed their training towards brute strength: *Maiden*'s was geared towards stamina. An all-female crew couldn't compete with males in terms of muscle. They had to find new approaches, and lateral thinking in many instances actually resulted in superior performance. For example, the *Maiden* members weren't strong enough to raise a spinnaker in over 55 knots of wind. Instead, they used a blast-reacher, which worked so well that sail modifications were made. The boat became stabler and easier to steer, which in turn lessened the stress on the crew: *Maiden* could be pushed to her limits with greater safety than with a spinnaker.

The prerequisite for the cohesion and development of any team is communication. This was an element into which Edwards poured great energy. Weekly crew meetings were held while money was being raised and the boat refitted. The plan was to stop the meetings once the project was firmly established, but in fact, they never ceased. The crew badly wanted to be continually updated on the project and its progress, as well as on each other and what was happening generally.

Communication alone, however, is not enough. Honesty is indispensable. If there were problems or differences among crew members, Edwards wanted them aired face to face and as soon as possible: there's no other way to alleviate grievances while continuing to work smoothly as a team. This is always vital, but especially in the narrow confines of a boat in which people will spend many months in cramped conditions. Resentments left to fester endanger safety, raise stress levels still further and lead to neglect of duties.

It's axiomatic that the team leader can't be exempt from the honesty. Edwards encouraged comments on her own performance as the necessary condition for her own honest critiques of the team. In general, she was determined to get input from all the crew. Like any good team-builder, she had set out to select the most brilliant and gifted people she could find. It makes no sense to recruit at this level and then to ignore the ideas and minds of such excellent colleagues.

Because the crew felt able to come forward and offer constructive suggestions in a positive atmosphere, many problems were solved with very little hassle or time-wasting. The vital ability to admit to ignorance without being made to feel a fool can only arise if trust and empathy exist between the team members. Creating that atmosphere is a prime responsibility of the leader. In the atmosphere built on board *Maiden*, all discussions, thinking and action became focused on a positive outcome: Edwards herself never entertained the possibility of failure, and her mind-set became that of the crew.

The vision and the mission were especially inspiring, of course, and she was surrounded by people equally determined to succeed. Edwards calls herself lucky in these respects, but the truth runs far deeper. However inspiring the thought of winning the Whitbread was to this all-female team, the moments of doubt and stress must have been innumerable. That's when the team looks to its leader, whose bearing and conduct at such moments can tilt the balance between success and failure. And more than the moment is at stake. If the members sense that the leader is still convinced and confident about the team's direction and prospects, the passing moment of doubt will be converted into a lasting boost to morale. Knowing this, Edwards used many techniques to maintain motivation, which wasn't easy during periods of setback, when their race position was lagging, when day followed day of bad weather conditions, when crew members were sick or suffering the effects of being so long away from home. Edwards used to keep bits of good news up her sleeve precisely for such moments.

Taking care of morale

Before the race, rebuilding morale meant taking the girls out for a crew meal, say, or showing them videos of the race. In the obviously tougher circumstances at sea, Edwards tried to keep the end result uppermost in everybody's minds. Reading out mileage results was crucial: the crew had to develop enough mental hardness to take the bad news as well as the good. If a team does not receive the whole picture, the credibility of any information collapses, and that of the leader comes into question.

It's dangerously wrong, to quote one example from our experience in management seminars, for a managing director to put an optimistic gloss on the prospects for bonus payments when he knows full well that none will be made. The natural inclination is to give only good news. Nobody wants to demotivate a management team, or any other group, by telling it the bad news. But that's one test of team leadership – and a good team proves its quality in adversity as well as success.

The difficult moments, though, shouldn't be created by internal inefficiencies. That's where good organisation – the key, as Edwards notes, to top-quality team work – plays its crucial part. On *Maiden*, the crew were well looked after in port: accommodation was good, hire cars were arranged, clothes were ready in their rooms, and toiletries and the right currencies were provided, along with an information pack about the country (including the nearest bars, restaurants and clothes shops) and details about the length of time in port and the work to be done before departure.

All the necessary spares were waiting wherever *Maiden* docked, thanks to a shore team so enviable that efforts were made to poach them. As it was, the Edwards team helped out many other crews. The excellent onshore organisation left the crew time for richly deserved rest and recreation. Edwards believed that a happy crew is a fast crew; that the more they enjoyed themselves, the more rapidly the boat would run when they moved off. One yachting journalist seemed to have got this message: he wrote of *Maiden*, 'not just smart tarts, but smart, fast tarts'.

Despite their speed, the women didn't realise their ultimate vision of winning the race. They came second. For the crew, that was a great disappointment, but for yachtsmen and women all over the world it was a magnificent achievement, an out-standing team performance. The basic principles to which Edwards adhered were well proven in practice, starting with the weight placed on the initial organisation and preparation. This enabled the team to spend ample time on learning, training and re-evaluating. On that foundation, Edwards could build honest and open communication; positive team focus on the final outcome; and high levels of motivation and organisation at sea and ashore during the race that matched the high quality of the initial approach. The crew exemplified the importance of being confident in your collective efficiency as a highly trained team, but also in your own efficiency as a highly trained specialist. Team-leadership is a speciality itself, and Edwards mastered the art to a high degree.

Without question, she was helped by her track record in bringing the project into any kind of reality. Every stage presented difficult challenges: distilling a skilled and motivated crew from the 300-plus applicants, raising the sponsorship despite a series of rebuffs, finding the boat, and making so effective a job of the planning and organisation. All that work on providing the foundations for *Maiden* earned Edwards respect. But once the team was formed, she had to set the standards and earn that respect all over again through her own behaviour.

Taking hard decisions

In any team, that means taking hard decisions. Very early on, Edwards sacked the second most important member of the crew, her first mate. If the leader believes that anybody on the team has become a disruptive influence, action must be taken. In this case, Edwards also sensed a direct challenge to her authority as leader. That made the decision inevitable, but no less difficult. Taking such decisions reinforces the leader's credibility: shirking them is even more destructive than the difficult personality who caused the problem in the first place.

Edwards didn't actually replace her first mate: she restructured the crew to cover the loss. The whole episode demonstrated great strength of mind. Throughout, that mental concentration – whatever the distractions and difficulties – stayed focused on the winning line and the vision of crossing it first. The focus of the leader and that of the team go hand in hand. That is fundamental in the relatively calm conditions of business, but life at sea in an arduous competition tests the basics to the limits.

In the claustrophic, pressure-cooker conditions of a racing yacht, the leader is as vulnerable as anybody else. Edwards could have become demotivated, demoralised and unfair in her treatment of the crew. That would have guaranteed failure. She stuck firmly to the six principles of team-leadership:

(1) Set the right tone, developing mutual trust and bonding.
(2) Allot specific roles, and make sure that those filling the roles get genuine satisfaction from their tasks.
(3) Communicate frequently and honestly.
(4) Involve the whole team in deciding every aspect of the project.
(5) Keep the team fully informed at all times – whether the news is good or bad.
(6) Create a blame-free culture: mistakes are made to be learned from.

These half-dozen points are simple enough. They are basics. The cry of 'back to basics', though, doesn't fit the needs of team-leadership. The right message is moving forward from the basics. Far too often in teams, the commonplace task of being good at basics is not commonplace. That is a good way to fail, but no way to succeed.

17

The New Copy of Xerox

Team-work is one of the rallying cries of the new management. Many of the results have become legendary, like the ultra-successful 1989 launch of the Land Rover Discovery, produced in twenty-seven months, roughly half the time needed previously for the typical British car. Tony Gilroy, the father of the Discovery, was so impressed by the project that he applied the same principles at his new job, chief executive of Perkins Engines, where by 1994 he had 900 project teams busily at work revolutionising performance.

What's new about that? The concept of project-based, self-managed team-working is as old as management itself. The mining industry worldwide, for example, could only have developed through the work of project teams under strong leadership. Often out on a geographical limb, combating fearsome difficulties of geology and climate, these teams accomplished heroic feats. They had to be self-managed, and they were multi-disciplinary, cross-functional, synchronous – all the fashionable elements of today's theory.

Gilroy's numbers, though, are new, and highly exceptional by earlier standards – but not by those of Total Quality Management. Rank Xerox, for example, appointed its Quality Improvement Teams (often cross-functional and drawn from several sites) wherever and whenever areas for improvement were highlighted. That included a QIT for management behaviour, taken on by managing director Bernard Fournier himself. His own behaviour isn't sacrosanct, either. Twice a year, the boss's own reports rate him on twenty-seven criteria. After debriefing discussions with his team members, possible improvements are proposed.

That's a basic principle of team-work: nobody's perfect – including the team leader – and everybody can be improved. The whole Xerox empire had compelling reasons for seeking self-improvement. As the 1980s began, the company fared badly when compared to surging Japanese competition: its indirect/direct cost ratio was double that of its competitors; it used nine times as many suppliers; assembly line rejects were ten times higher; product lead-times twice as long; defects per 100 products seven times as frequent. All these deficiencies, as noted previously, meant that unit manufacturing cost equated with the Japanese *selling* price.

The stark choice lay between total defeat and launching a programme to redesign the company from top to bottom. After nine years of continuous progress, the positive figures became as striking as the old negative ones. On the manufacturing side, defects per 100 products fell to a tenth of their previous totals, as did the number of suppliers. There was a thirteen-times improvement in the proportion of defective parts. These vastly improved figures underpinned remarkable rises in the vital statistic of quality: customer satisfaction.

Market share by volume, which had collapsed from a one-time near-monopoly to around 10 per cent, has recovered on a steady upward trend. That reversal of the Japanese tide is an achievement in itself. But so is the way it was done. Team-work proliferated all over Xerox, but Rank Xerox (the Eurocentric arm), moving in parallel with the American drive for corporate reform, has embraced an even broader concept – one in which the whole company seeks to work as a large, collective team, with every player working towards interlocking, shared objectives.

It's called Policy Deployment, and described by PA Consulting as 'a fully integrated top-down, bottom-up management system through which the two or three critical breakthrough targets and means are identified and implemented with the full participation and alignment of all managers' – and even all staff. This system cascades down from 'theme to objective, to target, to measures, to means'. Derived from what's known in Japan as *hoshin kanri*, Policy Deployment is the most pervasive aspect of the journey on which Rank Xerox embarked to combat the Japanese challenge.

The effort began under the title 'Leadership Through Quality' in 1983, and is not planned to end – ever. 'Quality is not natural,' says Fournier. 'If you stop pushing, in one year you would not recognise the company. You would lose a lot of strengths.' The corporate journey began, as noted in Chapter 6, by sending a team of line managers to Japan to discover the harsh truths behind the lower prices of their competitors. 'Facing up to those facts,' says *Fortune*, 'marked the beginning of Xerox's recovery.'

Note that *line managers* did the study, and as a team; they wouldn't have believed anybody else. That involvement of line managers is central to Policy Deployment. PD is designed to focus everybody's attention on the 'business priorities' – at Xerox, that means customer satisfaction, market share, return on assets, and employee motivation. Every employee in Rank Xerox has a personal 'Blue Book' (so-called simply because the first edition had a blue cover), which sets out the company goals, records the objectives and strategy for meeting the four business priorities, and lays down the 'vital few actions'.

Each business team, and each individual, has four or five vital actions supporting each of the priorities. As the set of specific aims and actions cascades down through all departments to the individual employees, they all know specifically what they are expected to achieve – and each has been involved in deciding his or her own part. Every individual Blue Book, from Fournier's downwards, has one section in common: the corporate aims. Fournier admits that the exercise 'looks a little bit heavy', but

*Managing director Bernard Fournier led Rank Xerox's
total quality teams.*

says that in reality 'it's not that heavy: people like to know what's
expected'.

Being aware of priorities

This last point is true of any team. PD has clearly achieved
a high level of awareness at Rank Xerox: When questioned
about their knowledge of the priorities, 98 per cent of the
respondents were 100 per cent correct. The approach is the
essence of all team-work: it seeks to bind together the purposes
of the individual and those of the organisation. By definition, this
can't be done in a regimented manner, and it can't be dictated
from the top. 'In addition to being a top-down cascade,' explains
Fournier, 'the closed loop also works from the bottom up.'

Each team puts on a presentation that recounts the obstacles
to achievement of targets. The quality questions then come
into play (What's the problem? What are the root causes?)

before the action plans are formed and followed up. In 1992 that follow-up achieved a more formal status. The idea behind 'Business Excellence Certification' is that each unit, working as a team, 'self-assesses' its progress on action plans along a seven-stage scale, ranging from 'nil-done' to 'world-class'.

Scoring 3, for instance, means 'some work done, results not yet visible'. Working out positions on this scale doesn't end at self-assessment. Then comes the certification visit when senior management examines the claims: 'You say you've achieved a score of 4,' might be asked on a particular count. 'Show us the evidence.' Does the unit, perhaps, think itself good in an area where actually the performance is accidental, with no foundations to sustain the improvement? As with individuals, so with their teams: the object is *continuous* improvement.

Advances on general quality measures and on detailed yard-sticks, however, are the *outcome* of such programmes, not their essence. The essence is human. 'Quality definitely drives you to go for more and more empowerment,' says Fournier, 'to diminish the number of layers and increase the span of control.' In 1993, fifteen people reported to him as chief executive officer; previously, when he was general manager in France, his team numbered only seven or eight. Self-managed work groups, he points out, lead to fewer managers, and this form of team-working has been spreading throughout the Xerox operating companies – as through much of world business.

The spread of self-standing teams is linked to the evolution of Xerox from copying to 'The Document Company', with copying only one of the several independent businesses that contributed to a 1993 turnover of $15 billion. The chief executive world-wide, Paul Allaire, is dedicated to the principle of a genuinely decentralised 'architecture'. In this construction, the managers down the line run distinct businesses. Though that means fewer managers in total, the key team leaders need a direct line to the ultimate boss, and vice versa.

Fournier's resulting number of reports would, traditionally, be thought much too high. One 1982 case is typical. When one great company acquired a thrusting new boss, he insisted that nobody should have more than six people reporting to him: his predecessor had nineteen. That's certainly far too large a number for effective team-working, but 'reports' don't necessarily form a team in the new, more horizontal style of organisation. At the top, there's generally a nucleus, an executive committee, whose numbers can often be counted on the fingers of one hand.

The ideal number for a management team varies according to circumstances – though, if you jumped to conclusions from the well-established Belbin classification of team roles, you would settle for seven: (1) coordinator (2) ideas man or woman (3) critic (4) implementer (5) external contact (6) inspector (7) team-builder. In fact, you can manage with fewer people, since some can perform two roles (or even three).

Making the team pull together

The main point, though, is that all seven functions must be fulfilled by somebody. Note that the functions don't include 'leader'. The team needs a leader, but that doesn't mean (as it too often does in practice) abrogating all seven functions to one person. That's the negation of true team-work. The major role of leadership is to ensure that all the necessary functions are being properly exercised, and to pull them together, so that the team truly functions as a unit.

That dovetailing is the justification for Policy Deployment. The process aims to counteract a constant threat: the more members there are in a team, and the greater the number of links, the greater the probability of people being sidelined and the more stultifying the task of coping with the sheer complexity that must result. The PD principle of having teams within teams within the overall corporate team is designed to keep things as simple as possible – and the proof of that pudding will be what happens at head office.

At Rank Xerox, the head office was once wildly unproductive: 'a lot of central time was spent managing the centre, not the company'. Under the new, reformed regime, Fournier was at pains to regroup the centre and to reduce the omnipresence of the former 'huge monster', which used to duplicate the functions of the operating units. After division into various groups, and clarifying roles to eliminate 'confusion between support and direction', headquarters became very small, leaving only some 150 people at Rank Xerox's international HQ in Marlow. You can hardly gainsay the philosophy that this enshrines:

(1) The exercise of authority is a two-way process.
(2) Head office cannot manage sharp-end operations.
(3) The shorter the lines of reporting, the better.
(4) Strategy is the responsibility of those who must execute it.
(5) Second-guessing managers on day-to-day issues is foolish in principle and practice alike.

The improvements generated by Xerox's long years of effort are plain. The real issue isn't the rights or wrongs of Policy Deployment or TQM; it's whether you can manage an organisation – any organisation – without making team-work its governing principle, teams its basic units, and shared objectives its guiding light. That guidance isn't a matter of words alone, although those of Rank Xerox's guiding light statement are unexceptionable:

> Quality is the basic principle for Rank Xerox. Quality means providing our external and internal customers with innovative products and services that fully satisfy their requirements. Quality improvement is the job of every employee.

So far, so good; except that you could substitute any other company's name for Xerox's. It's the specific behaviours which generate the results. For example, what do team members learn from each other, and what do teams learn from other teams? With operating companies across the world, Xerox has ample opportunity for useful comparison across its own frontiers. In fact, when managers do see where their peers are excelling, the 'buy-in' to change becomes much easier. Thus, in the vital matter of customer retention, Austria had the best practice, developed after looking at Belgium. 'They stole from Belgium and, in the spirit of continuous improvement, developed a much better practice.'

Great sports teams also interchange ideas and examples to improve both individual and team performance. That performance will be measured, as in business, by achievement against objectives. At Rank Xerox, 'continuous improvement in customer satisfaction' – including that of internal customers for internal services – is the unchanging target. Before the quality journey began, Rank Xerox had a 'market-oriented reputation, but we weren't market-oriented enough, not market-driven'.

Going for a major improvement in customer satisfaction was made a priority in 1986, with bonus payments linked to measures of satisfaction. Measured in various ways across five markets in fifteen countries, seventy-five parameters are involved. In 1989 the customers rated Rank Xerox first on only nine of these; the next year it was thirty-two, the year after that forty-five, and then in 1992 the score hit sixty out of seventy-five – on which Fournier commented drily that it 'still gives us some way to go'.

That is part of the essence of continuous improvement – the gap never goes away. Yet only three per cent of customers were left dissatisfied, and you can't get much better than that. To have a 97 per cent satisfaction rate among employees, however, is a much more formidable task: probably, nobody gets near it. The dissatisfactions expressed by Xerox employees are the same across Europe *and* the US: pay, communication, organisational change, career opportunities and job security.

There's a dilemma here. Insecurity is the enemy of effective team-work, because it damages morale. But teams are failing in their task (and won't have high morale, anyway) unless they act on the knowledge that, whatever the chosen activity, somebody, somewhere is doing better. Raising performance to that level will cost jobs: Rank Xerox and Xerox worldwide have shed tens of thousands of employees during the battle for survival. But leaving inferior performance to fester also loses jobs, because uncompetitive companies, by definition, can't compete.

Aiming at the achievement of constantly rising indicators and permanent improvement requires strenuous effort, which can look discouraging. In the right company, though, the effort only encourages more effort. In the wrong company, forget it. But there's one vital point to remember. *All* genuine total quality processes succeed. That's because they operate on the fundamental principle of identifying and correcting the causes of less-than-perfect performance – and doing so continually, across the board.

Team-work like that practised at Rank Xerox thus takes in everything: product, process, organisation, leadership and commitment. Former US Air Force General Bill Creech calls these 'The Five Pillars of TQM' (the title of his book). All five must be mobilised. Furthermore, they must interconnect in a way that permeates the whole outfit and influences all its members.

That's much easier to describe than to effect. In his book, Creech has plenty of praise for Xerox and its chief executive, Paul Allaire, but reserves final judgement. Just as the performance of England teams in more than one sport was hamstrung by top-heavy committee management, and by blinkered one-man leadership on the field, so corporate efforts to practise genuine team-work have been vitiated by what Creech calls 'centocracy' – Allaire identified this at Xerox as the 'structure, practices and values of a classic big company' which is 'staff-driven' and has an 'extremely functional organisation'.

Creech notes that 'we have more and more centocracies getting all steamed up over "teams" and believing they have the idea down pat. However, it's virtually always the *cross-functional, committee-like* kind they adopt – which leaves their centralised system and style otherwise undisturbed.' Allaire's object is to escape from centralism. With its organisation of separate divisions, of business teams within the divisions, and self-managed work teams on the front line, Xerox aimed to 'install a team-based, product-based, quality-oriented, decentralised management system and structure.' Will the effort succeed?

Today, there's no successful alternative. And the task shouldn't be as difficult as the corpocratic centralists find. As Fournier says, quality is not natural, but team-work is – see any company's history. The two-man team of Joe Wilson and Peter McColough created the greatness of Xerox, and such great teams often lie behind great companies. Partnership, the elemental form of team-work, is as powerful in business as rugby's unison between scrum-half and fly-half, or between the three back-row forwards. Absence of team-work is the unnatural behaviour. Remove the artificial barriers, and – as Rank Xerox proves – the natural results come flooding through.

18

Responsibilities and Results

Nobody needs to instruct sportsmen, in non-individual sports, to form teams: no team, no game. Even in individual games like tennis, golf and athletics, teams form – not only doubles partnerships, foursomes and relay teams, but whole groups of golfers, tennis players or athletes, competing under the same banner for prestigious international trophies. Cricket, highly individualistic, is also played in teams. Nobody doubts that the sum of a good team, in any sport, is greater than its parts.

The same is true of business. Top managers always, but often falsely, speak proudly of their teams. But in most companies, the leader is never a non-playing captain like golfer Tony Jacklin, under whose leadership Europe first took the Ryder Cup from the US. The business captain, the chief executive, not only plays, but plays from a position of unique strength. In Germany, he is more likely to be *primus inter pares*, first among equals, which roughly describes the England captain in rugby, football or cricket. But in business the British chief executive is far more equal than the others.

This runs counter to proven fact. Team-based organisation is far more successful than the one-man band. The most basic of the principles that have to be followed for teams to reach their enormous potential is that leaders must be genuine team-leaders

– and the necessary behaviour doesn't come naturally. As an American consultant, Erika Anderson of Proteus International, notes, 'At first it's hard to persuade them to let go of control. But once they become actively self-reflective, they realise they don't know all the answers. That sort of humbleness is very charismatic, because it makes the others on the team feel useful and powerful.'

Taking time to think

Her emphasis on 'self-reflection', or introspection, may seem odd in the context of leadership. But self-mastery is the key to mastery in any sport or management activity. Paradoxically, time spent on developing individual skills and attitudes pays off in terms of more effective work with others. One vital skill, as Anderson implies, is thinking about yourself. Yet managers complain that they lack enough time to think about the business, let alone their psyches.

This can't be true. The pressures of day-to-day work are never so massive that every last second is pre-empted by operations. Any expert on time-management can uncover great chasms of misspent time. Peter Drucker's neat catechism never fails. What am I doing that needn't be done by anybody? That could be done by somebody else? That can only be done by me? Honest answers will provide a surprisingly short third category. But this refers to activities within the manager's control. When working in teams, much activity is dictated by other members.

Help is nigh. Networked personal computers should not only discipline managers through diary programmes, but should also speed team-work by file-sharing, information retrieval and minimising meetings. Rank Xerox holds out hopes of dramatic change in the executive day from the present routine, which divides time in equal fifths between gathering information, communicating, organising, meetings and thinking. Instead, thanks to networking, the breakdown could be 10 per cent each for the first four, leaving six times as many hours for independent thought or team thinking.

Thinking time must be used, for reasons both corporate and personal. Research reported in *Fortune* suggests that lack of introspection raises executive stress and lessens managerial effectiveness. You need time to reflect and introspect in order to acquire vital abilities: objectivity, learning, self-confidence, responsibility, tolerance for ambiguity and paradox, balance in life, creativity and intuition, and subjugation of ego. Those attributes, all plainly good and essential to effective team-working, sound imprecise. Can the process of team-thinking leadership be tightened up? For a start, you must abandon the adversarial thinking which Edward de Bono attacked in *I Am Right, You Are Wrong*. One of his great escape routes is the 'six hats' method: six-hatted people follow different modes of thinking which are symbolised by different colours.

When a group dons white hats, everybody concentrates on what information is available, what's needed, how it can be obtained. Switching to green, all concentrate on developing new ideas, new possibilities. Wearing black hats, the same people apply caution and risk-assessment to their brilliant green ideas. Under the yellow hat, they look for benefits in a 'logical positive' manner. Blue-hatted, they study the whole thinking process – what are they thinking about and how? Eureka! thoughts are red-hatted: the team relies on intuition and emotions, with no requirement to justify any idea. Using the hats, the team brings all its intellectual horsepower to bear positively, instead of wasting time because one side is arguing with the other. As one chief executive ruefully admitted to de Bono, 'I used to wait until somebody said something with which I disagreed, and then jump on him.' With six hats, that's out. Thinking consequently becomes much quicker, and team-work more real.

Six hats has the added virtue of excluding one purpose altogether: victory over another team member. If the green hat has been ordained, say, you have to join in creative thinking. That takes politics out of the equation; you can no longer attack people by attacking their ideas. The Japanese, the world's most successful exponents of team-work, start here with an advantage: their intellectual tradition isn't adversarial. That's in marked contrast to the West, where the more powerful you are, the more you like to 'win' an argument.

In a good team, everybody wins. Differing views come forward, and good leaders, having listened to their exposition, sum up the consensus. De Bono's book *Parallel Thinking* shows how team thinkers can create parallel possibilities, different and possibly contradictory hypotheses, from which they produce a new design. Traditional analytical thinking says move from A to B as soon as possible. The parallel model is more akin to Japanese modes, where people don't know what they're thinking until they've heard and considered all the possibilities.

Ben Heirs, author of *The Professional Decision Thinker*, is convinced that much public and private error would be avoided if teams properly executed their prime function: thinking. Even the greatest individual intelligence has limits, and the ceilings of combined brainpower are much higher. As he says, if the team is effectively led, and its thinking processes properly structured, 'alternatives and their possible consequences can then be created and explored more fully and intelligently, without the debate becoming divisive, unfocused and unprofessional'.

Does that fit your last meeting, or even many that you have ever attended? If not, 'considerable damage and waste' probably resulted. Heirs stresses that leadership of the team is crucial, but that the skills involved are those most often neglected when picking leaders – or letting them stay in office. Lacking the ability (for which read training) to harvest other minds, the leader gravitates towards one-man-bandmanship.

One well-known female boss, for example, takes every single product decision. She's nearly always right, but in the process of being right, she destroys the ability of others to go beyond their present horizons. When Lee Iacocca abdicated the Detroit boss's godlike right of final yea and nay on new models, Chrysler took a giant step towards becoming America's most profitable car company. There was once a panel show entitled *Does the Team Think?* If it isn't a team, and doesn't think, you can't be surprised if disaster follows.

Today, moreover, it's a team or nothing. Remember that UK boss for a globe-girdling multinational who had some news for his top team. Henceforward, careers wouldn't progress from post to post, each more senior and better paid than the one before. Instead, roles and success would relate to skills – what the team members could do, rather than where they did it. That's the logical inference from the changing pattern of managerial work. As more and more time goes into multi-disciplinary project teams, task forces and the like, functional roles and hierarchical titles mean less and less.

This is nothing new in companies: technologists have always worked that way. The best available scientist or engineer leads the R&D project and then moves on to the next. Today management must increasingly operate in similar style, simply because it saves time, money and mistakes to have all disciplines involved from start to finish. Yet the great majority of managers still operate in their functional and hierarchical cocoons.

Many businesses rightly bring executives together for combined sessions to seek better strategies and leadership, and it's immediately clear that internal barriers impede realisation of generally shared and sensible aims. In that multinational example cited above, for example, there was one flaw: the executive team had never heard its leader's ideas before. As it happened, they agreed with the new strategic line. They should, of course, have been involved from the beginning. True teams are led from the front, but only in the sense that an orchestra is led.

Avoiding 'turf wars'

Artifical barriers between leaders and led are only one obstacle to true team-work. Inter-departmental and cross-functional rivalries – what Americans call 'turf wars' – are other serious hurdles, made worse by the fact that they are seldom overcome. They're known in sport, too. Try to persuade rugby forwards that they can learn from backs, or vice versa, and you'll usually get no more change than when persuading marketing to work (as it should) hand in glove with production, or either to co-operate willingly with finance.

The skills essential to the modern manager thus include the ability to work with other functional talents in teams, and to lead not by the authority of command, but by that of expertise. Team-leadership, paradoxically, includes knowing when to hand over the reins to others as their expertise moves to the fore. In games, this stems naturally from the functional demands. Only the quarterback can call the plays in American football: in rugby, line-out tactics are equally an expert function.

In the Pearl Harbor movie, *Tora! Tora! Tora!*, the decision to attack is discussed, in parallel-thinking style, by officers giving their opinions one by one, without the to and fro of Western debate. Then Admiral Yamamoto sums up the meeting and gives the go-ahead. The task of planning the onslaught, though, is entrusted to the fleet's best strategist, who happens to be a young lieutenant. And his plan then gets a going-over from the best critic, a captain, who finds it perfect. That's true team-work.

We previously mentioned that, when GM Europe was developing its Omega executive car, thirteen teams worked together, each containing all ten functions. A further crucial point is that project-leadership changed hands as different stages stressed different needs. Some managers now spend half their time in ad hoc task forces, tackling specific problems or projects whose success depends on deferring to the right expert at the right moment. Some experts play no greater part than the player who enters the Super Bowl only to kick at goal, but like his, the limited role may be vital.

All managers recognise the need to form small, self-managed, focused teams when a specific task must be completed. To take just one of countless examples, at Ciba, the Swiss chemical giant, a project designed to save millions on purchasing and warehousing costs demanded that a core of a dozen full-time executives be taken away from their former jobs for four years, helped by many part-timers. But why should the principle of horizontal, multi-disciplinary, cross-functional teams apply only to one-off projects? What about the continuing work of the business?

The challenge of restructuring

The guru-blessed tendency favours reorganising businesses into smaller sub-units, each given the fullest possible decentralised authority by a small, strategic headquarters. This goes hand in hand with the removal of unnecessary layers of management. That 'delayering' is the main cause of the new curse of executive unemployment. Delayering sounds an excellent idea, and so it is – provided that management processes (as opposed to the structure) are reorganised round the fewer layers. If processes stay unchanged, the layers may vanish, but the duties don't. As a report from Exeter University's Centre for Management Studies says:

> The removal of a layer of management which many companies have undertaken has meant that responsibilities from the moved tier have been reallocated to the levels above and below . . . the staff remaining have more responsibility, in some cases too much, which can lead to stress and inefficiency.

Nearly one in three of the companies subjected to Exeter's research had 'been involved in organisational changes' in the past three years. Many firms had indeed decentralised, but an equal number had moved in the opposite direction. Whatever the gurus propose, those who dispose have simpler thoughts. The decentralised business, eager for change, or forced into changing, centralises: the centralised outfit does the opposite.

Top management has no trouble in making a persuasive case for a move in either direction.

Much of this 'restructuring' has been done in haste to cut costs, and with no thought either for team-building or the long-term future of the business. Top managements react much like unthinking sports selectors, of which England's rugby choosers (in the pre-Cooke era) and Test cricket selectors (more often than not) are notoriously bad examples. The team loses, so heads roll – but not, of course, those of the selectors.

In the days before Douglas McGregor's Theory Y became the norm, the Theory X hire-and-fire method of obtaining improved performance was thought to be effective. But nothing demoralises teams more, in business or sport, than arbitrary execution. Changes are essential from time to time, of course, but unless they are understood and endorsed by those who remain on the team, the results may be counter-productive. Arbitarily 'downsized' or 'right-sized' companies may be leaner and fitter, but they won't have higher morale.

Nor will their leanness and fitness count for much unless they are part and parcel of a strong future strategy. The Exeter study's anxieties on this crucial point are supported by GMS Executive Leasing, whose Michael Dobson notes the 'insufficient attention . . . given to what the company's shape will be in two, five or ten years' time'. Will the traditional layered hierarchy, for instance, continue to make sense, even with fewer layers?

Managers agree on the need to break down barriers between departments by forming horizontal teams. They are less eager to contemplate the radical solution of breaking down the departments themselves. The concept of the 'strategic business unit' – the decentralised sub-unit mentioned above – is the antithesis of departmental management. What justifies the latter's continued strength? Why retain large central functions, from marketing and sales to finance, if the organisation is subdivided into discrete businesses?

Some sub-units, of course, are so large that they can readily breed bureaucracies of their own. The centralising tendencies are always at work, because top management likes to manage, and requires human machinery to help. But there's an extreme alternative. A few companies, like Sherwood Computer Services, have developed the task-force idea into an organising principle. The business teams organise themselves and substantially take charge of their own destinies.

At one investment bank, the IT department (normally one of the most powerful and self-contained functions) has been broken up in this way. Its members were dispersed to the different businesses, each of which is now armed with its own IT expertise. There's no reason why self-managed groups, each with full functional services, shouldn't be the building blocks of the organisation, and every reason why (to take a bad example) separate sales and customer-service operations should cease to be separate.

The company gains in flexible speed and shared experience what is lost in tidiness. Anyway, the tidiness can be illusory. In 1993 Volkswagen, under extreme economic pressure, was making rapid (though belated) progress on raising productivity and quality by better team-work in manufacturing. But all its other functions remained resolutely immobile. They simply weren't playing on the same team – or even, at times, playing the same game.

That is a gross failure of leadership, which raises a conundrum. The old principle had the virtue of clarity. As the sign on Harry Truman's desk said, 'The buck stops here.' There's something inherently unattractive about the idea that you can keep your head, and stay ahead, even after crass mismanagement. Justice seems to require that the team leader should pay the price of failure, even when it's not necessarily his own. But if the team is a genuine interacting group of equals, and any change should be handled with the consensual tact recommended above, shouldn't the leader be treated with equal respect?

Yet it's awfully hard to accept the protracted delays before self-evidently failed chieftains – at IBM, General Motors and Kodak, for instance – were removed. In these cases, like those where the founding fathers of fallen British stars have vacated the premises, board pressure helped force the departures. But what had the same directors been doing and saying while decline was gathering momentum? They could argue – as British political apologists have done – that where cock-ups are collective rather than individual responsibilities, the individual shouldn't carry the can.

In other words, if the Cabinet acts as a team, it's unfair to single out one member of that team, even the leader of the failed department, for the blame. In theory, that poor excuse applies equally in business, for the board, or management committee, is just as much (or little) of a team as the Cabinet. In practice, however, this is mythical. Many such teams don't function as teams: they are dominated by one or two figures, and the rest go along for the ride. In those circumstances, it's only right that, when the vehicle leaves the road, so should the driver.

But the object of managing, of course, is to win: not only to stay on the road, but to drive powerfully ahead. If the teams had truly functioned as effective working groups, far better results would have flowed, and the executions would thus have been unnecessary. It follows that the prime task of true leadership is to create teams which, in the final analysis, lead themselves to success.

VII

Visibility – How to Lead by Example

19

England's Visible Victories

Great leaders create an aura of visibility. Whether they are leading teams, companies or armies, they foster the idea that they are present and available at all times. Visibility runs even deeper. Great leaders have an empathy with their teams. The dictionary defines 'empathy' as 'the power of entering into another's personality'. Great leaders and their people develop a mutual understanding which is founded on the leader's ability to make others feel special and wanted.

Good visibility depends on setting high standards and developing what Field-Marshal Montgomery, as noted in the introduction to this book, called 'the atmosphere', which was the leader's first duty to create. This tone, this environment, enables the team (in this case, his Eighth Army officers) to fulfil its task (beating the awe-inspiring Rommel). To this end, managers, sports captains and generals need, as often as possible, to place themselves in the position of the people they lead. What do they require from the leader? What are they looking for? What would raise their performance? What would make them feel valued?

You learn many seemingly basic and obvious lessons from serving as a leader: in that, we're sure, business managers are no different to captains of England in sport. Rob Andrew, the England fly-half, pointed out one of the first lessons to Will

Carling within the first six months of his appointment. The situation was typical. Despite appearances, England get together as a team very infrequently. The old pattern consisted only of the weekend before an international, and then the Wednesday before the game, which left them just seventy-two hours to spend together before the match – not much time in which to build rapport between players, coaches and medical staff.

In 1988, it gave very little scope for a young – very young – captain, aged twenty-two, to create a style, a set of standards and an understanding of what was required from the senior players if they were to achieve the direction envisioned by the management. You easily become desperate to use the brief time to the full; spending it with a small group of individuals seemed like a good answer. It wasn't: it was a classic pitfall. Andrew quietly and politely pointed out to his captain that he had yet to sit next to a reserve player at any meal – and hadn't even spent much time with a number of team members.

This might seem unimportant, even trivial. But for a captain who was trying to create the right atmosphere, it gave completely the wrong impression – one of lack of interest in and concern for the reserves in the squad. This was something which had to be worked at hard, and without delay. It's an issue that you can't leave alone. You have to remind yourself of the importance and the need every time.

By moving around the squad, or the company, or the department, or the task force, you not only canvass opinions, detect moods and assess morale, you also have the opportunity to show an interest in every member and to treat all of them equally. On the 1994 tour of South Africa, it was thought a good idea to hold regular meetings with the most senior five or six players, the most experienced tourists. Carling took this a step further, dividing the whole squad into groups of similar size and trying to meet each of them weekly.

Innovation can come from inexperience

It's obviously important to plug into the thoughts and experience of the veterans. But every manager knows that it's often the inexperienced person who comes up with some of the most innovative ideas. This was certainly true of the greener tourists in South Africa, and the same applies to every team, in sport or outside it. Regular meetings with everybody also achieve primary visibility for the leader. A price must be paid, true, in loss of privacy. But Warren Bennis puts that matter in a nutshell: 'When a man or woman opts for a position of responsibility, he or she also surrenders their privacy.'

That lesson came across painfully during the 1991 World Cup campaign. England's last training session before meeting Scotland in the semi-final was held on the Friday morning. It was, as usual, a light run-through of the rhythms that the team hoped to impose on the game. The importance of the game only added to the usual tension, which was further enhanced by memories of the year before, when dramatic and unexpected defeat by Scotland at the same ground, Murrayfield, had cost England the Triple Crown and the Grand Slam. This is Carling's account of what happened:

Although I was focused on the training session itself, my mind kept on drifting to the evening, when I would be speaking at the team meeting. I was desperately trying to find a hook on which to hang my talk, a hook which would trigger the emotions of the squad and create the focused intent that we hadn't achieved eighteen months before.

With the session complete, I wandered off to do the required interviews with the assembled TV crews and waiting media people. As I went back to the changing room, the manager, Geoff Cooke, took me aside and asked, 'How do you feel? Do you think the session went well?' I was overjoyed with the quality of the session, but slightly puzzled by Geoff's question. Why had he asked it?

He explained that my head had been down the whole time. I hadn't made any comment to any of the players during the thirty minutes when we had been running. As a result, the squad had sat in the changing room afterwards trying to work out why I was upset, and what they had done wrong. I had underestimated how closely the players observe me and how much they read into my movements and apparent moods during the session. I had provided no encouragement for them.

The lessons for leaders are clear:

(1) Be aware of what you are doing, and what attitude you are adopting, at all times.
(2) Restrict your planning – and your worrying – to the privacy of your own room, office or home.
(3) If you find you have been delivering the wrong message, correct it at once (England, of course, won that game).

A more positive moment happened before the French game which decided the Grand Slam in 1991. The England side had finished all its pre-match rituals with a final team meeting on the Friday evening, and the players were relaxing in their different ways around the Petersham Hotel, where they always stay before the Five Nations home games. The side was almost desperate in its desire to win the Grand Slam after missing it the year before and losing the final game to Wales in 1989. Again, Carling tells the story:

I found myself sitting with Geoff Cooke at about nine o'clock in the evening. We discussed the mood of the squad, the level of confidence, my own worries and apprehensions, and whether I really believed we could win the game the next day. I did, but I still felt there was an uneasiness amongst the players – a lack of real confidence – probably because of the mental scars from the year before.

Geoff hinted that in some way I should just remind them how good they were as players and how good they could be as a team. I sat in my room and wrote on a piece of card for each player five or six lines, saying why he was exceptional, what he would bring to the team the next day, and why that would lead to victory. I slipped the notes under each of their doors so that it would be the last thing they read before going to bed.

The next day the notes were greeted with the usual derision by many of the players. They said they didn't really want to receive love letters from me the night before a game. But in the quieter moments that evening, celebrating after the victory, many of the side did wander over to say that the note had given them a little boost just before such a big confrontation. It's not something I remember as a personal achievement, but more as part of my role as captain, as leader, merely to remind the players how good they really are.

The incident also shows that visibility often hinges on significant detail. The players received a handwritten note. It had its effect because they realised that the captain had taken the time to sit down and write to each of them individually. The effect would not have been the same had the communication been impersonal. Typed general memos and E-mail don't have the same effect. The personal touch is essential to show people that you care. That doesn't always mean face-to-face contact, but it does mean spending some time on people as individuals and realising and acknowledging the special abilities which they bring to your team.

A great deal of importance should be attached to even seemingly trivial evidence of personal problems. For a sports captain that means, for example, dropping into the physiotherapy room when players are injured. An injury, however slight, causes anxiety. It deflects the player's mind from training and from concentrating on the build-up to the next game. The result is a certain amount of vulnerability and stress. While it's important for the captain to understand the nature and extent of the injury, it's even more vital to let the player know that you care, are aware of his situation and interested in his state of health.

On the field of play, different considerations apply when a player is injured. Of course the captain has to be at his side. Vital questions must be answered. How serious is the injury? Is a replacement needed? If so, the decision must be made quickly and any consequences communicated at once to the team. In a borderline case, you need to make a rapid assessment of the player's mental state. The captain and the player must decide between them whether the player can carry on. It's a more instantaneous, subjective analysis: there isn't time for discussion and thinking through the matter.

In general, the physio can pass on very useful information to the captain. England's Kevin Murphy has been hugely respected by the squad for many years. In the relaxed informality of the treatment room, many players off-load anxieties and paint a picture of how they see their form and their role in the team. This information can be vital to the captain, who should be continually monitoring the morale of his players. On many occasions Murphy has passed on the information that certain players are feeling vulnerable, are unclear about their specific role, or may simply need encouragement to take a positive view of some niggling injury.

Staying visible

The captain must also be visible in the most difficult scenario of all: when a player is dropped. The captain of the England XV sits in on selection, not only to express his own views, but to pass on those of the squad. When a player is dropped, he should always be able to sit down and discuss the decision with the captain as well as the management. The captain, after all, is a player like himself. He will probably find it easier to let off his frustrations and steam at the captain: the management, he may feel, might hold an outburst against him.

It's essential to treat a player honestly and to give him the specific reasons for his exclusion. In the first instance, this gives him a focus for his training and playing, and thus helps him to renew the challenge for his place. Moreover, the captain's concern shows a basic respect for a man who has played on the same side. No player will ever agree with his own deselection, but if he is to perceive the team management as honest and trustworthy, he must understand why he's been dropped.

By the same token, a player who is picked has his confidence boosted by knowing why. A common failing in management is to assume that promotion in itself is enough encouragement. On the contrary, players or managers picked for a new and more important job may well feel insecure and uncertain about their ability to make a success of their new role. They won't express those doubts, but this is a time when they badly need reassurance. The manager who has been moved downwards or sideways, of course, needs it even more.

Leaders must be at their most visible and approachable when people are at their lowest ebb, and they must be seen to take responsibility for their part in whatever decision has caused the unhappiness. At no point should you imply that you disagree with an unpleasant decision. Not only will this diminish the leader's own credibility in the eyes of the person concerned, but it also weakens the credibility of the entire management. A leader who doesn't face up to people at the bad times can never earn their true respect and trust.

Those managers who make poor excuses for their own invisibility ('not enough time', etc.) should try to put themselves in the shoes of those who want to see them. It's easy: all they need do is remember what they felt and needed when their positions were less exalted. All an England captain has to do, for instance, is to visualise what it was like when he was first picked for his country: how much anxiety he felt, and the attacks of nerves he experienced, even on first entering the team hotel. That visualisation arouses empathy, the core of visibility.

Rising to the top after years of experience only enhances the importance of being sensitive to the feelings of others, and showing that sensitivity. That demands becoming aware of the effect you have on members of your team; constantly trying to engender a positive, relaxed atmosphere; avoiding anything that will sow harmful doubts, especially when the pressures are mounting, as in the build-up to an international. Visibility is not, however, a one-off requirement: it's an all-time thing.

Visibility sets the example, establishes the tone and creates the atmosphere – Montgomery's word again. It isn't enough, of course, to see and be seen, as Monty was from his first day in command. In the 400-word self-introduction to his Eighth-Army officers mentioned above, Monty stressed nine other elements of leadership: two-way trust, team-work, clear objectives, equally clear communication, self-belief, back-up with adequate resources, insistence on good performance, humanity, and controlled aggression towards the opposition.

These attributes create 'atmosphere', and are reinforced by it and by each other. 'Atmosphere' equates with corporate culture: the innumerable cultural-change programmes now in progress are all endeavours to turn the Montgomery principles enunciated over fifty years ago into present-day practice: and that means all ten principles. Likewise, visibility is only effective in leadership when combined with the other nine attributes that, in a list very similar to Monty's, are the subject of this book. In team-work, it's one for all and all for one: so it is with the qualities of the true leader.

Vision, self-belief, results focus, courage, integrity, team-work, communicating, attentiveness, and commitment should form a seamless whole. But that unity can't be achieved without visibility, which is how the leader demonstrates his or her possession and exercise of all the powers required. As Monty did in that speech ('I am prepared to say, here and now that I have confidence in you'), you need as leader to remind members of the team how good they really are, and to show caring and respect for the people you are privileged to lead.

Leaders get nowhere by reminding people of their failures. You win by encouraging them to remember their successful experiences and to repeat those experiences in a consistent manner. For all that to happen, the leader must live the vision, 'walk the talk'. Vision and visibility share the same linguistic root. They are equally inseparable in true leadership.

Will Carling celebrates England's third Grand Slam under his captaincy – Twickenham, 1995.

20

Sex, *Sake*, and Soichiro Honda

The romantic image of the founder-millionaire wearing overalls, seen tinkering with some mechanical marvel in workshop or lab, is often reality. So it was with the late Soichiro Honda, in many ways the least typical of the post-war Japanese economic victors, but simultaneously the most visible archetype of Japanese success, though an eccentric one. 'Mr Honda,' said one baffled journalist, 'is a management executive who always wears red shirts and tells naughty stories when drinking.'

The drinking was important to Honda. In his early sixties, the great man admitted that he didn't understand computers. The fact that he couldn't keep up with the technology, though, was only one factor in his decision to take relatively early retirement. He also couldn't drink so much *sake* as before, while in sex his 'powers of doing and recovery' weren't what they had been.' And 'without sex and *sake*, I should quit the life of an entrepreneur.'

In contrast to Honda, Henry Ford didn't totally surrender power until death took over the decision, and he was notably abstemious in both wine and women. Yet Honda was known as 'the Oriental Henry Ford', and deserved the description. Like Ford, whose first business efforts were littered with failures and false starts, Honda learned the principles of efficient production quality the hard way. Out of fifty piston rings tested in Honda's first manufacturing venture, only three passed. Not surprisingly, the business failed.

His 1947 notion to make motorised bicycles with two-stroke engines adapted to run on pine-root extract was no more promising. Five years later, however, Honda came of technological age. With the Japanese market in recession, he invested $450,000 in German, Swiss and American machine tools, reckoning that they were the best in the world. He then 'reverse-engineered' the European bikes he was copying, taking them apart to see how they were made and discovering that their best was simply not good enough.

European manufacturers believed it was impossible to run motorcycle engines at 15,000 rpm, with even faster bursts. Honda not only proved that you could, but also started to win Grand Prix races all over the world. Super-design went with super-efficiency in production engineering. At Honda's motorcycle plants not a single storeroom existed for parts, raw materials, or finished machines: deliveries went in at one end, and finished bikes, up to one every seven seconds, moved straight on to double-decker trucks at the other.

Building the world's twenty-fourth-largest company (1993 sales, $35.8 billion) on the pillion of the motorbike is not only a prime economic achievement. It's also one that, before Honda demonstrated the method, would have been disbelieved, especially by the established British companies bearing once-proud names such as Norton, Matchless and BSA. In the Honda era, their decline and fall ended in pathos, with workers at the once-famous Triumph factory fruitlessly defying the management's efforts to close down the works forever.

Like those benighted British firms, the Japanese car establishment refused to take Honda's car plans seriously – especially when they saw his first, doomed model, which was little more than a covered motorbike. His vault, from a standing start, to number three in Japan (and number one in America) is all the more remarkable given that the opposition in Japanese cars was infinitely tougher than that of the biking Brits. Honda recovered

from his false start to build, very deliberately, a 'world car':
he undertook deep global research, wrote Robert Shook, into
'everything from road conditions to driving habits'. The result
was the Civic.

As in bikes, so in cars. Honda's strength was keeping ahead or
at least abreast of all the improvements to the car in his time, from
fascias and four-wheel steering to engine and braking systems –
even though, atypically for a Japanese company, the firm would
not buy in technology. As a top Honda man later explained,
'There are some technologies that we didn't have . . . But when
you buy technology it remains frozen, a foreign thing that is not
part of yourself, and in the end you don't know where to go
with it.'

It's hard not to see in this philosophy the highly visible example
of Soichiro Honda writ large. There's the indefatigable inventor
who (as with the non-polluting engine) prefers to create his own
technology because, if he leaves such tasks to other companies,
there will be fewer fields to conquer. The whole secret of Honda
was his direct participation in the life of the firm and its employees
– much too direct in the early days, to judge by one anecdote. A
bolt that had been tightened by a young worker made a few more
turns when Honda did it himself. 'You damned fool. This is how
you're supposed to tighten bolts,' shouted Honda as he hit his
employee over the head with a wrench.

While it is definitely visible, that intervention isn't how the
West pictures Japanese management. Honda's partner, Takeo
Fujisawa, fitted the pattern better when asked this question by
the head union negotiator. 'What do you think of the pay offer
you're making to us?' According to author Tetsuo Sakiya, Fujisawa
replied: 'The offer is so low, I think it's ridiculous.' The boss went
on to admit: 'It is our [management's] fault that the situation has
become such that we had to make such a low offer.' He predicted
that sales would pick up in March, proposed a new pay negotiation
at that time, and received thunderous applause.

Honda himself steered clear of industrial relations (wisely,
no doubt, in view of his penchant for hitting workers with

wrenches), yet it was he who stumbled on the management style which eventually got the company out of manpower messes for good. Honda got angry with 'workers who played baseball on the plant grounds', saying to himself, 'In collective bargaining, they complain about having to work too hard. But when it comes to playing baseball, they do it until they become completely exhausted, even though baseball does not bring a single yen to them. What kind of men are they?'

But then he thought:

I must recognise that man achieves the highest degree of efficiency when he plays. If someone says he works out of loyalty to the company, he is a damned liar. Everyone must work for himself. Even I work because I like working. I must create a workshop where everybody will enjoy working.

Which is what Honda proceeded to do, not only leading his men by example, but changing the example to one that suited both them and the company.

The Honda message

Visibility isn't only a matter of contact and example between management and men. That between managers and managers is also crucial. One of Honda's successors decided to move the executive suite from the customary top floor to the middle of the building so that senior management would need to spend only the minimum time elevating up or down. On that executive floor, there are no separate offices – not even for the chief executive. He sits in a corner at a round desk. The other executives are scattered about the enormous room, also at round desks.

Why round? So that anybody who wants can sit down for a discussion whenever he chooses. That's eminently practical. But you can't ignore the high and highly visible symbolism of this office layout. Taking the executive suite off the top floor signals that there is no exclusive, literally higher authority. Putting the emphasis on easy access to colleagues is a clear sign that involvement figures high in the corporate values. Placing top executives in an open office signifies the intention to have an open style, in which rank and status have no practical importance. The round tables indicate that decisions are only to be taken after full discussion among colleagues who are always on tap. The proximity of the desks establishes that lines of communication are to be short and easily opened. The classic Western office layout, based on the 'behind-closed-doors' principle, is the antithesis of visibility and delivers an utterly contrasting message.

The Honda message is entirely consistent with the visible example of its founder. In the 'sex and *sake*' valedictory quoted earlier, Soichiro Honda revealed that neither he nor Fujisawa had seen any operational papers or attended any operational meetings for the previous ten years. By playing no part in operational management, despite their enormous success and prestige, the two men enabled their successors to go beyond them. That was always their intention, as a banker discovered when he once addressed the pair as follows. 'I think you have an outstanding business going for you. I presume, of course, that you will eventually hand over the company to your sons.' They replied as one man, 'We have no such thought whatsoever.' As Honda explained, with a rhetorical question, 'If the company belonged to the family, who would have the motivation to work for the company?'

The unanimity of the partners, on this and other issues, was a powerful force in Honda's success and dates back to a 1949 conversation between Honda and Fujisawa. Fujisawa, then thirty-eight, informed Honda, four years older and already known as a brilliant inventor: 'I will work with you as a businessman. But when we part I am not going to end up with a loss. I'm not talking only about money. What I mean is that when we part, I hope I will have gained a sense of satisfaction and achievement.' A very Japanese wish, but a perfect expression of what business friendship means. They never did part, retiring by mutual agreement on the same day twenty-two years later.

You can get the flavour of their creation from a story about the initial build-up of Honda. It was based on a little, low-powered bike called Dream Type D. The name arose when somebody at a *sake*-and-sardine party to celebrate the prototype, remarked that it was 'like a dream'. Honda yelled out, 'That's it! Dream!' This story comes from an excellent book entitled *Honda Motor: The Men, the Management, the Machines*, by Tetsuo Sakiya.

Honda, though, made plenty of mistakes on the road from the Dream to the Civic and beyond. 'Success,' he wrote, 'can be achieved only through repeated failure and introspection. In fact, success represents 1 per cent of your work, which results only from the 99 per cent that is called failure.' The errors occurred even in the technology where he was most triumphant: engines. He obstinately insisted, against all contrary opinion in the company, that air-cooled rather than water-cooled engines were the future for cars. Finally, Fujisawa resolved the issue at dinner with his long-time partner. Here's Sakiya's fascinating account of the proceedings:

> They had not seen each other for quite some time and Fujisawa's mind was made up: 'If Mr Honda refuses a water-cooled engine, this would mean he is following a path different from mine. If the two of us cannot go in the same direction, our team-work will not function.' At the dinner, Honda told Fujisawa, 'The same thing can be achieved with an air-cooled engine, but I guess that's difficult for a man like you to understand.' Fujisawa replied, 'You can do one of two things. You can continue to serve as the president of our company, or you can join the engineers at Honda Motor. I think you should choose now.'

Honda looked unhappy to have to make such a decision, but replied, 'I'm sure I should continue to be the president.'

'Then,' said Fujisawa, 'you will permit your engineers to work on water-cooled engines, too, won't you?'

'I will,' Honda agreed.

Their conversation had lasted no more than a few minutes, after which the meeting turned into a party with both of them drinking *sake* and singing old folk songs together. The next day Honda went to the R&D centre and told the engineers, 'OK, now you can work on water-cooled engines.'

Although Honda was never seen to smile when anybody talked about water-cooling thereafter, his surrender was another marvellously visible example to everybody else. Remember, this was a highly combative, competitive man who hated to give in to anybody or anything, especially a rival. That characteristic, highly developed in the Japanese economy as a whole, has been a major factor behind their national success. In Honda's saga, the greatest example came in the motorcycle wars of the early 1980s.

This domestic Japanese bloodbath began with near-defeat. Yamaha's motorbike sales had pulled tantalisingly close to Honda's: 37 per cent of the domestic market against 38 – and you can't get much closer than that. There was a reason for the rise, as Yamaha's president shrewdly spotted. His words were reported by James Abegglen, a veteran Japan watcher and resident, and George Stalk Jr, in their book *Kaisha*.

At Honda, sales attention is focused on four-wheel vehicles. Most of the best people have been transferred [into cars]. Compared to them, our specialty at Yamaha is mainly motorcycle production . . . If only we had enough capacity, we could beat Honda.

Suiting the action to those words, Yamaha decided to match Honda new model for new model. Then it went for the supreme prize. In 1981 Yamaha announced a new factory that would within one year take the domestic lead; within two years the upstart would be 'number one in the world'. This was not a threat that Honda could brush aside. Its reading of the situation was as clear as Yamaha's: 'Yamaha has not only stepped on the tail of a tiger, it has ground it into the earth.' Honda adopted a

*Soichiro Honda's winning ways added car triumphs to
motorbike victory.*

new battle cry: 'Yamaha *wo tsubusu*,' which translates as: 'We will
crush/break/smash/butcher/slaughter/destroy Yamaha.'

The message got across. Whatever Yamaha produced, Honda
produced more, until the Japanese islands seemed in some danger
of sinking under the weight of unsold motorbikes.

In innovation, the counter-attack was even more dramatic.
In eighteen months, Honda introduced eighty-one new models, against only thirty-four from Yamaha. This understated the
full impact of Honda's devastating response. Its eighty-one new
models were accompanied by thirty-two discontinuations. Since
Yamaha could only manage three withdrawals, the upstart was
outgunned by 113 changes to thirty-seven. 'The customer,' says
Kaisha, 'was seeing fresh Hondas and increasingly stale Yamahas.'

After a year of blood, sweat and tears, the story had a happy
ending – for Honda. The group chairman at Yamaha observed
the wreckage and said, 'We plunged like a diving jet. My ignorance is to blame.' The Yamaha motorcycle boss who had started

the wars now saw reality: 'We can't match Honda's product development and sales strength. From now on I want to move cautiously and ensure Yamaha's relative position.' Personally, he didn't have the chance to pursue this more sensible strategy: he was out, and the great motorbike wars were over.

Those victorious product-development strengths are no accident. At Honda, the production of new models and new ideas is thought so important that it is seen as a young man's job. Development teams are selected to match the age group at which the new model is targeted, and engineers in R&D who haven't reached top status by forty are packed off elsewhere – just as Honda packed himself off when he considered that his prime usefulness was over. His successor, a mere forty-three-year old, in turn made way for a younger man ten years later.

As Rosabeth Moss Kanter has pointed out, a key to Honda's success was that its resident genius used to work directly on new products with the engineers. That was only possible because, as noted above, he and Fujisawa had delegated all operational responsibility. Soichiro Honda was thus free to concentrate on his vision of the future and to share it visibly with others. The corporate vision statement is like the founder himself, enormously practical:

(1) Quality in all jobs – learn, think, analyse, evaluate and improve.
(2) Reliable products – on time, with excellence and consistency.
(3) Better communication – listen, ask and speak up.

Developing a philosophy built on the experience of a practical engineer, the founding father had created a corporate culture that would go on working towards his objective – nothing less than becoming and remaining the world's best motor manufacturer – long after his own active days. His influence is still highly visible, as Honda was himself. And the visibility is inseparable from the success.

21

The Non-Managing Managers

The following four cases all have something in common – and it's powerful medicine.

(1) A plant in California became the most improved in Clorox's household products division after a woman manager asked the hundred workers to reorganise the operations. Her role was solely to ask a few questions as 'a team of hourly workers established training programs, set work rules for absenteeism, and reorganised the once traditional factory into five customer-focused business units'.

(2) A disposable nappy company has given five managing directors equal power. Each has a functional role, but they share reponsibility for major decisions, which always depend on consensus. (There's a venture capital firm which likewise insists on unanimity before making any investment.) Sales grew by 24 per cent in a year.

(3) When S.C. Johnson Wax moved towards self-managed teams, the human resources manager took a small staff down to the factory floor to teach management techniques like statistical analysis and 'pay for skills'. The time taken in switching a line from liquid floor wax to stain-remover came down from three days to thirteen minutes, thanks to a worker team. The Racine plant overall reduced its middle management to thirty-seven

instead of 140, and productivity went up 30 per cent compared to eight years before.

(4) The US outpost of France's Thomson electronics giant has a successful high-end line of TVs called Pro-Scan. Each member of a cross-functional team (from design, marketing, engineering and manufacturing) took turns as team leader while continuing to perform in his or her normal job. 'All the team members subsequently moved on to bigger and better things. Says [one], "It made us all better generalists."'

Such anecdotes should always be taken with a grain of salt, in the sense that somebody else's experience is never as valuable as your own. But the pattern of this new approach to management is clear enough. The manager's task is to make people offers they can't refuse, because they want to accept; and in circumstances where that acceptance will markedly improve the behaviour of individuals and groups. Today's best leaders don't lead in the traditional sense. Rather, they deliberately blur the distinction between followers and leaders.

The four cases outlined above come from a *Fortune* article which begins: 'Call them sponsors, facilitators – anything but the M word.' What's happening is nothing less than reform of the management process. 'Non-manager managers', in the magazine's terminology, manage by example: they are ceasing to function as part of an order-and-obey chain and becoming instead links in a process that binds everybody together – from top to bottom of the company.

It doesn't matter whether this sea-change is known as 'total quality' or by some other name. The need is to find approaches that will prove highly effective in changing behaviours at both the company and individual level. For example, one chief executive liked to chew out two colleagues each morning as a kind of second breakfast. Leading a total quality drive worked wonders on the business – and on the personal relationships of the boss. Relationships are always a cardinal factor in corporate performance, as the change in management style recognises.

The change from invisible boss to highly visible facilitator is one of enormous proportions. 'This is one of the biggest planned efforts to alter people's behaviour since the Cultural Revolution,' wrote one academic. He was describing developments at one of the world's largest companies, General Electric. Changing corporate cultures is notoriously difficult, with the emphasis on notoriously. The difficulty is much exaggerated by the notoriety. It's also true that a huge gulf exists between traditional management and GE chief executive Jack Welch's brave new world.

Welch is quoted as saying, 'We've got to take out the boss element.' In his vision, reported *Fortune*, 'Twenty-first-century managers will forgo their old powers – to plan, organise, implement and measure – for new duties: counselling groups, providing resources for them, helping them think for themselves.' As Welch puts it, 'We're going to win on our ideas, not by whips and chains.' Nothing here will be strange to exponents of what we call 'the management consensus'. Like Welch, the gurus of the consensus (meaning virtually every guru) believe you should:

(1) Involve employees at all levels in making decisions.
(2) Adopt 'best practice' ideas and methods from within and without the organisation.
(3) Attack every process and procedure in the company with the aim of simplifying, compressing, economising and improving.

Thus *Fortune*'s distinction between the old and new manager notes that the latter 'invites others to join in decision-making', while the former 'makes most decisions alone'. The one hoards information which the other shares. The passé manager is bound up in the cloak and chains of command. The new-style non-manager, in fully uncloaked visibility, 'deals with anyone necessary to get the job done'. That means colleagues, people in other departments, and people in traditionally lower spheres: the 'workers'.

As working methods become more intelligent, so the distinction between the worker and the manager (who presumably is also a worker) becomes even harder to sustain. Workers have long been known as untapped sources of valuable knowledge – like the Milliken textile man whose new boss, on a getting-to-know-you tour (a deliberate pursuit of visibility), mentioned a costly, longstanding technical problem. The veteran suggested a solution, which worked perfectly. When had the brainwave occurred? Long years before . . .

Tapping an operative's skill and experience makes indisputable sense, but non-managers go further. They ask operatives what help they need to perform better. This isn't namby-pamby stuff: the targets for improvement are, and must be, pitched high and taken dead seriously. But the changed approach alters attitudes and takes the first step towards long-term and lasting betterment. This isn't Utopia: rather, it's the hard-headed reality of hard-nosed companies like GE.

What are the attributes of the highly visible non-manager? They include sincerity, fairness, ability to motivate, readiness to recognise achievement and abilities in others, responsiveness, and making time available for others. They sound soft. The issue of softness disappears, however, when you consider the opposite characteristics: insincerity, favouritism, lack of motivation, poor or no response, and spending far too little time with the people on whose contributions you depend. In a sports team, these traits breed disaster: the same is true in business.

The command-and-control hierarchy is the only environment in which low-visibility management can survive. But many companies are now proliferating team projects, which can't be managed by order-and-obey methods. True, somebody has to keep the projects on track and on target, and this management contribution is vital: but 'facilitator' is absolutely the correct description of a role which is by definition temporary and obviously can't be fulfilled without participative, visible leadership.

The 'manager' job, in this and other ways, is becoming more visible, less stationary and more flexible. If that's true of the job, managers have to follow suit. Becoming visible, mobile and flexible demands optimising their own performance. Corporate

managers owe it to themselves and their co-workers to practise individual *kaizen*: continuous improvement. The admirable
American guru Michael J. Kami calls this 'self-renewal' and offers
an apparently intimidating 'personal checklist':

(1) Are you fluent in two languages?
(2) Do you read (a) one book a month, (b) four daily
newspapers and (c) thirty magazines?
(3) Do you attend one course a quarter?
(4) Are you out of the office half the time?
(5) Are you computer-literate?
(6) Do you possess multi-disciplinary knowledge?

Any manager who can answer half those questions in the
affirmative is exceptional. But all six positive responses are within
anybody's reach. Not only should each facility improve personal
effectiveness, but personal development is the foundation of
setting an excellent example. In top sport, good captains may
not match the world-class skills in their teams, but they will
lead, among other things, in the visible application and effort
they bring to developing their own games and their own skills
– including those of leadership.

Managing time effectively

Effective time-management is an obvious example. Shortage
of time is the main excuse which managers, good or less good,
offer for their low visibility, for their failure to see enough of
their people or to give them enough personal support. But poor
organisation of time, rather than inadequate supply, is the real
problem. In theory, the PC network will help: as mentioned
earlier, one IT study indicates that managers can hope to
save half the time they now spend in meetings, organising,
communicating and gathering information.

That would free 40 per cent of their hours for other priorities, like spending enough time with team members. It will still leave plenty of wastage, some of it self-inflicted: managers fritter away hours on totally unnecessary work, or work that could and should be delegated to others. They don't concentrate on what is exclusive and important to them, even when they have full control over their time – though that, of course, is rarely the case.

The organisation (for which read other managers) makes its own demands on the executive timetable. The more hierarchical and corpocratic the system, the more time will be pre-empted and wasted by procedure rather than process. Non-manager managers are interested in process exclusively, and in procedure not at all. The American consumer goods chain, Nordstrom, has a corporate manual which differs radically from those of other companies. Its first rule is an injunction to all employees to 'use your good judgement in all situations'. The second rule is: 'There will be no additional rules.'

This is the essence of non-managing: it saves executive time because the delegation is genuine and total. The facilitator visibly helps others to act on their own initiatives. The principle was demonstrated brilliantly by a speaker helping the Confederation of British Industry to launch its competitiveness campaign. After he had recounted the successes of his company (Short Brothers) in empowering workers to raise their productivity, a questioner from the audience asked how his firm could do likewise. 'Get out of the way,' was the answer.

Non-managers don't get out of sight, but they don't interfere or try to take over the process from those to whom it belongs. What applies on the shop floor is just as relevant in the office. In Barbara Tuchman's book *The March of Folly*, it becomes painfully clear that gross mistakes aren't made by fools, but by very intelligent people. There's no point in hiring bright people, or in selecting the best players, and then treating them in ways that guarantee stupid results.

One well-established path to this sorry end is the 'career structure', mapped out, not in terms of opportunities for achievement, but of steady progress up the ladders of seniority and hierarchy. One clearing banker, for instance, was heard to observe that modern ideas of career development, while splendid in themselves, didn't apply to his bank because a recruit's path to eventual retirement was planned from the first months of service.

These days, exactly the opposite career strategy is required. That's the only way to benefit from the extraordinary achievements that relatively young non-manager managers can generate when given their heads with full-frontal visibility – like that twenty-seven-month creation of the very successful Land Rover Discovery, or the eighteen-month construction by ICI Fluorocarbons of a plant that may have won the race to replace CFCs. All such examples show how highly visible, project-based, team-based management both uses managerial talent and develops it mightily in the process.

That is no surprise. To perform at their best, managers need opportunity and the space in which to seize their chances. If they are confined within 'structures' (career or hierarchical) they will conform rather than perform, manage rather than non-manage. Conformists will succeed to the summit in turn, and the conventional corporate wisdom will steadily clog the arteries. However much shareholders or top management may demand improvement, the necessary human material will already have been wasted. Decline and fall will follow – as it did at Hoover, the one-time king of European domestic appliances.

The misuse of human resources explains, but doesn't excuse, Hoover's greatest fiasco, in which deliriously happy shoppers swamped and almost sank the company with their response to its over-generous offer of free flights. Under extreme pressure to produce, the management went to extremes: the latest shambles came only two years after the US owners sent a special task force to Britain (under American leadership) to achieve 'rebirth, rejuvenation, stability and return to profitability' – a somewhat odd cocktail of objectives.

Companies can rejuvenate themselves continuously by promoting younger people, not to hierarchical ranks, but to team projects where they can create new birth, rather than rebirth, leading by example and visibility. Free-standing units, at home or abroad, offer the chance for younger people to run their own businesses within the corporation. Exploit that fact, and dynamism will replace excessive stability. Better still, the flow of excellently equipped achievers to the top will be the best immunisation against stupidity that any company could want.

The lateral rise

Multi-disciplinary, cross-functional task forces also provide focused and conspicuous roles that develop team as well as individual skills. The concept of vertical promotion thus gives way to the lateral rise. That sounds contradictory, but simply means finding the most exciting opportunity currently available, in which the task, rather than the organisational role, is the challenge and the chance. Already, successful task forces are being rewarded with stiffer assignments – not as teams (for they are always disbanded), but as individuals (witness the Thomson case reported at the start of this chapter).

Team winners and winning teams also need to be rewarded with money (a fact which has caused sports administrators endless and unnecessary problems). Since hierarchy is breaking down, hierarchical pay structures should be disappearing as fast as the middle manager's traditional role: sitting behind closed doors and passing messages up and down the system. The group which brings a new model to successful launch, on time and on cost, deserves exceptional pay for what will certainly have demanded exceptional efforts – and that's surely as it should be.

In most other walks of life, stars earn starry rewards instantly. Their reward is in the present as well as the future. Tomorrow's chief executives, and their colleagues, will have zigged and zagged their ways to the top. The zig-zag organisation will get the best of them – in both senses. It will get the best work from the best people, men and women with portable skills who can work effectively in any country and with all other nationalities, and who are conscientious as well as intelligent.

On that last combination, *Fortune* reports exceptional career progress among MBA graduates who scored well both on their high-numeracy admission test and on 'a composite of how hard-working, thorough, efficient, reliable and ambitious' they were. Furthermore, the highest fliers show an addiction to excellence in their personal pursuits, and exceptional achievement in previous projects is the most valuable element in the portable manager's briefcase.

But the environment is crucial. What if the company, like most, is light years away from the non-managing, high-visibility culture and persists in the set organisational ways that can be summarised as 'large company disease'? Honda's president has identified this crippling ailment in his own business. His remedy is one that, alas, must also be used with managers who can't adjust to non-managing in a new-style company. 'For those who are inflexible and refuse to do what they have to do, the only option is to fire them.' At one Scottish plant which went over to the new ways of managing, half the top management left, unable to cope with the new way of working life.

There's a highly symbolic example from GE which demonstrates the difference between this new world and the old. The company uses 'work-out' to uncover specific proposals for improvement from anything between forty to a hundred people, nominated by management 'from all ranks and several functions'. The work-out participants turn up for a three-day informal off-site conference under the guidance of an external facilitator. They form some half-dozen teams, each given part of the broad agenda laid down by the boss: say, to eliminate unnecessary meetings or forms.

On the third day, the teams present their proposals, which is where an equally interesting innovation appears. The boss, who may have a hundred or so proposals on the table, must decide on the spot whether to (1) agree, (2) refuse, or (3) demand more information, appointing a team to deliver the data by an agreed date.

The psychological pressure to agree must be heavy: in one quoted example, only eight of 108 proposals were turned down by a plant-services head. His own boss was present for the work-out, but the senior man lurked out of sight behind the manager, who thus couldn't seek signs of approval or disapproval. The boss was visible, in the sense that he was there, but he was invisible in that he wasn't interfering. He was managing, and also not managing – and that's the ideal, for good leaders and for companies which want to keep them. Non-managers won't stay where they can't non-manage.

VIII

Communicating – How to Open the Channels

22

Frank Dick's Roots and Wings

Great coaches no doubt differ in their styles as much as great athletes. But the coaches must all have one thing in common: they are great communicators. It isn't just a question of seeing what the athlete must do, but of persuading him or her to do it. Anybody who has seen Frank Dick speak on a public platform will bear witness to his skills as communicator to several hundred people: his skill at one-to-one communication also played a crucial role, not only in developing individual world champions, but in revitalising British athletics as a whole.

Today most people remember only the long string of glorious successes during Dick's reign as national coach: the middle-distance triumphs of Coe, Cram and Ovett; the sprinting of Christie and Regis; the decathlons of Daley Thompson; the hurdling of Gunnell and Jackson; the javelin-throwing of Whitbread and Backley, and many, many more. At the start, though, the international standing of British athletics was even lower than that of English rugby when Geoff Cooke took charge.

Athletics victory in the European Cup seemed as far away then as the World Cup final did to the rugby players before Cooke unfolded his vision. In an athletics competition the coach has to form a team by blending highly individualistic athletes who actually compete with each other in their individual events and only combine for relays. Working with different captains, Dick achieved miracles of communication in the big international competitions: spectators could *feel* the team spirit that was evoked and which plainly reinforced the athletes' own will to win.

Dick's prowess as coach and communicator has been widely recognised outside athletics. He has worked with such intense competitors as tennis star Boris Becker and racing driver Gerhard Berger, together with, most recently, a number of rugby players. Dick's years of experience have coalesced into startlingly simple, but far too infrequently applied, principles for coaching others to achieve success. He starts by denying a popular belief – that 'you have a coach or you hire a coach, and that's it for life. It's not like that.' What is coaching, then? Dick's answer comes not from sport, but from a wedding.

> I'd coached a boy who married a girl called Beatrice, the daughter of a titled Cuban family. I went to their wedding, and she said, 'Frank, I wish you in life the strength to give your children the only two gifts that you can.' Now I've got two daughters, and I thought, it's going to be expensive.

Dick asked if Beatrice were talking about a BMW or something: the answer was: 'The only two gifts you must give them are the roots to grow and the wings to fly.'

At a stroke, this young woman had summed up the entire development process. Dick believes that, whether you are a coach working with an athlete, a parent with children, a teacher with pupils or a manager with staff, it's the same. 'At the end of the day, when the athlete goes out into the arena, whether it's Twickenham or Wimbledon, he or she is making a total statement for himself or herself. It's their statement. The coach cannot be involved at that point.'

To Dick, the 'worst possible thing' is to see athletes looking up into the stand for their coaches, 'because you know they are not concentrating 100 per cent. They should be out there owning the whole problem.' The job of the coach, or the manager, or the parent, is to 'get into other people the strength to do the growing'. The mentor spends time on directing and coaching to achieve precisely that, and the next stage tests the coach as much as the player.

Letting go

> Once they've started to grow, and they're growing strong, there comes a point when you've not only got to have the skills, but the courage to push them away from you, to let them spread their wings. If you don't, you're hanging on to their wings, and you will hold them down.

Dick draws the analogy of the child learning to walk: 'Finally, there's a stage where you let them fall and let them pick themselves up.'

Everybody must go through these stages. Dick is adamant that 'you can't have a coach, a manager or whatever who never lets that person fall over'. The motive for holding on may be love, or the mentor's own dependency on the other person's dependency. 'There are parents, coaches and managers who don't really want the person to be able to spread his wings, otherwise they themselves don't feel needed any more.' They feel that their world has collapsed, 'that there's nothing more for you'.

Many managers have challenged Dick on this issue. 'If we make these guys good, what's in it for us for the future?' His answer is that, if their own superiors 'see that you can manufacture two, three or four of you, you're gold dust.' Dick's point is that any of the good guys might leave, but the boss won't 'want to lose you, because you can make more of you, and that's critical'. As he says, the work of the coach – in management as in athletics – 'is central to the whole business'.

The process is 'on-going, dynamic, changing, developing'. The philosophy of 'grab them and hold them for good' doesn't work.

When presenting to managers, Dick takes a quite different line. He usually tells his audiences: 'At the end of the day, the greatest compliment you can ever have as a manager, in the words of the Bette Midler song, is that "you're the wind beneath my wings".' The manager/coach sees his protégés spread their wings, smiles, and moves on to something else.

To Dick's mind, a good coach always takes his athletes through a definite process. Mistakes will be made along the way, but belief in the process, as well as the outcome, is crucial. How do you nurture the roots and grow the wings? When people first come to a coach, 'they are really pretty excited, because you represent the possibility of fulfilling their ambitions'. Giving them motivation or confidence therefore isn't that important. Here Dick uses a coaching style that he calls 'directing'.

The communication leaves no room for argument. You set the rules, saying, 'This is how you'll train on a Tuesday and Wednesday. I'll expect you to do this and this and this. Here's your programme – off you go. These are the rules that I live by.' The next stage is that motivation goes down. Confidence has started to rise because of the coaching process, but 'the fact is that no one in life ever improves as fast as they think they should'. As motivation consequently slackens, the mentor's style shifts from directing to 'coaching'.

This approach, says Dick, is 'a little bit softer'. He will give the athlete more help with fitting into the rules: 'I'll put demands on you, and then I'll help you to fit in.' At both the first two stages, though, Dick is in control. But then the athlete crosses a 'magic line' and enters stage three: 'Hey, I can see where I'm going now. I know where I'm going to get up. I've got my ambitions. I want to get there, and I want to get there fast.'

Mentors have to understand the peaks and troughs of this process. 'Motivation pops up and down with successes and failures.' Performance, says Dick, goes up in steps:

If you're going to develop people properly, there are going to be periods of stability, acceleration, stability. In much the

same way as you have day and night, and you need to sleep
and recover and regenerate, you need to push the work in,
and you need this balance all the time.

Stage four has arrived. At this point, the coach gives up the
reins: 'You are very much in control, and I support what you
are doing.' Then comes the dénouement: 'Finally motivation is
up, confidence is up, and I am simply there to give advice when
you need me.' The coach is now a counsellor, and the four-stage
process is complete, with the first two having provided the roots
and the second two the wings. 'Having spread your wings, you
come back to the nest or tree or whatever whenever you need
an expert.'

It takes great strength, as well as humility, for a coach to put
so much into his people and then sit back and allow them to take
the glory. But Dick believes that the ability to control your ego
is crucial in coaching. 'Ego must be controlled or the coach will

*Frank Dick's work as National Coaching Director saw Great Britain's
athletics performances transformed.*

never truly let go of his pupils and will thereby stifle their true growth.' The ego problem for the coach arises if he wants to be high-profile. Then: 'Of course, I'll always be looking over your shoulder when you're in the newspapers.'

But, Dick explains, it can't work like that, because the pupil will never feel clear of the mentor, and there'll be resentment of him or her at the end of the day. That's why it's difficult to work with athletes who are really going to spread their wings – 'rough diamonds', in Dick's nomenclature. Their athletic resources are very precious (hence the diamond). 'But they want to be mountain people, to get out of the valley, not to be equated with anybody else in life – they want to be different.'

Rough diamonds don't fit into moulds: 'The rough parts don't allow that to happen.' This poses a challenge to the mentor. 'Fitting you into a mould is desperately comfortable for me, because I can control you then.' That communicates the wrong message and contravenes the fundamental principles of the coaching process, which is 'not to control you, but to get the best out of you'. So the mould idea has to go. As for the rough parts, 'they are fine, provided they don't hurt other people in the team'.

Dick doesn't mind the rough bits hurting him, 'but if they start hurting other people, so that you don't have cohesion at the end of the day, then you had better start chipping off the odd rough edge'. The target is performance: a coach must have the confidence to measure himself on the performance of his charges. The fact that coaches rarely receive the plaudits misses the point. A coach's *raison d'être* is to nurture and encourage a great performance.

Its achievement provides immense satisfaction to the mentor who has been a key contributor to the success. 'It's how you measure yourself, that's the critical thing. You look in the mirror. You're only accountable to one person, and that's you, the guy in the mirror.' Dick was extremely upset in 1987 when the press 'had done a bad number on me because of Linford Christie and Daley Thompson'. The decathlon hadn't gone Thompson's way:

'He was injured when he went into it, and the view was that he should not have competed.'

The major press onslaught, however, centred on Dick having fallen out with Christie. 'I came back home, and my head had gone down.' He remembered a quote, though, about it not being the critic who counts. Dick's philosophy is that you must communicate honestly with yourself, asking: 'Did I give this my best shot? Could I have done it another way? Did I stand by my right set of principles? Did I put my ego in the way?' If the answers confirm that it truly was your best shot, well, 'there's nothing more you can do about it after that'.

Dick won't deny that he has an ego like anyone else, or that this raises difficulties.

> To start with, you think of coaching as a job, and because you see other people getting a spin-off from the work that you put in, I suppose it's tempting to think, 'Come on, let me got on to the front of the pitch.' And I was spoiled, really, because, being the chief coach for Great Britain, I was going to get a better profile, anyway.

Vitally, though, what counts is 'where your ego fits in, and how you adjust to the position – what's right for the athlete or the team, as opposed to what's right for you.'

Success = talent + motivation + confidence

It helps, of course, to work with extremely talented athletes like Thompson, although in fact Dick wouldn't count the latter among the greatest talents he's met. Nor would he call talent the greatest constitutent of success. Rather, success hinges on talent plus a mix of motivation and confidence. Too much talent can actually be a disadvantage, because everything comes too easily. You never learn to cope with failure, or what it feels like, if, in your evolving years, everything is a success.

When Dick began his athletics career, he recalls, 70 per cent of the gold-medallists from the All England Schools' Championship had left the sport within three years. The cream of the crop gave up shortly after entering the harsh world of adult athletics. The outstanding, talented athlete who had won throughout his schooling came up against the athlete with adequate talent, who had fought hard and won races, but who had also lost races, and probably had a healthier, more realistic experience of sport.

So which has the better prospects? The answer is obvious to Dick, but possibly not, he believes, to enough coaches – or enough athletes. All the great champions of Dick's time, like Thompson, Seb Coe, Steve Cram and Steve Ovett, had to fight their way through to the top. A great coach should look not just for talent, but for motivation and passion. The desire and hunger within an athlete govern the ability to bounce back and fight on, and spur the willingness to learn. You can always compensate for lack of talent; you cannot compensate for lack of desire or dedication.

The key is to create 'the right motivational climate'. Too many people, Dick believes, think of motivation not as climate, but as weather: you deal with rain or snow, specific situations, instead of creating the climate, the framework, within which your athlete can operate. As an example, Dick found when working with Gerhard Berger that the driver hated running, and communicated his hatred only too clearly. Like all athletes, though, he needed a high level of endurance to compete successfully. Dick had to find an alternative.

Berger turned out to love playing squash, which became the hub of his endurance training – no more miles upon miles of road-running. It's a neat example of how effective two-way communication between coach and player achieves winning results. Since Berger enjoyed squash, why make training a hated burden when it didn't have to be? Too often, coaches and managers think pedantically and predictably. Rather than seeking solutions to a problem, they tend to bulldoze through with a lack of communicative sensitivity that negates Dick's simple but eminently logical approach.

His method centres around building on people's strengths, what they are good at – 'and everybody is good at something'. people enjoy what they are good at, and do it competently. That's the foundation for good coaching: build a positive profile made up of strengths, and never do the opposite – concentrate on what people do badly. This flatly contradicts the common outcome of performance reviews in large organisations, which love to provide development programmes to cover the incompetences revealed by the appraisal.

'They never think of giving you a development programme for what you're good at.' Focusing on weaknesses gives the wrong message, providing negative motivation, while focusing on strengths is highly positive and recognises a basic truth: that people achieve in life through what they do well, not through what they do badly. Of course, weaknesses should be corrected, but not at the price of ignoring strengths. The mentor's role, using every means of communication in his or her power, is to create a positive, stimulating environment where success is continually recognised and reinforced, and where weaknesses are quietly strengthened.

23

The Technology of Information

'It's been a learning experience for me,' says Ben Rosen, 'the difference one person can make to a large organisation.' He's referring to Eckhard Pfeiffer, the chief executive of Compaq Computer – and the tribute is especially remarkable coming from a man of Rosen's immense experience as a venture capitalist. Pfeiffer proved himself the 'right leader' for a company in deep trouble by overcoming entrenched corporate resistance to a sea-change in policy: and Rosen has no doubt about the key to this success.

'The more you go down the organisation,' he says, 'the more of a job it is to get people to change. You really have to communicate.' A top executive, Gian Carlo Bisone, echoes this view. 'Eckhard really shared with us. There were a lot of sceptics.' Today a management communication group of 150 to 200 people from all over Compaq's world meets monthly to hear Pfeiffer explain his strategy in 'very clear terms', to question him, and to carry the message back home. During Compaq's crisis, these meetings were held weekly.

The gravity of that crisis in 1991 can't be exaggerated. Passing through general recession is testing enough, but having its own private recession in the midst of general gloom gave Compaq one of the sharpest falls from grace of any major company. Its first-ever quarterly loss in April–June 1991, however, was followed by recovery and resurgence swifter and fuller than has ever been made in any industry. Cutting jobs and costs was 'necessary, but not sufficient' to achieve this, says Rosen. The real driving force behind an astounding turnaround was a complete remaking of strategy.

The previous strategy had achieved equally extraordinary success. Compaq had passed $3 billion in worldwide sales faster than any company in history by concentrating on the higher-priced end of the personal computer market. By the end of 1990 there were one or two unfavourable trends – 'particularly the increase in market share of companies selling PCs on price'. But any fears expressed in the boardroom were 'allayed by management'. All businesses have problems at any given time, and at first nobody suspected that the rise of the cut-price clones heralded fundamental change.

The first Compaq officer to spot that sea-change was Rosen himself. His special position as non-executive chairman, which derives from the role of his venture-capital firm, Sevin Rosen, in Compaq's genesis, played a crucial part in the company's rebirth. Unusually, the small board (eight members) includes only one executive: the CEO. The board's ability to take an independent view is far stronger than in the typical company, where executives in general, and the CEO in particular, dominate the board.

In what he saw as Compaq's looming crisis, Rosen felt free to circumvent the CEO (and principal founder), Rod Canion, by sponsoring an independent, two-man mission to discover how quickly and cheaply the company could produce a counter to the clones. The time and cost were both much lower than planned by Canion, who knew nothing about the mission. Though 'brilliant and extremely competent', the CEO was unwilling to change the strategy and systems that had served Compaq and himself so well. He had to leave – and four other corporate officers went too.

Before Canion's fall, Pfeiffer, a German, had been transferred from Europe, where his build-up of Compaq had contributed vitally to group growth. Born in 1941, Pfeiffer spent twenty years with Texas Instruments, ending in top jobs in corporate marketing and marketing strategy. He masterminded Compaq's international expansion after joining the original executive team in 1983. Remarkably, he is the only member of that thirteen-man group who is still with the company.

That fact is evidence in itself of the unprecedented volatility of this industry. The timing of Pfeiffer's move to Houston from Munich was fortuitous: the head of North American operations had retired young to breed horses. Pfeiffer, who has an American MBA, was thus on the spot, serving as chief operating officer, when the need arrived to replace Canion, who was ousted at a now-famous, fourteen-hour board meeting on 24 October 1991. The day before, the first-ever redundancies had been announced, and a meeting with Wall Street investment analysts was scheduled for two weeks later.

There wasn't 'much time to provide the answer' to Wall Street's legitimate questioning – in Pfeiffer's words, 'Would Compaq go down the tube or would I bring about change?' The pressure of external communication, though, enforced a key element in tackling any crisis: speed of decision. Two weeks was all it took for Pfeiffer and Co. to redesign Compaq from top to bottom. Their aim wasn't short-term salvation, however, but long-term success.

Like speed, opting for a growth strategy was crucial. Cut costs when sales are static or falling, and you may eliminate losses. Cut costs when sales are rising, though, and you get a double whammy: in two years, sales per employee doubled to 1993's huge $716,000. That year's profit levels (narrowly a record at $462 million) were left far behind in the next twelve months – net income doubled as sales increased by over half. Pfeiffer was as surprised as anybody by the speed and scale of the turnaround, but both flowed directly from that fortnight of compressed, total rethinking.

What he communicated to the analysts 'was exactly what was

implemented all the way through today'. Crisis had come about because Compaq, blinded by vast success, was locked into its 'financial model', based on lowering prices by somewhat less than rapidly falling unit costs and thus maintaining nice, fat gross margins of 45 per cent. The company's chosen criteria showed well in the six months to March 1991, so Compaq was 'not attentive enough to other signals' – notably the rising market share of rivals like Dell and the myriad smaller IBM clones.

Concentrating on the high end, Compaq insouciantly became the high-cost producer. The consequent crisis was fully shared by the dealers on whom it depended. They, too, badly needed communication and reassurance. At the nadir: 'The world around us,' says Pfeiffer, 'was so confused, in doubt, lost.' The dealers, unable to sell the over-priced Compaq lines, asked, 'What do you want us to do?' The only answer was to slash prices on 'high-cost products to keep our customers' while forcing through the foundation of Pfeiffer's new Compaq: an entry-level, low-margin line designed to sell profitably at prices that matched those of the low-cost competitors. It would also act as the base of a vastly extended range.

Pfeiffer told the analysts that, in addition to its traditional high-end products, Compaq 'would meet all other product requirements'; that positioning and the creation of 'low-cost capability' would 'expand our reach into all sectors', and enable Compaq to be 'fiercely competitive'. That 'fiercely' gave the rethinkers some pause, but Pfeiffer used it all the same. True, it was the antithesis of Compaq's previous comfortable stance. But Pfeiffer's top team had exposed the weakness of that position by 'a very comprehensive analysis of what went wrong, putting aside all denials and all excuses'.

That is a third key to the perfect turnaround: (1) speed, (2) growth strategy, (3) soul-searching, or 'interior communication', which, like all communication, depends on absolute honesty. Pfeiffer's group didn't look at the obvious symptoms of failure, but at the 'root causes' of weakness – and strength. The question 'What are our strengths?' came up with some encouraging

answers. They included 'all that product and engineering capability, global manufacturing and presence, brand recognition
and loyalty', plus a strong cultural base – a 'can-do attitude'.

Pfeiffer's task was to build on and 'leverage' these strengths.
Here he faced an immediate, urgent and searching test in the
new, low-priced line. Ben Rosen wanted the life-saver before
the first quarter ended in 1992. This urgency left Pfeiffer with
no option but to break with Compaq's past: an independent
business unit (Project Ruby) was set up, well away from other
activities on Compaq's glass-and-steel campus in Houston. 'One
champion, completely tuned in' was given a free hand to pick
his own team.

Richard Swingle was told to 'show the way to the lowest cost
in the industry, whatever it takes'. As Pfeiffer says, the rush
to end-March shipment 'almost precluded the obvious step of
putting engineers to work' and thus getting imprisoned in the
company's old mind-set. So 'we pursued OEM sourcing', buying
in all components. Only five or six weeks into the crash project,
though, a fundamental conundrum appeared. Could the far
cheaper PC still be called a Compaq?

Talking to customers

The team, which didn't think so, adopted a brightly coloured
design that looked neither like a Compaq nor anything else
on the market. But Pfeiffer was deeply concerned about the
customers. A fundamental difference between the old and
new Compaq, according to Rosen, is another vital aspect of
communication: 'We changed the whole customer satisfaction
approach. Before, we never talked to customers.' When Pfeiffer
initiated a dialogue, major buyers told him what they wanted:
'Do what you're doing, only competitively, and give us what we've
been asking for.'

They didn't expect a clone from Compaq, and how could a
non-Compaq Compaq fit the strategy of building on the corporate strengths? Shortly before Christmas, Pfeiffer was presented

with a batch of component purchase orders to sign. 'I just couldn't do it,' he admits. On the flight back home to Munich, intuition and analysis alike convinced him that the planned product 'wouldn't save our factories and our employment base'. At the risk of demotivating the team, he 'switched gears'. The object was still a low-cost, low-priced PC, but within a range covering every performance point all the way to the top, where Compaq had pioneered client-servers for networks.

Pfeiffer had to disappoint Rosen on time: the new PCs couldn't appear until 15 June. Before that, though, main-dealer reaction, especially to a vague price of 'under $1,000', was ecstatic. When the ProLinea finally appeared, at $900, it was Pfeiffer's turn for ecstacy. A flood of orders ushered in a new era and in many ways a new Compaq. The cost base tumbled down as output shot up: the company was on its way to producing at five times the 1991 rate in the same square footage with the same number of people, at costs down amazingly from 31 per cent of revenues to 13.5.

Achievement of this order, visible to everybody, is powerful communication in itself. The scepticism mentioned by Gian Carlo Bisone could hardly survive this explosion of efficiency. Anyway, it was effectively lanced by the extension of Compaq's severance programme (needed initially to reduce labour costs) to volunteers. Those uncomfortable with the new era departed, and 'within six to eight weeks the number of sceptics fell pretty much to zero'. That echoes the famous Montgomery communication exercise on taking over the Eighth Army: 'If anyone thinks it [beating Rommel] can't be done, let him go at once.'

Exceeding goals

Those who stayed had the excitement of achieving 'almost impossible' goals – and often of exceeding them. One member of Project Ruby, Bill Ramsey, was told to drive down material costs by no less than 30 per cent, and to prove that what became the ProLinea could be made in-house, rather than in the Far East. That was 'very important'. Had the team not proved 'that we could build at a competitive price internally', the work would have gone offshore, and the new Compaq might have been stillborn. As it was, 'what we learned ran across the company' – another exercise in practical communication.

So was Pfeiffer's choice of goal. Often vision and mission statements are inspiring, but insufficient; not precise enough to act as target and spur. That didn't apply to Pfeiffer's commitment to become world leader in personal computers in 1996. His ambition once sounded wildly optimistic for a company which, at its previous peak of profits, trailed IBM's market share by 3–1. The trebling of market share since then, though, took Compaq into the lead, at least temporarily, in 1994 – two years ahead of a schedule that now looks highly conservative.

Britain was first to meet the original turnaround target. The whole of Europe followed, then America. Whether or not this lead was to hold in 1995, beyond primacy lies the aim of building what Pfeiffer calls 'a significant leadership position' – much further on than the odd percentage point. A business, says Rosen, that 'was a portable company, then a PC company' has plainly moved into a new zone; it is now 'a computer company', capable of meeting any needs from the fast-growing home market to the corporate territory once occupied exclusively by mainframes, mostly from IBM.

These are not opportunities that could have been taken with equal speed and success under a founding regime which, in only ten years, had become more conservative, 'less experimental'. But despite Pfeiffer's remarkable success, the crisis that might have laid Compaq low leaves a crucial question. Could it recur? Rosen's answer is an unequivocal yes. He adds, however: 'Having been through it once, we're less likely to get complacent. We're much more on guard, much more willing to make changes.'

The dangers of becoming smug, arrogant and complacent must increase when a company is 'riding high, as we are now'. But Rosen points to a difference which could well prove to be a saving grace. What happens if performance – in the marketplace, say – diverges from the plan? In the past, dishonest interior communication held sway: 'If we saw differentials we didn't like, we would explain them away.' Two little words almost always betray this common and pernicious failure of inner strength: 'Yes, but.' For instance, Canion thus explained away IBM's success in beating Compaq to the punch with a PC using Intel's 486 micro-processor. *Yes*, IBM announced first, *but* when the chip came into full production, Compaq quickly took the market lead. 'Now,' says Rosen, 'we try to avoid denials' – and to act swiftly to remove differentials and their root causes. IBM played a more general role in Compaq's old culture of denial: 'We denied that we had any other competitor.'

That has utterly changed since 1992, when Compaq removed the price umbrella that used to protect the clones. They have been left with 'little to sell on', which explains much of the company's sales surge. Stealing from the clones helped make Compaq easily the 'fastest-growing computer company in the world'. As Rosen wrily points out, expanding sales in 1993 by 75 per cent from a $4 billion base was 'non-trivial'. The 'most formidable competitor prospectively', though, remains the old enemy, IBM.

The latter's costs are still high, however, 'which will limit what they can do'. Compaq's sales per employee are approaching four times those of IBM. The giant is struggling with a culture change that has already taken several years, compared to the nine months or so which remade Compaq. The IBM PC company has been struggling through technological and management upheavals to make a profit from an allegedly 'unmanageable' proliferation of models. Pfeiffer's range is just as broad, though with more commonality. 'It is manageable,' he says unemotionally, 'but you need a whole new set of tools and processes.'

This is the 'can-do culture' at work. Provided that it keeps low-cost, low-price leadership, Compaq looks more vulnerable to industrial and economic downturn than it is to any competitive threat – although, as Pfeiffer says, you can't exclude wrong products (as Compaq found recently with a line of laser printers that was rapidly axed). The most serious threat, however, lies within. 'You always run the risk of "we have it made – we're unbeatable"' says Pfeiffer.

Such complacency was at the root of the company's crisis. To prevent a recurrence, the five pillars of the turnaround triumph will be required continuously: speed, a strategy of growth, focus, the decisive 'can-do culture' (even Pfeiffer hadn't thought Compaq could 'execute so well, with so broad and enthusiastic an acceptance') and 'intense communication', in Pfeiffer's own words. Much of the excellence in execution and acceptance, along with the stunning speed and smashing success of the turnaround, can be attributed to that intensity. The ace communicator adds a powerful thought about communication, though: 'In hindsight, it's never enough.'

Chief Executive Eckhard Pfeiffer took nine months to turn Compaq round triumphantly.

24

Upping the Organisation

All sportsmen know that the basic essentials of their game can be expressed in very few words. The greatest squash player of all time, Hashim Khan, needed just one page and nine points to record a lifetime's experience of the game he dominated. These pidgin-English principles, expressed in a mere sixty-seven words, are key. We have added analogies for business that are just as critical for excellence as Hashim's points are for squash.

(1) *Keep eye on ball*. Concentration on the objective is an essential element in all success.

(2) *Move quick to T* [the position on the court from which you can dominate the play]. Seek the position of greatest strength and comfort.

(3) *Stay in crouch* [the position from which it is easiest to spring into action]. Be ready to act at any time.

(4) *Take big step*. Think and act big, if that's what you want to be.

(5) *Keep ball far away from opponent*. The golden rule of competition is to avoid head-on conflict wherever possible; to bypass the opposition.

(6) *Have many different shots ready so opponent does not know what you do next*. Exactly so.

(7) *Do not relax because you play good shot . . . better you get ready for next stroke.* Exactly so again.

(8) *Soon as can, find out where opponent has idea to send ball.* Know your competitors, and act on your knowledge.

(9) *Have reason for every stroke you make.* Always think before acting.

What's the essence of the credo? Is it the words, the communication? The words convey a *process*: that's why they would have more force and effect if demonstrated, delivered and enforced on a player personally by the great man. All sports coaching rests on the same principle of precepts translated into action. Management coaching is no different. In trying to improve performance, both words and action are required: communication is both verbal and visible.

To put it another way, if more effective actions producing much better results are not flowing, communication has not been achieved in any meaningful way. This isn't to diminish the value of words, whose role is exceedingly important. We earlier mentioned a study on the long-term performance of twenty companies which were committed verbally to 'values': they had expanded their net income twenty-three times, while America's gross national product had managed to rise only two and a half times in the same period.

But the proof of the pudding is in the numbers: values that don't add value, you might well say, are valueless. Organisations have no values, no culture: people do. As in all societies, traditions are handed down, while physical assets, factories and offices no less than cities and landscape, influence how people behave. But behaviour is the crucial outcome of culture. You may communicate verbally about 'a high degree of attention to the customer, sensitivity to the individual inside the company, dedication to quality'. But these are meaningless concepts unless they are translated into, and proved by, behaviour.

IBM's Louis V. Gerstner mentioned the above trio as aspects of the company's culture that he valued and had 'created' in his previous roles at American Express and RJR Nabisco. He added, though: 'I'm not interested in the part of the culture that defines processes as opposed to values. I don't want anybody to tell me about the processes.' The truth, however, is that processes enshrine culture. Change the process by which operational managers are judged, for example, and you communicate in ways that radically change their behaviour.

At IBM, people working in the research 'culture' once had as top priority communicating with their peers – 'being published in scholarly journals'. The new regime communicated a different message. 'Now they have to specify how their work will help the company.' The result, says *Business Week*, is that IBM's research labs are picking up their own developments and running with them: controlling a start-up in 3D super-computer graphics, for example, or actually manufacturing special lasers for telecommunications.

That's a clear case of process changing culture and doing so for the better. The initiatives taken at Jack Welch's General Electric likewise communicate the gospel of change through effecting it. An example is work on projects such as mapping and redesigning the manufacturing process for a jet-engine shaft. Here GE workers were able to turn a total tangle into an orderly pattern, and to double production speed, by their own intelligent efforts. GE calls this 'process mapping', and it's a very powerful, basic tool, not just for efficiency, but for morale too.

Much the same analytical technique can redesign entire 'business systems', after finding out where cost and time are most spent and most wasted. You can then design detailed plans for reducing or eliminating both cost and time. GE also uses 'best practice' – looking for the best ideas from other organisations and adopting and adapting them for its own purposes. Sensible sports teams and individuals do the same: the example communicates, and the communication is turned into action by adopting the improved process, whether it is a high-jumping technique, a soccer formation or a golf swing.

Look at service champions for further confirmation. What

does 'high attention to the customer' mean? Process. There's a marvellously effective store operation in the US that has demonstrated the point while growing its earnings per share by 42.5 per cent annually for ten years. The processes used for this do-it-yourself chain, Home Depot, include many 'cultural' features that are special to this particular company, like having no commissions on sales. This is to ensure that small customers are treated with as much consideration as large ones – again, effective communication through and leading to action, to process.

In other respects, while most giants could subscribe to Home Depot's cultural principles, such as training, meticulous recruitment and having employees as shareholders, such cultural elements can't make enough difference without another vital ingredient: Field-Marshal Montgomery's 'atmosphere' again. The word was used to describe what others might mistakenly think to be the sum total of culture. In the right atmosphere, though, people are bound to the company by love of their jobs and loyalty to the culture, as they were at IBM in its old and palmy days.

Tom Watson Sr used every communications device, including corny songs at pep rallies, to boost IBMers' morale. The Home Depot bosses do the same: at 6.30 one morning every month, *Breakfast with Bernie and Arthur* (the two bosses) is relayed live over closed-circuit TV to nearly all the 45,000 employees. The dominant refrain is to contrast 'Where do you go if you want a job?' with 'Where do you go if you want a career?' (enthusiastic screams of 'Home Depot'). The razzmatazz conceals a deep truth about management priorities: the difference between a job and a career is fundamental.

Putting people and their lives first has to come top, because nothing can be executed save through people. 'Right-sizing', for example, will be far better done if the employees are involved, not as a final thought, but as a first. In one high-tech company, job cuts were approached culturally, as a total quality exercise. The object was to ensure that only dispensable posts went; that all necessary strengths were left intact; and

that everybody agreed with the decisions and their implementation.

Cut down on meetings

That exercise, which involved heavy two-way communication,
is a *process*, but one that helps to create, nourish and sustain a
creative culture of change. Management's overarching priority
is to do precisely that, and it isn't easy. Readiness to change
can never be taken for granted. Take unnecessary meetings.
In theory, meetings are excellent communication devices: in
practice, as every manager knows, they can cast more darkness
than light on issues. But it's not only the whole meeting that may
be superfluous: unnecessary individual attendance at meetings is
just as serious a time-waster.

One consultant had a client company which suffered badly
from the 'he's-in-a-meeting' syndrome. He wisely suggested that
all executives be given a rubber stamp they could choose to use
on memoranda or agenda convening meetings. Its message read:
'I see no reason for me to attend this meeting. Please let me know
if my presence is considered essential.' Top management showed
interest; but it didn't buy any rubber stamps. The consultants
also suggested that senior management should agree to come
to the office every Monday, keeping the whole morning free
of meetings and their doors open. Everybody could then be
certain of the chance to communicate, and with luck get the
answers and decisions required, for at least that one half-day
every week. This brainwave suffered exactly the same fate:
nothing doing.

That kind of organisational, bureaucratised knee-jerk reaction
is precisely what reformed processes seek to make impossible.
Such processes drive into people's consciousness (and thus the
corporate culture) the idea that communicating and accepting
practical suggestions is part of the way the company manages.
They do it not by exhortation, but by example. The best example,
of course, is that of the 'best practice', mentioned above as part

of GE's vitalising kit. The approach is so simple that its neglect is amazing.

All well and good, but have these efforts at practical communication changed the culture enough? Not according to Jack Welch himself. He believes that it will take ten years to transform an established hierarchical culture into a horizontally organised grouping. GE will then employ participative, successful people to whom change is a natural order in which the role of managers is to facilitate and communicate rather than command and control. Ten years? Is that long haul unavoidable? The danger of accepting too long a view was well expressed by the new man at IBM, Lou Gerstner, soon after he took over: 'The adjustment period that IBM has been going through in trying to deal with changes in its markets is now carrying into its second or third year. The longevity of that change is as dysfunctional as the seriousness of the change.'

Delay communicates a deadly message: you needn't do anything – yet. The longer you take to implement a change process, moreover, the more likely it is to be overtaken by events. On taking over Coca-Cola, chairman Robert C. Goizueta wasted no time over the first element in any change process – finding out where you're starting from:

> You make a chart. Across the top you put your businesses . . . Then you put the financial characteristics on the other axis: margins, returns, cash-flow reliability, capital requirements. [Some,] like concentrates, will emerge as superior businesses. Others, like wine, look lousy.

The latter, naturally, you sell. The message to the good businesses is that they are expected to perform by your selected yardsticks, which are crucial means of communication. Change agents look for the critical success factors, seeking to link performance measurements to strategy. To quote one US executive, 'If you're going to ask a division or the corporation to change its strategy, you had better change the system of measurement to be consistent with the new strategy.' Since WYMIWYG (what you measure is what you get) applies, a central task of change agents is to pick those dynamic measures which will best communicate the company's objectives, financial and non-financial.

Change masters like Goizueta succeed, while other CEOs (like John Akers at IBM) fail, because the successes insist on a proper management process. That no longer means a well-structured hierarchical pyramid. In the flatter, horizontal, fluid organisation, excellent communications are still needed for command and control, but they don't take the form of 'order-and-obey' instructions. Rather, people with clear respon- sibility are expected in turn to give clear responsibility to others.

The process of communication becomes a continuous loop, in which feedback leads to action which leads to feedback which leads to action, and so on. Without that process, change can't be achieved. And without change, you can't establish what Kalchas, the London strategic consultants, calls 'total organisation capa- bility'. To find out whether you possess that capability, ask yourself: Are priorities effectively ordered? Is decision-making of the highest quality? How efficient is execution? Inadequate capability shows itself in observations like these from the senior managers of one company, who seem wholly baffled by botched internal communications:

'I will tell you why I cannot get things moving. I can never get the right people together at the right time, and when I do the action step is another meeting, or let us set up a working committee or something, but I can't get action.'

'I have so many people to speak to to get a decision that it takes ages and I'm exhausted at the end of it. I can't do that on every issue.'

'I have got two major problems in trying to get to grips with the business myself: I cannot get the right data and when I do, eventually, force what I need out of the system, it's inconsistent or unreliable.'

These fairly standard communications gripes, as Michael

de Kare-Silver of Kalchas points out, actually indicate 'process roadblocks'. The moans reflect obstacles in the way of prioritisation, decision-making and efficient execution. Remove the communications roadblocks and you change the 'culture' and improve the total organisational capability. Kalchas found a wholly different, much more effective culture at another business in the very same industry, which generated managerial quotes like these:

'We don't have meetings that are not decision-making.'

'Everyone helps out if someone is behind on a profit target, as we'd all suffer otherwise.'

'I cannot recruit any additional manpower without the approval of the president of the company.'

'It's simple – *we all know what we're shooting for and what our individual responsibilities are in getting there.*'

We have stressed that last sentence because it enshrines the guiding principle around which all good communication revolves. In this particular company, staff, skills, style, symbols, systems and controls, and the shared values are all used to communicate and achieve the desired business results. Kalchas found that, 'before we do anything', three questions are invariably asked:

(1) Do I need to do this?
(2) If yes, how can I do it at no extra cost?
(3) Now it's done, how can I do it at less cost next time?

The questions are excellent, although we would improve the first: as phrased, it invites the answer no. A more positive rephrasing would be 'Why do I need to do this?' But the trio establish what kind of capability the company is seeking (the ability to achieve optimum cost-effectiveness), and the whole corporate system communicates the importance of that drive. For instance, managers are rewarded with money for achieving profit goals; they receive public recognition for cost efficiencies; they suffer public embarrassment for cost inefficiencies.

Don't just talk – act

Obviously, the installation of these approaches in the first company in this odd couple would enormously change the 'culture'. But acceptance is the greatest change of all. Somebody, or some group of people, has to determine and communicate that the firm is going to change – and show it by instituting new processes. That's axiomatic to the Welch regime at GE. In many organisations, though, the communicators write and talk too much about changing the 'culture', and do too little to turn worthy thoughts into valuable deeds.

The problem starts with the word itself. 'Culture', in the sense of the organisational norms of a business, has a very recent meaning: the word used to refer only to 'improvement or refining by education and training', coupled with 'the intellectual side of civilisation'. Every company does have a distinctive nature, a set of traditions, often dating back deep into its past, which can be broken only by sharp discontinuity. This must happen if the traditions have become embedded in obsolete or inefficient systems.

One of the best antidotes is to look, listen and learn (i.e., communicate) *outside* the company. The outside world offers important lessons from which you can benefit. 'Not invented here', a stupid excuse for rejection in many companies, should rather be a recommendation. When GE looked outside, its major discovery was exactly what this chapter has been stressing: that winners concentrate on process, on *how* you manage – rather than on function – *what* you do.

Likewise, good communications concentrate less on what media are being used and more on how people are aligned with the collective purposes. The overall object is to improve processes continually in a culture which becomes self-generating and self-regenerating. That's the ideal of the management consensus. It can be realised, but only through process, not just by preaching. Get procedures and structures out of the way so that what really matters – process and behaviour – enables everybody to learn what's going on and why. Then the company must win. If, of course, you also 'keep eye on ball'.

IX

Attention – How to Listen and Respond

25

Brearley's Ashes

You couldn't pose a more severe test of captaincy than this. You take over in the middle of a five-match series, with the side already trailing behind tough opponents – the Australians. Your predecessor as captain is still in the side, which has played unconvincingly in the previous two games. The enemy scores 401 runs in the first innings. Your own side's batting performance remains feeble, and England have to follow on, more than 250 runs behind. Do you have any chance of winning whatsoever?

The answer has become sporting history. Mike Brearley's team, playing at Headingley in 1981, recorded perhaps the most remarkable victory ever on an English Test pitch. In terms of runs and wickets, the victory was achieved by the man Brearley replaced as captain – Ian Botham. At first thought, the idea of the deposed leader giving one of the greatest all-round performances of all time in the very next match seems out of the question. But in the wake of his resignation after the Lord's match (he wouldn't have been reappointed, anyway), Botham had given an unequivocal vote for Brearley.

'The best captain in this country,' Botham said of a man who 'I've always admired.' To rub in that admiration, Botham called Brearley 'by a long way the best captain I've played under'. Like all great leaders, Brearley seemed 'to bring out the best in everybody around him', creating in the side the 'willingness to win – everybody wants to do well for him'. During that historic success at Headingley, you could sense Brearley's influence just by watching him on the pitch – quick to congratulate, but never effusively; or on the dressing-room balcony – pointing to Botham with the message, after his wonderful century, to stay on and score more.

Yet in hindsight Mike Brearley isn't wholly happy with his style of captaincy or leadership. In an ideal world, he would have been more consultative. Not for him the flag-waving, over-the-top bravado of some leaders, or the quiet hard-man style of 'Do what I do, not what I say.' Brearley always wanted an honest and open environment for the England and Middlesex cricket XIs, one in which everybody would have an input on the crucial matters of direction, style and at times even the composition of the team.

He's a great believer, in theory, in using all your resources, which must include all the available minds. In practice, however, he doesn't think that he lived up to his ideal. In honest reflection, while he listened to other attitudes and ideas, if he didn't like what he heard, he ignored it. He didn't, he believes, try to understand and certainly not to incorporate views with which he disagreed. That sounds like extreme inattention. Yet the cornerstone of Brearley's brilliantly successful leadership was the opposite: true attentiveness.

The welfare of the team

He was able to get the best from his teams in the way Botham acknowledges because the players believed in his genuine concern for them as individuals and players, and for the welfare of the team as a whole. The key was his total commitment to the success of players and team alike, together with lack of concern for his own image, performance and benefits. He made time for others as individuals and was attentive to their requirements – something which, on their own admission, many business managers fail to do.

Whether this is caused by bad organisation, shyness, aversion or laziness, it's a serious failing. As General MacArthur once observed, the greatest asset a leader can have is the care of the people under his command and the ability to show that care. This must, of course, be accompanied by technical mastery of the job, and Brearley was without question an astute tactical captain who had served a long and fruitful apprenticeship in the game.

In his childhood and early cricketing career, Brearley would follow his father (once an excellent club cricketer) round the club grounds, listening to his thoughts on the game and discussions of its finer points. He remembers digesting and analysing his father's comments on field positionings, bowling changes and the general tactical evolution of the game. Research into past tactics, study of current ones in world cricket and a striving for tactical innovation – for staying abreast, preferably ahead, of current ideas – became the foundation of Brearley's own approach on the field.

Off the field, the roots of success were found in Brearley's desire to understand his players and hence their interaction as a team. It was almost a matter of curiosity. How did each player view the game tactically? What was each one's psychological make-up? Brearley spent an inordinate amount of time, especially on tour, on communicating with his players, whenever and wherever he could: changing room, field of play, anywhere. Within that communication, a great deal of his time was spent listening.

On tour, he would sit with players individually – a habit initiated on his first trip to Australia – and discuss how they saw their tour going, how they perceived their own form, what they were contributing to training and deriving from it, what they thought about selection, how they would change the side. Details of the hotels and facilities came into the talks. Did they have any ideas on how to improve any aspect of the tour? The principles, he says, are clear: listen with an open mind, and assimilate what you hear: never dismiss anything out of hand, even if your gut reaction is to disagree.

Brearley recalls one lunch, on his first tour as vice-captain in

India, never an easy country for visiting cricketers. He spent the meal with the great spin bowler Derek Underwood, discussing in detail the latter's outlook on cricket. Brearley was fascinated by the Kent man's views on field placings (especially for his own bowling); what he thought about the batsmen he faced; who he liked (and didn't like) to bowl at; his favourite grounds, and which end he preferred on those grounds; what time of day he liked to bowl, and for how many overs in a spell. All this detail went into Brearley's memory bank. It was acquired in a very relaxed manner, not in interview or appraisal style, but as a discussion between equals from which Brearley could draw immensely helpful tips for use during future campaigns. This essentially humble approach allowed Brearley to build up a massive fund of knowledge about the available players and how they thought about and reacted to different situations, different teams, different players, individual grounds.

As we have seen, leading in international sport and leading in business have much in common – including the fact that victory and defeat are often finely balanced, and may well hinge on a single big decision. In that amazing Headingley Test, Australia required a mere 130 runs for victory. They began badly when both Botham and Chris Old took early wickets. But the turning point was Brearley's decision to switch Bob Willis from one end to the other. Running in like a man possessed ('Out of this world,' said commentator Richie Benaud), Willis proceeded to take 8 wickets for 43 runs.

The greater the knowledge of the decision-maker, the more intensive his preparation, the more likely the balance is to swing in his favour. You can reach your decisions in lofty and lonely isolation, but that guarantees a lower level of knowledge and preparedness than leading in concert – which isn't just the modern ideal, but the modern necessity. Business has become too complex and specialised for one person, however able, to play the whole hand: you need partners.

Similarly, a cricket captain depends wholly on the special talents of others. Brearley knew that very well: he also knew the importance of keeping himself available and his mind open to all avenues of information, to ex-players and to respected members of the media. On tours he found it vital to build a good relationship with another key source: the physiotherapist. The physio spends many hours with the players, and when they are with him, they may sometimes be slightly depressed and down, slightly vulnerable. As we saw in Chapter 19 with the England rugby team, players tend to talk to and confide in the physio, and such conversations can provide a deep store of knowledge for a captain.

Some problems don't arise from passing moods, but from basic situations: how to deal with the older, experienced players, for example. Many times Brearley had to face a familiar question: when do you drop the veteran in favour of the young enthusiast? How long do you keep the cynical older player in the side simply because you don't want to admit how much damage he's doing to morale? How many chances do you give to the player of great reputation who for some reason is no longer delivering? How long should you keep hoping that his return to form is just around the corner?

In this area, Brearley as Test captain was lucky to have experienced these problems early in his Middlesex captaincy. The side was highly experienced, verging on the mature. For all its experience, though, the team was struggling. Not only were results unsatisfactory, but his messages weren't getting through. The fairly widespread resentment of the changes being introduced was led by the older, established players. When three or four of these players had lost their places to younger, more open-mided ones, the form and morale of the side were transformed, and the county went on to a very successful run.

Good leadership depends on respect

That was the moment when Brearley realised how much courage a leader really does need. It takes courage to make hard decisions about people and face up to older players too set in their ways to accept necessary change. But nothing damages morale more, or so effectively undermines the environment you're trying to create, than that. The stance he took may not have made Brearley any friends, but he understood from that moment that good leadership is not about seeking popularity. It is about being respected. Hard but fair decisions lay down the path to respect, which is clearly what Brearley achieved – once again, Botham testified to the regard in which Brearley was held, not only by him, but by the other players in that 1981 side.

Brearley, however, never did solve the problem presented by one particular player – Phil Edmonds, the talented but temperamentally difficult spinner. Like Brearley, he is Oxbridge-educated, very eloquent, with very strong views on how cricket should be played. Edmonds felt that Brearley never gave him the benefit of the doubt, not only when selecting sides, but also in field placings for his bowling and even the length of his bowling spells. Brearley tried a variety of tactics, every ploy he felt possible, in an effort to bring the best out of Edmonds and incorporate him into the team. There were long face-to-face discussions covering all the tricky subjects: Brearley would give his views on Edmonds as a bowler, as a player, even as an individual. The captain tried anger and confrontation. At other times, he would ignore Edmonds completely. Nothing worked. Brearley believes that this player never trusted him or believed what he said.

In consequence, he thinks he never got the best out of Edmonds as a player, let alone as a person. This failure contrasts sharply with his ability to obtain stunning results with Ian Botham. You might think that the two Oxbridge men would have had far more in common and would find it easier to form a winning combination, but it was the Brearley–Botham axis that produced the chemistry and the results – and Brearley thinks he knows one reason why: there was no competition between them. Brearley offered no challenge to Botham as an individual, which wasn't the case with the intellectual Phil Edmonds. Botham was an outrageously gifted cricketer, but wasn't known for long thoughtful moments or introspection. Brearley's cricketing gifts were of a lower order – and as a batsman in Test cricket, much to his own chagrin and puzzlement, he didn't live up even to those talents. He is, however, a deep thinker, and in handling Botham he showed the true qualities of a brilliant leader.

Brearley could challenge Botham in a non-threatening manner. He could provoke him with astute, pointed comments. In the 1981 series against Australia, the turning point came, not with Botham's thunderous batting at Headingley (which he followed with another devastating century at Old Trafford), but with his bowling at Headingley. Botham hadn't performed well with either ball or bat in the previous matches, getting the dreaded pair, two noughts, at Lord's, where he returned to the pavilion in humiliating silence. But now his captain kept Botham on and on. The result, even though Australia amassed a large total, was an excellent analysis of 6 wickets for 95 runs. Brearley played a key role in rebuilding Botham's confidence. He was even prepared to rile the player into improving his bowling by calling him 'the side-step queen'. That was after watching him run up – or, to be more precise, amble up – on the wrong line. Not many men would dare call Botham a queen, but Brearley could interact and bond with the all-rounder because (in contrast to other Botham captains) there was no antagonism or competition in their relationship.

The victorious series against Australia has gone down in history as Botham's Ashes, but they were Brearley's, too. While Botham's astonishing hitting and explosive bowling were the stars of the show, it shouldn't be forgotten that the new captain won splendid and unexpected performances from many others, such as fast bowler Graham Dilley and spinner John Emburey as batsmen, and, of course, Bob Willis as a lethal strike bowler. A team that under Botham had under-performed excelled itself for the new captain. The side included the Yorkshire opener Geoff Boycott, a man of tremendous and prickly pride, who could also have presented a problem. Again, because Boycott as a batsman wasn't challenged by his captain, the relationship was manageable.

He could give Boycott the reassurance he constantly sought, and Brearley cleverly used the rest of the team to bring the Yorkshireman down to earth whenever he became unbearable. As a side issue, Brearley believes that Boycott, with his direct and almost abrasive style, would have led Phil Edmonds more successfully. He would have been less sensitive than Brearley to Edmonds' mood swings.

Brearley's unequalled achievement as England's cricket captain can be distilled down to his consistent team-first philosophy. The team was everything to Brearley, and its members knew that well and accepted it totally. He made every effort to be fair and open with the players and to involve them wholeheartedly in the team's strengths, weaknesses, opportunities and threats. If leaders don't pay close attention to their team members, they will fail: and attention is by definition personal.

In fact, Brearley believes that the personal attributes of leadership, rather than the technicalities, are crucial. Personal issues caused him problems and anxieties and, in his own candid appraisal, his failures. By the same token, sensitive handling of personal issues explains his success. That Headingley victory in 1981, and the subsequent clinching of the series, depended greatly on the contribution of a captain who, as a player, produced relatively little in the way of runs or even catches.

The extent of that contribution can be gauged by a vital moment at Edgbaston, a remarkable match in which bowlers dominated, with no batsman on either side passing 50. Brearley took a key decision when the game seemed lost. Australia needed only 151 runs to win, and were two-thirds of the way home with 5 wickets left. At that point, Brearley gave the ball to Botham, and recalls: 'He didn't want to bowl.' Botham admits that 'I wasn't too keen', but he did as his captain asked – and proceeded to take 5 wickets for 1 run in one of the most devastating spells ever seen in Test cricket.

Afterwards, Botham admitted revealingly that, had he remained captain, he probably wouldn't have put himself on to bowl. But Brearley's ever-attentive mind had spotted how Botham's confidence as a bowler had surged – he was really 'going in hard', as the Australians found to their cost. That sense of timing, of knowing, not only the right thing to do, but when to do it, is the hallmark of the great leader. It springs from the same attribute that explains why Botham and his team colleagues found Brearley to be a great captain: he paid attention to his players, and used what he learned to gain their respect and, even more important, their best performances.

Mike Brearley, the consummate captain, offering a few words of advice to Peter Willey and Graham Dilley during the Third Test against Australia – Headingley, 1981.

26

The British Airways Take-Off

Only four of the world's top companies are singled out by two toughly critical management academics for having both 'reinvented their industry' and 'regenerated their strategy'. Of the four, only one comes from the UK: British Airways. The authors, Gary Hamel and C.K. Prahalad, base their book *Competing for the Future* on the proposition that reinvention and regeneration are the only ways of winning the competitive battles to come – and their praise is mighty pleasing for Sir Colin Marshall.

Marshall has been in command of BA since becoming chief executive in 1983 when he was fifty years old. Although he has never been to university, let alone business school, he brought to BA wide experience in international business. After going into the merchant navy at eighteen, he started on the management ladder as a Hertz Corporation trainee in Chicago and Toronto, and obviously showed extraordinary promise. General manager in Mexico at the age of twenty-six, he was assisting the corporation's president a year later. At twenty-nine he was running the UK and Benelux operations.

From there, Avis poached Marshall to head its European operations. He was chief executive worldwide when the Avis business was taken over in 1979, and moved briefly to the Sears Holdings retail group before joining BA. What has happened there under Marshall to earn Hamel and Prahalad's plaudits? The reinvention and regeneration, they say, have produced 'unfailingly high standards'. BA constantly searches for areas that 'can add new levels of customer service that yield more in terms of loyalty and price realisation than they cost to create'.

The airline offers free mileage programmes, 'but more as a bonus and less as a bribe' – one of several comparisons that the authors make between BA and its transatlantic rivals. The authors saw Marshall as engaged in a competitive race against Robert Crandall of AMR (American Airlines) and Stephen Wolf (then at United) 'to create the world's first truly global airline'. Other potential runners, such as Pan Am, have been eliminated – and who would have rated BA's chances against the industry pioneer before Marshall took charge?

The dream that Marshall pursued for BA, privatised in early 1987, was that it should become 'the world's favourite airline'. Hamel and Prahalad call such an energising dream ('often something more sophisticated, and more positive, than a simple war cry') a 'strategic intent'. The rapid improvement in BA's customer rating (to best transatlantic airline in 1992, according to *Business Traveller*) represents the realisation of the dream, the turning of intent into action. The academics believe that BA is 'one of those very few airlines that people would actually go out of their way to fly'.

This may mean only that Hamel and Prahalad are two exceptionally happy customers passing on their good experiences, which include the innovative 'elegant arrivals lounge at Heathrow', where passengers disembarking from red-eye flights can shower, shave, smarten up and breakfast ('heaven-sent'). But there's serious strategic intent behind all these frills. BA needs to 'protect its margins and avoid deep discounting'. So you target ways of contributing the most to 'customer value': or you 'leverage' resources by targeting them 'in the areas that make the most difference to customers'.

You can only find out what makes that difference by listening to those who know: the customers themselves. Another highly regarded American academic, Richard Pascale, also believes that BA's 'service ranks among the best' and links that with the fact that

'it is one of the most profitable airlines in the world'. The programme
which launched BA on Marshall's ambitious way was called 'Putting
People First'. Writing with two co-authors, Pascale told readers of the
Harvard Business Review that Marshall 'began leading British Airways
down that road by going to those who dealt closely with customers
and asking them what needed to happen'.

Responding to needs

Flowing from these inquiries, the necessary action turned
out to cover 'everything from making sure that the concourse
lights were always on to seeing that meals on short flights were
easier to deliver and unwrap'. Action taken included placing the
airline's operations under the marketing arm, to ensure that 'all
operating decisions would start from a concern for the passenger'. Paying attention to the customers and responding to their
needs is fundamental to modern management. It fundamentally
changed BA.

British Airways' Chief Executive, Sir Colin Marshall.

The necessary attentiveness is a demanding, but vital discipline. As Charles R. Weiser, BA's head of customer relations, wrote in the magazine *Customer Service Management*, 'Who wishes to further a relationship in which one partner never hears, nor takes note of, the other?' Weiser stresses that the obvious element, getting it 'right first time', which is the ideal of good service, depends on a second element: 'service recovery' – correcting what goes wrong, as something inevitably will. Service can never be perfect, and only feedback will enable faults to be found and cured. So you need both elements to obtain the customer loyalty which generates traffic – and profit.

BA now has 'a listening post plan' which Weiser describes as 'a concerted effort to encourage customer feedback'. The airline found that ease of contacting BA was one vital dimension: the other was the customers' own willingness to complain. Plotting these dimensions in a simple matrix identified four classes of customer:

(1) 'Walking Wounded'. These people could complain, don't, aren't happy, but stay loyal.
(2) 'Champions'. Complainers who find you easy to contact become active in helping to provide better quality and information about the market. They stay loyal, too.
(3) 'Missing in Action'. You lose these customers because of poor communication or because they simply don't bother to complain.
(4) 'Detractors'. They complain, but find you unresponsive. They defect, and are 'very vocal to others regarding service'.

Champions not only stay loyal -- many of them, like the American academics quoted above, will tell others about their good experiences. But detractors are more likely than champions (or 'apostles') to vocalise their feelings, so studies show, on a ratio of 11:6. Bad-mouthing is thus much easier to arouse than helpful feedback. So BA had every reason to launch a 'customer retention philosophy' under the title 'Retain, Invest, Prevent'. The initials are distinctly unfortunate, but RIP is nevertheless the way to keep your customer loyalty alive.

You couldn't find a better guide to true attentiveness than Weiser's four-point exposition of how to 'retain the customer as job one'. As he says, the customer's needs turn out to be very straightforward:

(1) *Apologise and own the problem.* No denial, no blaming, just saying sorry and taking the customer's side.

(2) *Do it quickly.* Customer satisfaction falls sharply if a reply takes longer than five days.

(3) *Assure them it's being fixed.* You may not be able to supply an instant solution, but you can and must reassure the customer that something satisfactory is being done.

(4) *Do it over the phone.* People are delighted to hear a real human being taking the three steps above – BA gets a 95 per cent satisfaction rating with customer retention efforts over the phone.

A complaining customer is informative gold dust – provided you use those four steps. But BA needed to invest heavily to cope with 'the customer contact iceberg' (it cost £4.5 million just to create the 'customer analysis and retention system': the acronym – CARESS – is much happier, and the system eliminates all paper). The iceberg's a real problem for all organisations. BA found that 68 per cent of customers never talked to the airline at all; 10 per cent got through properly (and four-fifths of these became champions); but the customer-retention people never received the messages of another 24 per cent. What you must do is 'lower the waterline', proving to more customers that their care has really been taken to heart.

BA's 'Putting People First' programme gave great attention to creating that vital concern in individual employees. As Chris Lane of TMI, the company which installed the programme, has observed: 'Everyone has their customer service stories, good or bad, but they have a common theme – the benefit of individual attention.' But what persuades individuals to pay attention to the customers – or, more commonly, stops them from doing so? Lane stresses that managers 'have a quality customer-care duty to their own staff, as well as to those who provide the corporate income more directly'.

Too often, though, companies make 'the mistake of focusing their efforts only on members of staff who have direct contact with customers. This strategy has almost always failed in the long term.' Colin Marshall had no doubt that this truth applied to BA. Back in 1983, the year he moved in, he said: 'We want to persuade our staff that their colleagues are people too, and that the way staff treat each other is just as important as the way they treat the customer.'

BA has provided striking proof of the benefits of paying attention to your own indirect people in an area where direct contact with the passenger is furthest away: engineering. It's a very large business in its own right, managed by Alistair Cumming, who became director of engineering in the year of Marshall's arrival. The merger of BOAC's and BEA's workforces had brought total numbers down from 14,500 to 8,000. Productivity had duly risen sharply, but nobody could have called BA Engineering productive. It was beset by bad working practices, often enshrined in union agreements. Then an apparent miracle happened.

In fact, 'magical' is the word Cumming uses for the breakthrough numbers of 1991. In a very hard year, the reduction in engineering costs went 'beyond my wildest dreams'. The total underspend was a thumping £38 million. Even though drawing a precise cause-and-effect line is impossible, probably half the gains came from higher productivity of labour. And the major cause is clear enough. The management, in effect, went down to the shop floor and asked the men two questions. What are we doing that's preventing you from doing a better job? What are we not doing that would help you to work more effectively?

Importantly, management listened to the answers, and even

more importantly, acted on them. Management wanted not only to save costs, but to turn the organisation, to change its culture from one which satisfied neither management nor men into a successful business which satisfied both. All operations, however good, can, of course, be improved. In most cases, though, the gap between present performance and potential is enormous. BA simply refused to accept that the gulf in engineering couldn't be bridged.

As with satisfying customers, what BA wanted to achieve with its engineers depended heavily on emotion. When the emotion is positive, anything becomes possible. Let negatives into the air, and everything becomes much tougher. One highly negative example that Cumming discovered on taking over was a pile of unserviceable undercarriages. They occupied a third of the floor space, and were blamed on capacity bottlenecks. The problem could have been dealt with by sub-contracting, but shop stewards had an effective veto on putting work outside. With full backing from Marshall, Cumming acted firmly to restore management rights in the matter.

Nothing illustrates the huge gulf between then and now than another sub-contracting story. On the face of it, overhauling its own seating seemed senseless for BA, exactly the kind of work that could be done better by outside contractors. The work stayed at Heathrow – but not because the unions, or anybody else, said it must. The men, given the chance, simply proved that their costs were well below those of all two dozen outside contenders.

Between 1983 and 1990, however, the result of management's determination to manage was turbulence, including a much-publicised strike. Management, together with the professional engineers, literally ran the airline for the best part of a fortnight. But Cumming was convinced, in the aftermath of the stoppage, that 'very determined management' could only go so far. To sustain further progress, BA had to win the employees' positive involvement and support. Achieving a totally different relationship, though, would demand a totally different approach from middle managers – and that was the biggest challenge.

At Aircraft Maintenance, the largest chunk of Engineering, the consultants began by going down to the shop floor in January and February 1990 and seeking answers to five key questions:

(1) Are there any quality issues?
(2) If so, how are they picked up and transferred?
(3) If they are picked up and transferred, how are they dealt with?
(4) If they are dealt with, what working mechanism is used?
(5) Is the environment supportive of change and the new behaviours required?

The analysis found plenty of internal quality issues, but since they weren't picked up or transferred, they were never dealt with. The last three questions were therefore redundant. There was an iceberg effect here, too, as in most companies. However good the channels, very few employees say what they think. The customer-retention principles apply. First, invest in attentiveness. Above all, management must take responsibility for defective operations (the great W. Edwards Deming placed 85 per cent of the responsibility for all failures on management's shoulders).

Second, act quickly – and decisively. Unspecific messages are no good. Hard, clear proposals and practices are needed. William Hextall, the Kepner–Tregoe consultant who led the BA project, emphasises that 'pragmatic, nuts-and-bolts total quality' was the necessary order of the day, using ostensibly 'hard' processes to achieve 'soft' objectives. The programme was on the face of it not cultural at all. It consisted of defining areas where K-T's well-established tools could be used, supplying the tools, coming to solutions – and carrying those solutions through.

Plan – do – check – act

Basically, you find out what's wrong; discover why; decide how to correct the fault; watch out for possible trouble ahead. That closely fits the philosophy of Deming's famous cycle of plan, do, check, act, which is also the guiding light of customer retention. But Kepner–Tregoe has a fifth vital element: 'managing involvement', which means ensuring commitment through involving the right people. That demands paying attention – the consultants designed the project round what they heard and saw, using interviews, observations and some number-crunching.

The benefits were wonderfully illustrated at Heathrow's Terminal 4. Traffic growth demanded more engineers. The extra numbers couldn't all be accommodated in one place. How best to divide the workforce between two sites? Management could have planned the split and issued orders, risking almost inevitable uproar. Instead, the problem was turned over to a volunteer total quality group led by a foreman. The excellent outcome, in Cumming's words, 'was a dream beginning to come true'.

The dream isn't *not* managing; rather a *different*, truly attentive way of managing. BA's view is that this more effective way probably takes no more time, though it certainly demands more patience. That is the only downside of the switch from giving directives to 'facilitation and getting to understand'; to 'encouraging and helping'. There will still be failures, of course. Just as customer-service quality is never perfect, so working relationships within the firm are never fault-free. But finding the faults is the way to improvement.

At Engineering, the biggest identifiable gap (identified by the men themselves in a survey) was in the man–manager relationship: specifically, paying two-way attention. Time and again, in companies good and bad, big and small, the same item is the largest area of complaint: nobody tells us anything, or nobody tells us enough. Staff felt they still got much of their information from rumour, that their contact with managers was far too little, that their efforts weren't sufficiently recognised, that they were not listened to.

Cumming's response was to tell managers literally to take their coats off and spend every Friday afternoon in the workplace. A strict and intelligent code of conduct governed these sorties. This included: don't argue or get involved in argument, listen as much as you speak, don't mix business with pleasure (i.e., don't just socialise and ask about the wife and kids), and always follow up on what's discussed.

Paying attention to internal staff and paying attention to customers have certainly transformed BA's reputation and performance, but such major improvements merely establish another task. The next stage is to do better what is already done well. It's never-ending work, and the basic principle never changes, either. Behind the scenes or up front, in Cumming's words, 'You've got to enthuse the people who do the work. You can't light a bonfire at the top. It only happens if you light the fire at the bottom.'

27

What Management Quality Means

Quality is a word from which few managers can hope to escape for long these days. That's not quality meaning 'goodness, beauty, luxury, brightness or excellence' (to quote guru Philip Crosby), nor even meaning a product free from fault. Fault-free products result from true quality, though: paying unceasing attention to the continuous, measured improvement of all processes – those of service as much as those of manufacture – and responding fully to feedback from the people being served.

Managers must lead this improvement in more senses than one, for management is a service itself. Unlike the lilies of the field, managers do toil, but they don't do much in the way of spinning. However, their toil is as susceptible to improvement as anybody else's, starting at the straightforward levels (very important in quality work) of on-time performance and responsiveness. Thus one top manager, compiling a list of personal quality criteria, included punctual arrival at meetings and answering his phone within five rings.

He asked for feedback on his quality performance from colleagues. At first they looked at him askance, but before long, they were all using similar lists. Consequently, one day everybody arrived for a 9.00 a.m. meeting by 8.45. So they started there and then – and finished before the meeting had officially begun. Don't imagine that such standards are trivial. One chief executive we worked with was apparently unreachable by phone, thought nothing of arriving half an hour late without apology (even for meetings with outsiders present), and often paid no attention to his subordinates' proposals.

By no coincidence, that boss nearly ruined the company with awful one-man decisions. He was rightly deposed. The better manager, with his checklist, had grasped two essential truths. First, just as athletes can raise their games, every manager can raise his or her own quality of management in ways which are instantly apparent to others, and on which others are the best source of help. Second, all quality programmes must be led from the top: personal example reinforces the initiation and follow-through on which success depends – and success has eluded all too many earnest seekers after quality.

That's partly because they haven't emulated one successful seeker, the Belgian steel-wire firm Bekaert, which began its total quality programme not on the shop floor, but in the boardroom. As any honest director will tell you, many companies pay more attention to the quality of the board's lunch than to that of its processes. What's the purpose of the meetings? Is it the right purpose? Does the process enable the right purpose to be translated into effective action in the speediest, most efficient way?

Further, how is the board helping the managers to change from giving orders to 'counselling groups, providing resources for them, helping them think for themselves'. Though that's General Electric's Jack Welch speaking about the future, this is no pie in the twenty-first-century sky. It's a precise description of the manager's role, at all levels, in quality companies with genuine quality of management. That in turn depends on listening to what everybody involved in the whole activity has to say. Then you enlist their support – as in total quality management (TQM) and business process re-engineering (BPR) – in devising and implementing better ways of getting results. James Champy (see

Chapter 15) blames failures in BPR not on poor support lower down, but on 'poor alignment of management'. Three of his colleagues expand on what this means:

'The changes inherent in re-engineering – the reinvention of the company around key processes like order fulfilment, for example – are so radical that they cannot happen without the co-operation of all the major functions in the company which are affected by the effort.' Before that alignment can even be launched, however, you've got to get 'absolute agreement' from the executive team on a couple of key issues. They need a vision of how the company will operate in the future 'so powerful that it creates a competitive advantage in the marketplace'. That vision must also be 'so strong that it motivates the team to bridge the unknown gulf from the current ways of operating to the compelling new view of the business'.

The team must also be dissatisfied with the present: 'The team must have the common view that the current way of doing business will weaken – perhaps even put at risk – the company's future.' The two-part necessity is no different from Geoff Cooke's formula for lifting the England XV from the slough of the Eighties to its unprecedented run of success. It hinges on involving people in efforts to achieve improvement by asking for their help and paying attention to their concerns.

That's the essence of TQM. Companies engaged in this method may well embrace all the other fashionable waves in management technology, especially BPR, and the closely related benchmarking, which seeks to match or excel the best standards in any other organisation for particular processes. All these approaches lead to various forms of participative management, in which the entire team tackles problems and comes up with solutions – and results.

The operative word, again, is 'results'. There have been all too many management fashions, fads and theories, but total quality differs in kind, not least in this emphasis on achievement. That's not all. Unlike, say, management by objectives, with which there are similarities, total quality is a philosophy, built around attending to, responding to and using the talents of individuals, alone and in teams. Unlike most philosophies, though, total quality is eminently practical.

Put like that, how can any sentient manager argue against the quality ideals? They can't – which means that opposition has to centre on the practice, and on the several TQM failures (notoriously, two American prize-winners, Florida Light & Power and Wallace, which fell flat on their TQM faces). But specific failure doesn't invalidate a management philosophy any more than specific success validates a theory.

Beware of tactical errors

TQM, though, doesn't purport to be theoretical. It's a practical methodology for continuously improving all business processes. But does that include the processes which determine the future of the firm? At both the US total quality flops, top management took fundamentally wrong decisions. However much every process in the business has been improved, the higher echelons can swamp all the gains with, say, one ill-advised 'strategic' swoop or gross tactical error.

For example, *Business Week* reports that the vacuum-systems unit at Varian Associates improved on-time delivery from 42 per cent to 92 per cent. The pressure to meet the deadlines, though, stopped the staff from answering phone calls from customers, who retaliated by taking away market share. As it happens, failure to reply to phone calls and letters (the ultimate in inattention and unresponsiveness) is a common and especially infuriating fault of many companies which avow their dedication to quality. But that isn't the most serious form of inattention. Why wasn't customer satisfaction being properly tracked?

The same question can be asked of Federal Express, a quality prize-winner, which also put the emphasis on speed, with the result that misdirection of parcels rose as promptness improved. Each error cost a disastrous $50 to correct. Another delivery operation, United Parcels Service, also hustled its drivers for speed, only to find that customers valued talks with the drivers more than quickness and that the harassed fellows no longer had the time to talk.

Unless attention is properly directed, management can't know what the customer or the employee wants, or what the latter can do in response to the former's needs. Moreover, while the three companies no doubt involved employees in making the abortive changes, none of them (unlike Sir Colin Marshall at British Airways) made sure that somebody consulted the operatives about the value of the changes to the customer. Unless management quality is much higher than in these cases, the best-intentioned of quality efforts must misfire.

As noted, some leaders (not only Bekaert, but Motorola) have recognised this from the start, beginning with an exercise on the quality of the board and its working processes. Others (like Royal Mail) have included crucial areas, such as how they determine strategy, later in the day. Sooner (very preferably) or later, the top must right itself, if management sincerely wants successful reform. But whether they change themselves or not, and whether they're driven by logic or customer insistence or (foolishly) fashion, many more boardrooms will be choosing some kind of quality route.

That being so, managers had better brush up their quality knowledge. They're likely to need it for the sake of their careers – and for that of the whole British economy. Poor attention to customers, employees and processes, and inadequate response to clear evidence of deficiency in all three areas, has had predictably bad consequences for economic growth. That is almost taken for granted: not one eyebrow was raised by a fairly recent, unpublished DTI report that found British manufacturing's management to be inferior – along with its products and productivity. That was in 1993, but the same message has been delivered by report after report ever since the end of the Second World War. Even during the war, so Corelli Barnett's research has found, manufacturers were steeped in sin. Is the sin original? Does some genetic disorder in the British, their education system, their class structure or their history doom their factories to incompetent management? That theory is no more valid than the idea that English rugby teams could never beat those from the southern hemisphere.

Our visits to several companies have uncovered managements which, by modern, intelligent and hard-working means, have improved operations to world-class standards. Some are service companies, but that doesn't affect the issue. The proportion of 'manufacturing' employees actually engaged in manufacture has fallen even faster than the share of manufacturing in the total economy. The fact remains that individual managers and firms, within the overall gloom, shine out – and would shine in any country.

Don't make excuses

A possible argument, however, is that the supply of able, attentive, responsive managers is so limited that a few lucky employers nab the best while most companies make do with dross. That theory requires a corollary: that too much talent (of which Britain must have the normal share) gets siphoned off into other sectors. Finance and the civil service are the usual candidates. But confidence is not inspired by the City's long record of disasters – like spending £400 million on a Stock Exchange computer system that never worked, and never could.

As for the civil servants, the summit of their profession is the Treasury, which can't escape its share of blame for the national under-performance. The mandarins, true, can fairly blame the politicians – which leaves hardly any sectors where the brightest and best can claim the brightest and best results. In sport, though, you rapidly learn that making excuses and blaming others doesn't win matches. The same is true in economics. What distinguishes the world-class, right-stuff Britons is that their companies are pointed in the right direction.

That will have been achieved by successful leaders who, both inside and outside the organisation, have asked, listened and taken action. There's no other way of developing the correct ends and means, of developing focused, motivated and productive people who agree to the ends and have mastered the means. If the players/managers either don't know what's expected of them, or disagree with the demands, or can't cope with those demands, the team/company will be defeated.

In business, if the whole organisation is heading fast down the wrong lane of the motorway – a bank over-lending to property companies, say, or a government defending sterling at DM2.95 – nobody's reputation will survive the crash. The trouble is that, much too often, crashes appear to be required before organisations alter course, just as often it's only humiliation that spurs sportsmen to mend their losing ways. For instance, Rolls–Royce Motors in 1993 pushed through a praiseworthy drive to modernise its methods and reduce its costs – but only under the spur of horrendous losses which had almost crippled its parent, Vickers.

The actions that had become desperately essential were always desirable. Why weren't they desired – and carried out – much earlier? The answer is that, with sales topping 3,000 lush Rollers annually, as they once did, lush profits also rolled in. But what if the reform programme had been executed during those good times? With the break-even point forced down to the present much lower levels, Rolls–Royce would have generated the cash to finance what was equally essential for long-term survival: new model development.

British products and productivity have fallen behind, not because managers were unable to keep them ahead, but because they weren't asked to do so by 'the company'. But what's the company? Other, more senior managers. It's far better for them to be embarrassed into changing direction by impertinent juniors than by incontinent losses. Pay attention to those actually doing the work, and you will invariably find that major savings are possible.

James Champy cites an insurance company which took twenty-four days to issue a standard policy. The actual process took between ten and thirty minutes. The delay arose because thirteen to fourteen HQ departments took a hand in the transaction, another set of departments in the field also got in on the act, and overlaying functions were required simply to find out where the policy had got to in its meandering journey around the organisation. Had their heads been put (or knocked) together, everyone involved would surely have perceived the system's total nonsense.

Eliminate inefficiency

Total quality argues that, once inefficiency has been spotted, it must be eliminated. In most companies that doesn't always happen, of course. Departmental bosses can dig in their heels and protest that nothing in the defective process can be changed without endangering the whole company. In fact, that's exactly what's at stake – the whole company. Such horrors don't happen in isolation. They are symptoms of systemic failure and have to be treated as such. Tracing the problem back, TQM-style, to root causes will surely unveil a counter-productive culture of checking and double-checking, overmanning and over-regulation, bureaucracy and form-filling.

Champy won't countenance any of that: 'There should be only three levels of hierarchy in a re-engineered organisation,' he says. At the top are the enterprise managers. Below them are the people/process managers, who control the rest – all of them 'self-managers'. There may also be 'expertise managers' responsible for specific areas, mostly to do with technology of all kinds. In other words, the re-engineer seeks to install an organisational form radically different from any that is likely to exist. We recently worked in one insurance company, for example, which had fifteen levels of hierarchy.

But where does re-engineering stop? What if the standard insurance policy is an inferior product? What if the range of policies being offered is too narrow, or too broad? What if the whole sales operation is geared to maximising turnover and commissions, rather than to fundamental values? The last question is especially painful for British insurers who, in their rush to grab personal-pension business, notoriously unleashed armies of ill-trained ruffians who misled the customers. The result has been not only acute embarrassment, but heavy fines and the very real threat of huge compensation payments.

If strategies are misplaced, the company will fall into the trap of doing the wrong thing for the wrong purpose. Even if it is done in the right way, little good will result. That's what happens to firms which, to use a Champy phrase, are not 'living in the future'. The greatest danger of even the best re-engineering is that managers will concentrate so hard and so proudly on the operations they are currently changing so radically that they will succumb to management's biggest weakness: living in the present, and sometimes in the past.

To break away from that mind-set requires no less a sea-change in attitudes than TQM. The criticism and professed disillusion with both TQM and BPR really stem from reluctance to undertake top-to-toe revision of the corporate being. Without question, the analytical skills and executive ability needed to manage British firms to world-class standards exist in quantity. By the same token, there was seldom any shortage of top-class players in the long doldrums of English rugby. If the quality doesn't match the quantity, it's because leaders haven't got the best from the highly capable and usually experienced people around them. Being truly attentive and responsive to other managers – and to everybody else in the business system – is the essence of interaction and the pre-condition of top management's own success.

X

Commitment – How to Settle for Success

28

Inside Jonah Barrington

At Jonah Barrington's school, pupils were encouraged to play all sports, and he delighted in the lot – cricket, rugby, football, tennis, badminton, swimming and the squash that was to make him world-famous. He relished the opportunity. Looking back, he feels privileged and lucky. He regrets that children now tend to specialise or are asked to specialise far too early in their lives. In Barrington's view, for any good sportsman or woman to develop, they need exposure to the whole range of activities. Not only will that develop their co-ordination, but different sports tend to evoke different reactions in eye and hand. Channel somebody into one specific sport, even into one specific event, at a very early age, and you may limit his or her potential. There are obvious parallels with management. The broader the experience, in terms of both functions and operations, the better equipped the manager becomes for the truly testing moment: when all his or her commitment must be focused on a specific and important task.

Jonah Barrington's future task wasn't at all apparent in those sporting schooldays. He wasn't the greatest of students: the classroom bored him, and only the sports field was thrilling. There he could express himself and his energy: in the classroom, he couldn't excel – or didn't. Nevertheless he managed to get to university in Dublin, but here again, he says, 'outside attractions' tended to deflect him from his work.

The extreme pursuit of these outside attractions and influences gave Barrington a terrific time. It was a rich experience – no doubt too rich: he was eventually sent down. It was then that he stopped to think. In his own words, Barrington realised that he had 'messed up' in most aspects of his life, and that he needed to commit himself to total focus in one area to become a success. He had always felt that to be possible; he just hadn't set himself any targets, or formed any firm commitment to any activity.

Squash, he says, was almost the last possibility he investigated. He felt he lacked the requisite ability or achievement in any other sport, and he was definitely not a Seb Coe, someone who had fastened on the sport he loved when very young. The choice must have been influenced to some degree by Jonah's brother, who was a county-standard squash player. In any event, once Jonah had focused himself on squash, it gave him intense enjoyment.

The sport he grew to love also grew to become his obsession and sole focus. His ambition, his dream, was to make himself world champion. It was a whole-life commitment. He set about clinically and systematically gearing all his training and all his days to achieving that aim. Barrington studied every aspect, not only of squash and squash players and the court, but of every other sport, to see what he could learn, what facets might enhance his performance.

He was probably the most dedicated trainer ever seen, certainly in squash, and perhaps in any sport. The technique of the game itself had made little advance since the Khans of Pakistan, led by the great Hashim, had shocked all opposition by their speed and power. Nobody had thought about the basic fitness requirements on court or had compared squash preparations (which consisted almost entirely of just playing the game) with training methods from other sports. Barrington, however, looked at everything.

Acquiring what doesn't come naturally

If athletes trained at altitude, why not squash players? How did gymnasts train to achieve their phenomenal flexibility? He scoured all possible sources of improvement and information. There was a very powerful reason. It's an understatement to say that Barrington wasn't the most talented squash player in the world. To achieve the ambition to which he was committed, therefore, he had to use that very commitment: to out-train, out-practice, out-think and even out-diet the opposition (he used to be a great believer in nuts and raisins).

What didn't come naturally would be acquired: he would force himself to become the best-prepared, the fittest, and thus the best squash player in the world. When he turned professional in the late 1960s, Barrington wasn't motivated by money for its own sake. He needed all his time to focus his whole being on the long climb of improving his squash. His commitment to perfecting his game was truly professional, anyway. The rest of the sport was dominated by amateurism: that couldn't co-exist with the pursuit of excellence.

Barrington was following the same route that Jack Kramer had used to create the professional tennis circuit. The idea that squash players could emulate Kramer's circus seemed far-fetched at the time, but Barrington had the confidence to take that risk: the end would justify the means, and others would follow him along a path which would improve the sport and bring it to a wider audience. That would increase income, not only for himself, but for the sport as a whole.

This vision, confidence and commitment made Barrington the architect of a huge increase in public interest in squash. As he expected, the other leading squash players did turn professional; as he planned, Barrington himself did become the world champion, though he had to beat brilliant players like the great and supremely talented Australian Geoff Hunt to do so. Hunt has paid unstinting tribute to Barrington: 'Given the same circumstances [Barrington's relatively late start in squash

Jonah Barrington's wins at the British Open (above, 1974)
changed his sport.

and limited natural ability] I could not have achieved what he has done.'

Hunt had 'no doubt that Barrington ... introduced a new concept of physical fitness into squash. His extreme methods, which included training at a high altitude in Kenya before he defeated me in the final of the 1972 British Open Championship, have made him probably the fittest man in the world.' Winning against men like Hunt was an extraordinary feat in itself, but it's the way in which Barrington motivated himself after becoming world champion that epitomises his dedication, commitment and focus.

He wanted desperately to stay world champion. His motivational technique was to build 'false' barriers, difficulties which had nothing to do with performance on court. He would make himself angry because challengers around the world were getting better treatment from their squash authorities. Others had better facilities and a governing body that would help and enhance, not hinder and mar their prospects. The great anger and frustration Barrington felt about the squash establishment in Britain were deliberately used as a motivational tool. They helped give him a psychological edge over his opposition. He would go on court as the self-appointed underdog, put under greater pressure than his opponent by his lack of similar opportunities to prepare for competition. The supposedly impoverished environment reinforced his desire to train harder, work harder and play harder – and better – on court.

He wasn't, of course, suffering from any serious disadvantages, but he believes that building that 'false environment', creating barriers for himself to climb, was crucial in sustaining his achievement as world champion. His ability to feel hard done by resulted not in self-pity, but in still greater commitment. In this frame of mind, to him competitors were trying to take away his living, trying to take away his money, seeking to deprive Barrington of the rewards for which he had sacrificed everything. His reaction – again – was to raise his commitment, drive and preparation higher still.

Those words 'higher still' applied literally to his altitude train-ing. Once, when Barrington had to play high up in Zimbabwe, instead of staying in England to prepare at sea-level in the comfort of London, he sought the necessary edge over his competitors by training and playing at altitude before arrival. The profile of squash was then so low that Barrington was able to sneak out to Africa to train and arrive in Zimbabwe without the local competitors realising what he'd done. His private knowledge that he had been training at altitude in a spartan environment gave Barrington a huge psychological boost, a massive mental edge. Opponents who believed that, this time at least, they were fitter and better prepared had a shock. During the games, Barrington could see the disbelief in their eyes when he didn't tire. He still remembers his tremendous satisfaction at outwitting his opponents and winning.

You couldn't have greater evidence of commitment than this episode – going to Africa, enduring a very basic existence for five or six weeks on his own and forcing himself through severe additional training to get an edge in just one competition. To maintain his position as the best in the world, however, Barrington needed other ways to overcome his relative lack of ability, especially compared with the naturally gifted Pakistanis. He had to work harder to get the best possible angle out of every shot; he had to practise more to make sure he understood all the angles in the court.

His knowledge of this restricted space became total. Barrington's almost scientific approach to the application of angles, speed and trajectory was coupled with his training to maximise physical output and effectiveness on court. As he travelled the world for years, solely to play squash, to become and remain world number one, he continued to learn. In other countries, how did they train? How did they play? Was he missing out on some innovation off or on court? Opponent after opponent was worn down as Barrington exploited his powers to outlast them in long rallies, using an uncanny ability (to quote the admiring Geoff Hunt) 'to keep the ball along the side walls and at the back of the court with accurate lobs and drives'.

As we noted earlier, his commitment to winning was so great that it radically changed the way squash was played and the way the game was structured. By recreating squash as a professional game, he opened the eyes of the world's top players to their income-earning potential. The professional circuit required someone like Barrington (a 'very robust character', says Hunt) to become a viable business. As the Australian observes, Barrington is 'amiable and amusing, but he can also be quite ruthless in pursuing his own interests, and he is not afraid of controversy'. His absolute focus and commitment not only attracted other players, but also sponsors, whose money was essential to enable the circuit to function. As the players could afford more time to practise and hone their skills, the game naturally improved and became a more attractive spectator sport.

The general awareness of the game was vastly increased by the improved image on court and the enhanced ability of the new generation of full-time players, who combined natural talent with Barrington-like fitness. Like many successful British athletes, though, Barrington doesn't believe that the national culture encourages the tremendous commitment required to achieve number-one status and to stay there. In sport as in management, the British often seem to wait for adversity to stir them into action. Plainly, it makes far better sense to insist on excellence, to strive for perfection, and to seek the best standards at all times.

That way you avert crisis and demonstrate true professionalism, as a manager or as an athlete. And Barrington came to embody the ideal of committed professionalism. It wasn't everybody's ideal: Barrington felt that he was almost ostracised, not only in squash committees around the world, but by many in the media. One article in *The Squash Player* even attacked his achievements with fitness: 'He accepted the conditions imposed on the game aerobically by Afridi Sikhs of the North-West Frontier, and approached it as an aerobic activity rather than a racket sport. While conceding that he virtually had to in order to win, I submit that he has probably killed the game as a result.'

As events have shown, this prognosis was arrant nonsense. The game remains triumphantly alive. But Barrington's single-minded pursuit of his goal, being best, seemed to his critics un-British, if not downright unsporting. Barrington turned even the critics to his advantage, however. Their attacks stimulated the competitive urge and helped to generate the desire and focus – even the anger – he needed to perform to his maximum ability. The more he succeeded, the more time he spent on preparation, analysing his performance and training, studying his competitors and their methods, and continually looking for valuable innovations.

Confusing the foothills with the summit

Again, the management parallels are striking. Far too many top managers behave as if reaching their senior posts is the summit: in truth, it's merely the foothills. Yet they train less, prepare less and plan less. That adds up to massive under-commitment, not only to the company, but to their own careers. The top manager who has ceased to learn is headed for failure; the top athlete who has stopped learning is headed for defeat. Barrington did exactly the opposite. He trained harder and longer, and did more homework, both on himself and on the opposition. The harder he trained, the harder he forced himself to the limits of his own endurance: thanks to him, the aerobic level (the processing of oxygen to muscle tissue) has been raised at least three times in top squash. He takes tremendous pride in the belief that nobody else in the sport has pushed him or herself so far. The object wasn't simply to establish his own extreme limits, but to ensure that he was fitter than any opponent.

Without that basic commitment, the obscure Dublin under-graduate who had been thrown out of university would never have metamorphosed into a world champion. He was, he admits, 'a loser'. What turned him into a winner, the best in his sport? First came the choice of field: squash was woefully under-exploited and unrewarding for the players, but that very fact provided the opportunity for a breakthrough. Second was Barrington's total commitment to his choice, fuelled by the urge to surpass his brother, who was successful, not only at squash but also in his career. His brother was the family's golden boy, and Jonah something of a black sheep.

The consequent creation of a champion is more inspiring and instructive than the sagas of athletes who have preternatural gifts. To became world number one, Barrington had to defeat opponent after opponent who had greater talent, but who were outsmarted by the Cornishman's dedication, determination and drive: in a word, commitment. These adversaries also trained hard and prepared carefully for their matches, but he trained harder and planned more effectively.

In 1973, Geoff Hunt was determined to avenge his defeat by Barrington the previous year. He raised his normal (or rather abnormal) succession of eight quarter-miles, run in seventy to seventy-five seconds with only a minute's rest, to no fewer than ten. He added eight 100-yard sprints, and then did ten more quarters. All this took about an hour, and shows the extremes to which opponents had to go to match Barrington's fitness. But the work-outs didn't work: Hunt lost in the semi-final, and Barrington beat the winner to retain his title. As Hunt conceded, it wasn't only Barrington's dedication to fitness that brought success: it was 'determination'.

Another powerful lesson for managers is that Barrington's campaign was based on thorough investigation of other sports and training methods – he certainly knew how Hunt trained, but he also looked outside squash. Often sportsmen and women, like business people, develop tunnel vision. They become obsessed by their own sport, their own sector of industry, their own specialisation. Dread phrases like 'not invented here' and 'we've never done it that way' shut out the most accessible and valuable source of new ideas and new methods.

Such killing phrases were never in Barrington's vocabulary. He sought knowledge from every other area of competition, not only from observation, but from the players and coaches themselves. His sponge-like ability to soak up desired information and turn it to his advantage; his fierce competitive spirit; the way he drove himself on through erecting false barriers to progress; his creation of a harsh personal environment: all these were forces which enabled him to sustain his excellence on court. But above all, to stay ahead of the competition he had to think ahead of it, anticipating and innovating all the time. That's the ultimate commitment, and the ultimate winning way.

29

The Entrepreneurial Giants

All companies today want to stay or become entrepreneurial. But what are the attributes of the entrepreneur? The most convincing list by far was assembled by Geoffrey A. Timmons in an article published by the *Harvard Business Review* in 1979. He found that entrepreneurs required the following nine qualities:

(1) A high level of drive and energy.

(2) Enough self-confidence to take carefully calculated, moderate risks.

(3) A clear idea of money as a way of keeping score, and as a means of generating more money still.

(4) The ability to get others to work with you and for you productively.

(5) High but realistic, achievable goals.

(6) The belief that you can control your own destiny.

(7) Readiness to learn from your own mistakes and failures.

(8) A long-term vision of the future of your business.

(9) Intense competitive urge, with self-imposed standards.

How do these attributes stack up against the actual careers of great business founders? We found nine entrepreneurs whose key success factors fitted the nine qualities, but all of them were bound together by a common tie. They were deeply, thoroughly and permanently committed to the enterprise in which they passionately believed, and all the nine attributes represent facets of this commitment.

Miguel Torres showed enormous **drive and energy** as he created an empire from a small family wine company in Penedès. He took control aged twenty-three, and never wavered from his aim of making Torres synonymous with Penedès, and Penedès the match of any wine-making region in Spain. In 1940 he began rebuilding the family *bodega*, switching from bulk selling to promoting the Torres brand, using now-famous names like Sangre de Toro, Viña Sol and Coronas.

In the 1960s, Torres took the equally important step of planting non-traditional grapes (starting with Cabernet Sauvignon and Chardonnay) and using modern wine-making techniques. His expansion created Spain's largest independent wine business, and very possibly the world's biggest producer of fine branded wines, selling 17 million bottles annually – and 7 million more of brandy. The firm remained under the founder's autocratic hand until his death at the age of eighty-two in 1991.

His commitment was total: witness a wartime journey to America, when U-boats prowled the Atlantic, to sell his products and learn brand marketing. After the war, he piled wine into a battered old car and crossed the Pyrenees to establish further markets outside Spain. To fulfil his ambitions, he bought vineyards endlessly, in huge quantities, while simultaneously, and, just as tirelessly, perfecting production techniques.

Torres believed that the best way past obstacles was straight through them. He often trampled over regulations, and had no use for bureaucrats – witness one parting shot at a group from Brussels: 'If you achieve half that you promise I will be pleased.' The intense personal drive of this diminutive man couldn't allow any Torres wines to sell under somebody else's label. In his eighty-five markets worldwide, his refrain was always the same – 'First they must taste my wine.' His labels were his

principal means of promotion, and dynamic enthusiasm was his
main management technique. It works wonders.

Torres owed much to his oenologist son, Miguel, just as Bill
Hewlett owed much to David Packard, and vice versa. The
Hewlett–Packard story (see Chapter 11) exemplifies all the
self-confidence required **to take carefully calculated, moderate
risks**. Cautious risk-taking expanded the company to 1993 sales
of $20.3 billion, profits of $1.2 billion and assets of $16.7 billion
– or 31 million times the pair's start-up capital.

Even Dave Packard didn't have a clearer **idea of money as
a way of keeping score, and of generating more money**, than
William Morris. Yet Morris was no financial genius, nor, for that
matter, a skilled mechanic or brilliant engineer. He started his
first bicycle workshop in 1893, aged only sixteen, with capital of
£4, and seven years later took on both motorbikes and a financial
backer. That partnership broke up; the next, intended to expand
Morris's new line in cars, went bankrupt.

Starting again, Morris rapidly built his reputation and business
in car repairs: by 1943 Morris Garages was also Oxford sales
agent for several makes. Their unreliability and high repair costs
gave Morris his great idea: producing cars that would beat the
competition on both counts, with no extras on top of the basic
price – £165 for the first Morris Oxford. It launched Morris
(later Lord Nuffield) on his way to becoming Britain's leading
car-maker.

He cemented that position after the Second World War,
first with the Morris Minor, the all-time national best seller,
and second by merging with Austin. Morris had an infinite
capacity for taking financial pains. In the 1921 slump his acute
understanding of the relationship between volume and cost saved
the day, and the firm. With output down from 276 to seventy-four
cars a month, Morris cut the Cowley's price by nearly a quarter,
despite protests that profits would collapse to £15 a car. Sales
soared to 361, and profit to £50. The repeated price cuts (he
created a 1931 sensation by launching a car at £100) were based
on meticulous costing, supervised personally. He also insisted

on having a detailed financial report every Friday, coupling this rigid score-keeping with an equally tight control over capital employed. Yet he believed devotedly in ploughback as the engine of growth, and never doubted the crucial importance of his financial policies in creating his success. He wrote in 1924: 'I owe very much – more than I can tell – to sticking to them.'

It took Gottlieb Duttweiler even longer than Morris to find his commercial feet and to demonstrate his great **ability to get others to work with you and for you productively**. Born in Zurich in 1888, Duttweiler founded Migros in 1925 when he was thirty-seven. His idea was to undercut the food retailing oligopoly by working on halved, 10 per cent margins. 'I could only have revolutionised the food business through finding a clever partner – the Swiss housewife. I put forward an ultimatum: either she took part in a new, simpler sales system, and then we both could win, or she could cling to her old habits, and I would shut up shop'. The Migros motto, 'More goods and less hassle', worked like a charm.

Before opening stores, Migros sold from street corners. The housewife-partner had to turn up at the right time at the right street corner for one of Dutti's vans, and to buy a limited range, starting with only six items (rice, sugar, pasta, coconut oil, coffee and soap), all unbranded. To simplify pricing, he sold his packages at unvarying price points. If market prices rose, he simply adjusted the weight downwards, and vice versa.

Duttweiler thus pioneered many common features of today's supermarkets, from own brands to discounts for bulk purchases. He died in 1962, still in absolute command, having converted Migros into a co-operative twenty years earlier by giving away shares to his customers. He commanded loyalty from his staff as strong as that of his customers. 'There is nothing so deeply contenting for employers,' he said, 'as the sense of harmony with co-workers: there is also no better pledge for the success of working together.'

The **realistic, achievable goals** of Marcel Dassault (born Bloch) were literally sky-high. An aeronautical engineer, he became

Europe's premier aerospace tycoon. Unhappy with the propeller of a plane on which they were working, Dassault and Henry Potez began making their own. The Eclair was a success, and the partners promptly designed their first plane, a two-seater fighter. Peace forced his retirement, but when government interest in military aviation returned, so did Dassault.

A stream of planes followed: air ambulances, fighters, bombers and transports. In 1936, when the industry was nationalised, Bloch pocketed 17 million francs, and went back to making propellers. During the Occupation, this business was seized by the Vichy government, and Bloch spent several months in Buchenwald. He was liberated in 1945, aged fifty-three, and went on to design personally the military aircraft which made him one of France's richest men.

In 1986, the year of his death, the Dassault–Bréguet group won almost half of all overseas orders awarded to the French aviation industry: that year it delivered 4 billion francs worth of military aircraft, nearly double the 1985 total. Dassault's enormous wealth, and his intimate relations with the state, made him a figure of constant controversy. He used journalism to advance his interests, founding *Jours de France* and taking it to a 4 million circulation. His ambitions, like his planes, flew high in everything he touched.

Like his heroes, Edison and Ford, Dassault combined technical genius with powerful business instincts and disdain for the 'impossible' – like enjoying development costs, on one estimate, only a sixth of American figures. He consolidated this advantage by extensive sub-contracting to minimise his dependence on production. He gleefully recounted the many times (nearly always) when his aircraft beat the prototypes produced by nationalised competitiors. So long as he made the machines the military wanted, Dassault could present the state with the offers he loved: 'those it couldn't refuse'.

Akio Morita showed his belief that he could **control his own destiny** early in Sony's history. The firm had created the first transistor radio, which Morita took to the US. The Bulova watch company came up with an order for 100,000 units, worth several times Sony's capital, on one important condition. The radios had to carry Bulova's name. Morita wouldn't agree. The Bulova man was astounded. 'Our company is a famous brand name that has taken over fifty years to establish. Nobody has ever heard of your brand name.'

Morita replied: 'Fifty years ago your brand name must have been just as unknown as ours is today. I am now taking the first step for the next fifty years of my company. Fifty years from now I promise you that our name will be just as famous as your company name is today.'

Three decades on, Bulova is just another watch brand, whereas the Sony brand's reputation for quality carries enough weight to attract premium prices and underpin assets which today total more than $41.7 billion.

Morita, born in 1921, founded the business in 1946 with Masaru Ibuka, backed by only a few hundred dollars of family capital. The first significant product was an American-inspired tape-recorder. In the 1950s, however, Ibuka found the newly invented transistor at Western Electric, and immediately licensed the new technology for a down-payment of $25,000. The first pocket transistor radio, launched by Sony in 1957, started the company on its upward trajectory.

By 1990, it was the world's fifty-first largest company, thanks to breakthroughs like the Walkman, the video cassette-recorder, 8mm video and many others. Ibuka supplied the technical brilliance and Morita the marketing genius. He thus chose Sony as both company and brand name because 'that way we would not have to pay double the advertising cost to make both well known'. And Morita has always called the Bulova decision the best he ever made.

Camillo Olivetti had many opportunities to **learn from his own mistakes and failures**. Even in 1930 the firm, founded in 1908, was relatively small, employing 700 people to produce some 13,000 typewriters. His untrained employees and tiny capital were typical in an Italy with no mechanical engineering tradition.

He also had to battle against severe external difficulties, in both war and peace.

Very prudent in his finances and expansion, Olivetti, according to his son Adriano, was basically a good engineer – 'intelligent and tenacious'. That alone wasn't enough to combat the Americans, who then dominated the industry. Olivetti was distinguished from the pack by his aesthetic ambitions. Not only did his advertising set new European standards; so did the airy layout of the Ivrea factories and, above all, the product design.

The M1, devised after an American visit, took three years to develop. Olivetti claimed that it stood out 'for the unified taste of its design, which is ahead of all previous examples'. In fact, many mistakes were made. Olivetti himself admitted: 'We are still obviously in an early phase of technology: the mechanisms on view are still numerous and they are more juxtaposed than co-ordinated.' However, he always used the failings of one design as the springboard for the improvement of the next.

Trial leading to error leading to success also advanced the advertising from 'ingenuous and often bombastic language, with the relationship between image and copy still uncertain, to brilliant posters, using well-known artists to emphasise speed and the new social status of the typist'. Leadership in office machinery stemmed from learning, in one description, 'to survive the bleak moments without jeopardising the future of the company, but each time consolidating its position, thanks to a willpower and clarity of objectives that never flag'. Camillo spent the last years before his death in 1943 designing and building new machines with a group of his old workers.

Ruben Rausing's **long-term vision of the future of his business** extended beyond the grave: as a last-wish injunction to his heirs, the inventor of the Tetra-Pak insisted that they should not diversify the core business he had created beyond packaging beverages and other liquid food. Rausing had invented his tetrahedron-shaped container in the 1950s, solving a major technical problem: how to package liquids like milk aseptically so that they could be shelved for long periods without refrigeration.

Major publicly owned corporations shy away from reliance on one product. But Rausing, keeping his business entirely private, saw that his invention had the potential for enormous growth. Tetra-Pak became the world's largest paper packaging business, with revenues of $5 billion from 109 countries. This enormous geographic spread followed naturally from the insistence on sticking to the single product. To grow, therefore, Rausing and his sons, Gad and Hans, had no option but to take the geographical route and expand vigorously outside Sweden.

In markets such as Spain, Italy and Japan, the taste for milk pasteurised under very high temperatures created huge volume for a product facing virtually no competition. In America, where the milk market proved unsuitable, fruit juices provided rapid growth. With such large volume, the efficient concentration on one basic product also means very low production costs and very high margins. On one estimate, it cost Tetra-Pak only 6 to 7 cents to make cartons that sold for 10 cents in numbers exceeding 60 billion a year.

In its single-mindedness, the company has turned aside business from detergent, shampoo and other non-food firms. But in 1990 the multi-billionaire heirs paid £1.5 billion for the Alfa Laval dairy and food-processing equipment company. A third of the cost came from their own cash. That's the reward for having a long-term vision – and sticking to it.

The German engineer Robert Bosch was no less intent than the Rausings on realising a long-term vision and on achieving near-monopoly status. In the age of fuel injection, one of his successors could boast that for European car-makers the 'only alternative to Bosch is Bosch'. That flowed from an **intense competitive urge**, which was accompanied by **self-imposed standards** so high that they still deeply influence Robert Bosch's successors.

As he wrote in 1919, 'It has always been an intolerable thought to me that someone should inspect one of my products and find it inferior. I have therefore always tried to ensure that only such work goes out as is superior in all respects.' Born in 1861, Bosch opened his 'workshop for precision and electro-mechanics' aged twenty-five. His big breakthrough came in the early 1900s, when his technician developed the high-voltage magneto ignition which, combined with the first Bosch spark-plug, initiated a new era of internal combustion engines.

His competitive urge took him by 1918 into manufacture of all the electrical equipment for cars, from electric starters to lighting systems. He believed 'from my experience that nothing can be harder than for a company to continue and remain progressive without competition'. That thought spurred his drive for ever higher standards: 'You can only compete against efficiency with efficiency.' It was demanded from his suppliers as well as his staff.

The latter benefited from Bosch's humanitarian social ideas: he introduced the eight-hour working day and the five-day week as early as 1906. He also vested control of the business (now the world's fifty-ninth largest, with sales of $19.6 billion) in a foundation dedicated to public and social purposes. His rigorous standards led Bosch to anticipate many of the key features of total quality management, including supplier partnership. As he said, 'A good supplier is more important for me than a bad customer.'

The power of the nine attributes is evident from all nine careers, which, of course, don't exemplify only one apiece. The qualities form a cohesive pattern whose separate elements require each other, and all of them can be developed by determined, committed individuals and companies. In fact, that's the test of commitment. If you are deficient on any of the nine counts, will you work to remedy the weakness and turn it into a strength?

There's an equally important follow-up. Will you sustain that commitment over time? Look at the careers of these nine entrepreneurs and notice how many of them strove until middle age to achieve major success – and then intensified the drive thereafter. Commitment over time is the tenth attribute. Without it, you'll never make the most of the brilliant nine.

30

The Zen of Success

Is striving strictly necessary? Westerners think of commitment in terms of climbing mountains, vying with others, applying (to quote the Prussian general and master strategist Karl von Clausewitz) the 'maximum exertion of powers'. In war and sport, the need for immense effort and superior resources is self-evident. They must be directed, true, by superior strategy, for which read thought, and at least equal mental vigour, for which read will; but battles and games won against vastly superior forces are rare.

The mighty (like the All Blacks at their all-conquering peak) make themselves mightier still by the application of their power, and not by its sheer weight alone. As every rugby player knows, it's mass multiplied by velocity that breaks the defence. Like war, sport is a very useful source of inspiration for business success. Virtually all the moves can be fully documented and observed in retrospect. The armchair strategist or coach can spot where all errors were made, where the golden opportunities were missed.

But the differences are as important as the similarities, not least in the rarity of total defeat in business. Managers talk of 'blowing the opposition out of the water', but defeated opponents may not only stay in the game, they can rise anew from the depths. The dazzling comeback of the down-and-out is a Japanese speciality – witness the rise of Komatsu to world power in earth-moving machinery as just one convincing example of commitment in adversity.

Left to die by its own government, Komatsu built an astounding rise on the war-cry of '*Maru-C*', or 'Encircle Caterpillar', its seemingly invincible American opponent. Such Japanese victors seem to epitomise Clausewitzian warfare. No effort is spared. With terrifying thoroughness, these deeply committed companies press on until the opposition has melted away. Yet these supreme strivers come from a culture whose most influential philosophy is the antithesis of striving.

The core of Zen is meditation. Its heroes are not men of action, but teachers, artists, poets and dreamers. While Zen literature revolves around self-improvement, the ultimate objective of improving the self is to obliterate the sense of self altogether. 'Success' is enlightenment, which to Westerners is both incomprehensible and nothing to do with any worldly success.

The black-and-white Western mind insists that worldliness and spirituality are opposed; that they are different worlds. The idea that you can succeed without striving is also foreign to the puritan ethic: whatever their nominal religion, most Westerners are Calvinists at heart. If you believe that high success is the reward of the righteous for hard work, the Zen approach sounds like Eastern gobbledegook.

Having the right attitude

What would a Western trainer do, for example, if he had a wrestler named O-nami (or Great Waves) who, despite wonderful strength and skills, loses every public bout – beaten not by better wrestlers, but by his own fears? Exhortation and effort would almost certainly be the remedy. O-nami would not, for sure, be advised to spend the night in a temple, living up to his name mentally: 'You are no longer a wrestler who is afraid. You are those huge waves sweeping everything before them, swallowing all in their path. Do this, and you will be the greatest wrestler in the world.'

By morning, the waves in the wrestler's mind have swollen gigantically, drowning the temple in 'the ebb and flow of an immense sea'. The beautiful book *Zen Flesh, Zen Bones* says:

> In the morning the teacher found O-nami meditating, a faint smile on his face. He patted the wrestler's shoulder. 'Now nothing can disturb you,' he said. 'You are those waves. You will sweep everything before you.' The same day O-nami entered the wrestling contests and won. After that, no one in Japan was able to defeat him.

The East-West conflict is less real than it seems in this anecdote. The wrestler's objective was still total commitment and maximum success. Every sportsman knows that mental attitude is as important as strength and skill in achieving success – that's the essential message of this book. And the wrestler actually was stronger and more skilled than his opponents. The Zennist, like any sporting champion, seeks to master two things: his art and himself. Great Waves had succeeded in the former, but not the latter.

Nobody who saw Kurosawa's *Seven Samurai* will forget the swordsman, first seen sparring with a belligerent opponent, who refuses to accept that he has been outsparred and insists on fighting for real against his rival's wishes. Forced to fight, the latter kills his challenger in an amazing slow-motion sequence. The senior *samurai*, looking on, comments that the victor lives only to perfect his art. Commitment indeed. Japanese literature is full of similar stories about unwilling champions compelled to put down unwise challenges.

The object of the martial art *aikido* is to develop the inner force that, writes Michael Random, 'can easily master brute force'. Ueshiba Morihei, founder of modern *aikido*, failed 'to convince one powerful adept of *karate*'. The adept declared: 'I don't care what you say. I weigh 80 kilos, and if I hit you, you will fly 6 metres off the ground.' The smiling, 57-kilo Ueshiba begged to differ, but the *karate* champ insisted on a public duel.

Ueshiba bared his chest and the opponent ran up and struck

him a violent blow, but 'he might as well have hit the air. The master stood looking calmly at him, not blinking an eyelid.' Begged to try again, 'the young man ran up again and hit out with all his strength. This time the master remained as motionless as the first time, but the karate expert shrieked with pain. His wrist had been broken.'

After using non-resistance to absorb the first blow, Ueshiba had 'produced a rebound' of his opponent's energy to the power of ten. While that sounds like nonsense from a scientific point of view, we wouldn't want to test our scepticism in practice. The lesson is that perfection is an end in itself, from which success can indeed flow; but that the person who over-commits, who tries to bully success into being, to force it to happen, will always be defeated by the opponent who is more in harmony with what Ueshiba would call the 'universe'.

To relax while applying the 'utmost exertion of powers', to try by not trying, to resist by not resisting – all these concepts are familiar to Western thought. The phrase 'he's trying too hard' is common enough; athletes of the highest class 'tie up' in a race and lose their vital rhythm. The basis of avoiding the trap, of keeping your neck intact and your wrist unbroken, is that perfect mastery of the art – what you are doing – and of yourself – the person who is doing it.

The combination won't be achieved unless you take time out to think, to contemplate, to acquire the 'serenity and self-mastery' which are the apparently paradoxical objectives of the Japanese martial arts. Serenity is hard to reconcile with breaking someone's neck with a single blow. The ability to reconcile opposites without turning a hair, however, is basic to Zen and provides a basic strength to Japanese management – not because of any mystical values, but because paradox is fundamental to business life, and to all life, for that matter.

Organisations and individuals must continually make trade-offs, sacrificing the maximum in one dimension for the sake of a better overall result. You can't simultaneously plough back the maximum investment into new plants, machinery, technology and products and show the maximum short-term return on capital. You cannot, as an individual, serve both God and Mammon with equal devotion – at least, not if you're an orthodox Westerner.

The Japanese find no difficulty in the God–Mammon paradox or the investment–profits conundrum. Since return on capital is depressed by high investment, which they account a higher good, they cheerfully concentrate instead on return on sales. Their reckoning, eminently sound, is that so long as profit on sales is maintained or increased, the other ratios will look after themselves – and that anyway it's long-term profit that counts if you're committed (as they are, passionately) to the long-term future.

They refuse, moreover, to agree that Mammon has no part in the spiritual life of man. Nobody has chased the money-changers out of their temples. Rather, the money-changers have created their own. Japan's premier industrialist for decades was Konosuke Matsushita, who began making plugs and sockets in Osaka just as the First World War was ending. His National Panasonic brand became a worldwide symbol of the Japanese advance in consumer electronics; the plug-maker, through its JVC subsidiary, tore the world market in video cassette-recorders from Sony's hands.

Matsushita, a multi-billionaire, set up his own college to teach and research 'a new philosophy of government and management based on a new conception of man'. The initials of his monthly magazine, *PHP*, stood, not for any management or business nostrum, but Peace, Happiness and Prosperity. If you're like Matsushita, you are committed to seeking external success through the successful development of inner resources and to combining the two to provide material and spiritual benefits to the external world, which in return rewards you with still greater success.

The programme translates easily into Japanese business philosophy. You conquer markets and the competition by developing and strengthening all the firm's resources to provide goods and services that so benefit the customer that you can conquer markets and the competition, and so on. It's the most benevolent of circles (benevolent, that is, if you're not the competition). The development of corporate and individual skills fits perfectly into the circle of commitment.

Perfectly is the perfect word. When Japan's superior product quality first hit the West, the response was to equate it with harder work by a docile work force. But what is higher product quality other than higher deployment of skills? The decisive strength in this success – for quality has been a most powerful weapon in the commercial drive of the Japanese – is the commitment to perfection, a quest brilliantly demonstrated at Toyota.

The business was originally built by a patriotic manufacturer of sewing-machines who didn't like seeing all the motor vehicles in Japan foreign-made. For most of its pre-war career the firm flopped: the first truck broke down on the way to its first public airing; its successors broke down in the hands of unhappy purchasers. After the war, when the badly blitzed plant had been heroically restarted, Toyota suffered from still worse breakdowns, in its own operations.

As the Arthur D. Little book *Breakthroughs!* recounts, in 1949 'Toyota management started to run out of operating cash. Inventories grew, salaries were cut, and finally, for Japan, the unthinkable happened. First, rank-and-file Toyota workers were laid off. Then the workers went on strike.' The rise from this grisly failure to astounding success owed much to an inspired production boss, Taiichi Ohno. His philosophy could not be simpler: 'I feel strongly that the word "work" refers to the production of perfect goods only. If a machine is not producing perfect goods, it is not "working".'

On that foundation, Ohno erected the Toyota production system, in which built-in sensors stopped machines whenever they began to malfunction: the machines were operated by human beings who could likewise stop the line when imperfections occurred. This *jidoka* is a literal application, in large-scale manufacturing, of Zen perfectionism. The analogy goes far. Like a great Zen master, Ohno became a revered sage, whose students were 'the apostles of Mr Ohno'. The sage or *sensei*, moreover, used Zen indirection to achieve results.

Ohno once found a bunch of defective cars. He removed the keys from one vehicle. It couldn't be driven away until the key cylinder had been replaced. Then he took the keys from another car, but left a note to say they were in his office. When the foreman showed up, he was told to find and bring back the first car, wherever it was. In the ensuing shouting match, Ohno yelled nothing except, 'Bring back that car!' Finally, the foreman said, 'Well, I will take a day off tomorrow. We'll do everything we can to find it.'

At that point Ohno relaxed and said, 'That's all right. Never mind that car. You can go.' This elaborate play-acting, which has innumerable Zen parallels, was designed to force the foreman to divine and learn the real lesson: no more defective cars. To the Westerner, this seems absurdly roundabout. But Zen teachers believe that enlightenment comes only from within. Yell at somebody for producing defective cars, and you won't change his habit of mind. Yell about him not bringing back one car, and you force him to work out the real fault.

The deepest learning and commitment arise not from teaching but from absorbing – witness the would-be swordsman, in another story from *Zen Flesh, Zen Bones*, whose master, Banzo, tells him never to speak of fencing, never to touch a sword. After three years of doing chores, Matajuro Yagyu has learned nothing. 'But one day Banzo crept up behind him and gave him a terrific blow with a wooden sword.' Like Peter Sellers with his Japanese manservant in the Pink Panther movies, Matajuro never knew when another attack was coming, but by constant, instant dodging 'he learned so rapidly he brought smiles to the face of his master. Matajuro became the greatest swordsman in the land.'

Much the same thing happened to Takashi Oyama in the early 1970s, when he wanted to study pottery under the immortal Shoji Hamada. After six months in which he was merely entitled to watch, Oyama was allowed to do the thankless, unpaid task of kneading the raw clay – for a whole year. It was eighteen months before he was allowed to sit at a potter's wheel, and even then Hamada 'taught' Oyama nothing in words or explanations. But the young man became one of Japan's most successful potters.

There's a similar story, again, about Ueshiba Morihei, the master of modern *aikido*, mentioned earlier in this chapter. Over five years, his master gave him just a hundred days of very expensive teaching. The clue lies in the swordsman story. When Matajuro, the pupil, first asks how long his lessons will take, Banzo says ten years. When he asked how long it will be if he works intensively, the master's answer is thirty years. Pressed still further, Banzo says: 'In that case, you will have to stay with me for seventy years. A man in such a hurry as you are to get results seldom learns quickly.'

Accepting fluidity

Western managers complain about the inordinate delays and expenditure of time as their Japanese counterparts make up their minds. Once a decision has been taken, though, the Japanese are committed to acting with a speed and determination that can leave Western partners breathless. But there's no hard and fast set of Japanese principles to help Westerners achieve equally successful results. The whole essence of Zen is that nothing is hard and fast, that everything is fluid.

It's a state of mind. That's where true commitment starts, with the acceptance of fluidity, of change within the unchanging, of the combination of opposites. Move on to the value of taking time out to think – about yourself, about what you're doing, about life, about the organisation, about the long-term future, about whatever means most to you – and regard time spent in reflection, or meditation, as time well spent, even if no material results follow. They will, eventually.

Use time in which nothing is happening to set the scene for making things happen: watch, look at and absorb the events and the people from which or whom you can learn. Don't hurry this process, or try to hasten anything that can't or shouldn't be hurried. And think of yourself always as both pupil and teacher

– the more you learn, the more you can teach; and the more others learn from you, especially by example, the more valuable their work will be.

Also, never forget that what people realise through their own efforts, convictions and commitment gives them greater strength. Allow people time to make their own mistakes and their own successes, in which you will inevitably share. Insist on perfect performance – or on trying to achieve it – for yourself and others. Finally, look back over this very bald rendering of Zen, and note that the precepts are precisely those that progressive Western firms are seeking to apply. There's nothing foreign here, nothing mystical; nothing but common sense and common humanity.

The Eastern spirit, however, gains enormously from the sense of unity that binds everything together and helps provide the confidence to strive for success by relaxing, to seek external victory through inner strength. Again, it's a lesson which should be familiar to Western managers and sportsmen and women. The most successful periods in the histories of the most successful companies and teams come when the culture provides an especially strong unifying force, when everything 'fits'; when commitment is total. The peak periods of achievement for individuals also tend to be those when they are most in harmony (a very Zen concept) with themselves and their environment. But the Japanese didn't achieve their economic miracles without the mixture of worldliness and spirituality that is beautifully demonstrated by our last story from *Zen Flesh, Zen Bones.*

The great warrior Nobunaga attacks an enemy force which outnumbers him by ten to one. That's no way to win. But Nobunaga turns to the spiritual world for help. He stops at a Shinto shrine and tells the troops that, after praying, 'I will toss a coin. If heads come, we will win; if tails, we will lose. Destiny holds us in her hand.' He prays silently, then tosses the coin. It comes up heads, and his soldiers, inspired by the omen, shatter the enemy.

'No one can change the hand of destiny,' says his attendant. 'Indeed not,' replies Nobunaga, showing the coin he tossed. It is double-headed.

Bibliography

Brown, Mark *The Dinosaur Strain: The Survivor's Guide to Personal and Business Success* (Element Books, 1988)

Creech, Bill *The Five Pillars of TQM: How to Make Total Quality Management Work for You* (Truman Talley/Dutton, 1994)

de Bono, Edward *Parallel Thinking: From Socratic Thinking to de Bono Thinking* (Penguin, 1994)

Dixon, Norman *On the Psychology of Military Incompetence* (Jonathan Cape, 1976)

Dyer, Dr Wayne W. *Your Erroneous Zones* (Avon Books, 1977)

Gale, Bradley *Managing Customer Value: Creating Quality and Service That Customers Can See* (The Free Press/Macmillan, 1994)

Gershman, Michael *Getting It Right the Second Time* (Addison-Wesley, 1990)

Hamel, Gary, & Prahalad, C.K. *Competing for the Future* (Harvard Business School Press, 1994)

Hammer, Michael, & Champy, James *Reengineering the Corporation: A Manifesto for Business Revolution* (HarperCollins, 1993)

Harvey-Jones, John *Making It Happen: Reflections on Leadership* (Wm Collins, 1988)

Harvey-Jones, John *Getting It Together* (Heinemann, 1991)

Heirs, Ben *The Professional Decision Thinker* (Grafton, 1989)

Hunt, Geoff *Geoff Hunt on Squash* (Edited by Alan Trengrove,

Cassell, 1974)

Kanter, Rosabeth Moss *When Giants Learn to Dance: Mastering the Challenges of Strategy, Management and Careers in the 1990s* (Simon & Schuster, 1989)

Kelly, Kevin *Out of Control* (Fourth Estate, 1994)

Khan, Hashim *Squash Rackets: The Khan Game* (Souvenir Press, 1967)

Kouzes, James M., & Posner, Barry Z. *Credibility: How Leaders Gain and Lose It, Why People Demand It* (Jossey-Bass, 1993)

Kushel, Gerald *Reaching the Peak Performance Zone: How to Motivate Yourself and Others to Excel* (AMACOM, American Management Association, 1994)

McKenna, Regis *Relationship Marketing: Own the Market Through Strategic Customer Relationships* (Addison-Wesley, 1991)

Nayak, P. Ranganath, & Ketteringham, John M. *Breakthroughs!* (Rawson Associates/Macmillan, 1986)

Pinchot, Gifford, III *Intrapreneuring* (Harper & Row, 1985)

Pfeffer, Jeffrey *Competitive Advantage Through People* (Harvard Business School Press, 1994)

Random, Michael *Japan Strategy of the Unseen: A Guide for Westerners to the Mind of Modern Japan* (Thorsons, 1987)

Reps, Paul (*Ed*) *Zen Flesh, Zen Bones* (Penguin, 1971)

Sakiya, Tetsuo *Honda Motor: The Men, the Management, the Machines* (Kodonsha, 1982)

Semler, Ricardo *Maverick! The Success Story Behind the World's Most Unusual Workplace* (Century, 1993)

Senge, Peter M. *The Fifth Discipline* (Doubleday, 1990)

Wendt, Henry *Global Embrace* (HarperCollins, 1994)

Picture Credits

Index

Page numbers in *italics* refer to the illustrations